THE FIRST BOOK OF

VEGETARIAN COOKING

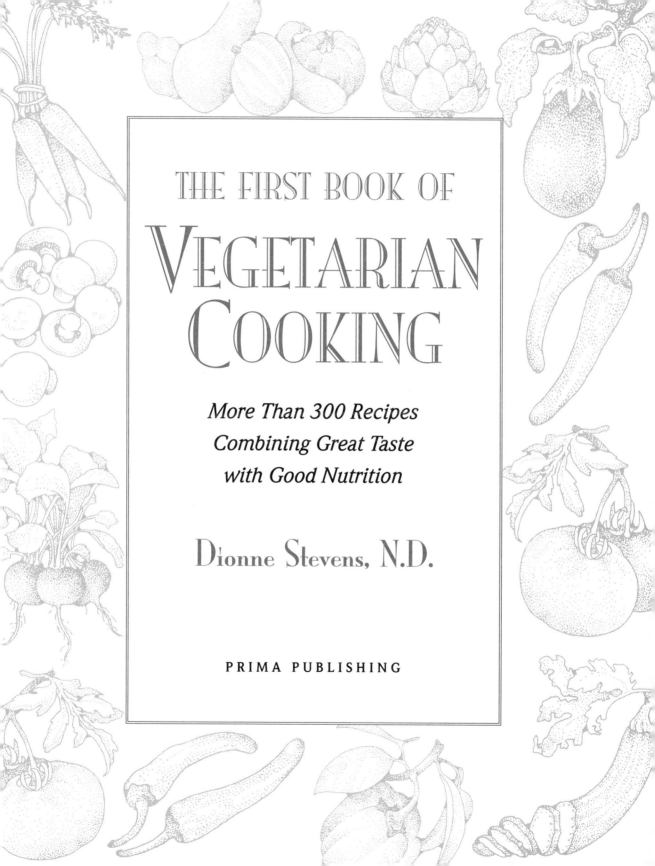

THE FIRST BOOK OF
VEGETARIAN
COOKING

*More Than 300 Recipes
Combining Great Taste
with Good Nutrition*

Dionne Stevens, N.D.

PRIMA PUBLISHING

Warning—Disclaimer
Prima Publishing has designed this book to provide information in regard to the subject matter covered. It is sold with the understanding that the publisher and the author are not liable for the misconception or misuse of information provided. Every effort has been made to make this book as complete and as accurate as possible. The purpose of this book is to educate. The author and Prima Publishing shall have neither liability nor responsibility to any person or entity with respect to any loss, damage, or injury caused or alleged to be caused directly or indirectly by the information contained in this book. The information presented herein is in no way intended as a substitute for medical counseling.

Library of Congress Cataloging-in-Publication Data

Stevens, Dionne
    The first book of vegetarian cooking : more than 300 recipes combining great taste with good nutrition / by Dionne Stevens.
       p.   cm.
  Includes index.
  ISBN 0-7615-0624-1
  1. Vegetarian cookery.   I. Title.
TX837.S774 1996
641.5'636—dc20   96-21943
                                          CIP

96 97 98 99 00 01 AA 10 9 8 7 6 5 4 3 2 1

Printed in the United States of America

Nutritional Analyses
A per serving nutritional breakdown is provided for each recipe. If a range is given for an ingredient amount, the breakdown is based on the smaller number. If a range is given for servings, the breakdown is based on the larger number. If a choice of ingredients is given in an ingredient listing, the breakdown is calculated using the first choice. Nutritional content may vary depending on the specific brands or types of ingredients used. "Optional" ingredients or those for which no specific amount is stated are not included in the breakdown. Nutritional figures are rounded to the nearest whole number.

How to Order
Single copies may be ordered from Prima Publishing, P.O. Box 1260BK, Rocklin, CA 95677; telephone (916) 632-4400. Quantity discounts are also available. On your letterhead, include information concerning the intended use of the books and the number of books you wish to purchase.

Visit us online at http://www.primapublishing.com

Contents

Preface

Coming from generations of restaurateurs, my love affair with food seems only natural. I think I was weaned on a restaurant steam table, started cooking at the grill in my preteens, and continued to help out in the kitchen for many years. As a result, I have collected cookbooks that I read as if they are novels. If I am in a foreign country, the first thing I do is visit a bookstore looking for cookbooks featuring local cuisine. I don't know which I love most: to eat, cook, or travel?

Because of this love of good food and an avid interest in nutrition, I obtained a degree in Naturopathic medicine. Later I held a position teaching nutrition and weight-loss for an international weight-loss organization. I realized then that a vegetarian diet was the healthiest to follow.

I became a vegetarian. So, the first thing I did was to buy a vegetarian cookbook. Well, let me tell you, I thought I had stepped over into the twilight zone. A large number of the ingredients I had never even heard of—TVP, what in the world is TVP? It took me a few weeks until I located it at a health food store and found that TVP is textured vegetable protein.

Many cookbooks later, I wondered why the recipes did not have foods and tastes with which I was familiar. I wanted to eat well but not feel deprived. *The First Book of Vegetarian Cooking* is my solution. I have taken familiar recipes and foods and converted them into more healthful dishes through ingredient substitution or elimination. You might find a few ingredients that seem strange to you, but try them—you will like them!

Some people think vegetarians lose weight because they only eat vegetables. Wrong! Most vegetarians eat all kinds of foods, and many of them are loaded with fat. It has been very difficult to find lowfat vegetarian foods, but it's getting better. The manufacturers still have a long way to go, however you will find most of my recipes very low in fat.

I hope this cookbook will help you make the transition. If you are not already a vegetarian, don't clean out your refrigerator and pantry; replace your foods as you go with the healthier alternatives.

Food *can* be your body's medicine: healthful, lowfat, and delicious.

May this book bring you joy and wondrous health.

—*Dionne Stevens*
Tampa, Florida

"And God said, Behold, I have given you every herb bearing seed, which is upon the face of all the earth, and every tree, in which is the fruit of a tree yielding seed: to you it shall be for meat."

—*Genesis 1:29*

Preface

Acknowledgments

Many thanks to my husband, Brian,
for his encouragement and assistance.

Vivian Crawley for getting me started.

In memory of Angelina Campbell.

Introduction

You have a choice between mainstream medicine and the older, proven, usually less invasive forms of treating the *cause* of your disease and not the symptoms. More and more people are turning to herbal medicine, homeopathy, acupuncture, vitamin therapy, chelation, and other natural forms of healing. Each day we hear of startling results obtained from these organic, natural cures. We have become aware of what "modern medicine" is doing to our bodies. As we reconsider a traditional approach, it is natural to look more closely at the food we eat. After all, "we are what we eat." Our scientists now tell us that animal products cause cancer, heart disease, and myriad other diseases. This is the reason for *The First Book of Vegetarian Cooking*, a painless transition to healthier eating through diet. You will find many of your favorite recipes with a change here and a change there and voilà you have a healthful version of an old-time favorite.

What Is the Difference Between a Vegetarian and a Vegan?

A vegetarian does not eat meat, fish, or poultry. Vegans are vegetarians who do not eat any animal products, including milk, cheese, eggs, or any other dairy products. Some vegans do not even eat honey because it's an animal product.

Why Be a Vegetarian?

The reasons for vegetarianism can range from health, world hunger issues, ecology, religion, spiritual enlightenment, compassion for animals and their suffering, to economics and the belief in nonviolence. More and more people are seeing the link between diseases like cancer and meat consumption. Vegetarians have lower rates of heart disease, high blood pressure, some forms of cancer, diabetes, and obesity.

How Can a Vegetarian Get Enough Protein?

How many times have I heard that question? The answer is simple: Vegetarians can easily meet the protein requirements through such sources as legumes, tofu, nuts, seeds, tempeh, peas, greens, whole grain breads, potatoes, corn, and sea vegetables. Protein is found in most plant foods. It was once thought you had to combine certain foods to obtain a complete protein, but we now know this is not necessary. The body will make its own complete protein as long as your diet is varied, and enough calories are consumed throughout the day. Americans eat excess protein which can lead to calcium excretion and loss of bone density.

If You Don't Eat Dairy Products, How Do You Get Calcium?

Some vegetarian sources of calcium include dark green leafy vegetables such as broccoli, collard and mustard greens, kale, and turnip greens. Bok choy, beans, fortified tofu, and rice and soy milks are also excellent sources. Studies have shown that vegetarians absorb and retain more calcium from foods than nonvegetarians. For example, approximately ½ cup of milk has

119 mg of calcium, ½ cup of raw kale 135 mg, tofu 205 mg, parsley 130 mg, and collards 117 mg.

The Alternative Lifestyle

To achieve the healthier "alternative lifestyle" it has been recommended by experts to *eliminate* the following products:

- ☞ White flours—pastas, breads, biscuits
- ☞ Refined sugars
- ☞ Products with caffeine—sodas, chocolate, coffee
- ☞ Dairy products
- ☞ Meats, including chicken and fish
- ☞ Products containing aspartame
- ☞ Products containing MSG
- ☞ Table salt
- ☞ Limiting alcohol consumption to wine

Can a Vegetarian Diet Extend Your Life?

It is unfortunate for us that 90% of the medical schools in the United States do not require one single course in human nutrition for medical doctors. Could this be the reason why doctors only treat the symptoms of a disease and not the real cause?

Take for instance cancer; many cancers are directly related to what we eat and our lifestyle. Cancers of the colon, rectum, breast, stomach, intestine, mouth, voice box, pancreas, liver, ovary, thyroid, and bladder could be prevented in 50 to 90% of the cases with proper nutrition, as it could help prevent heart disease and stroke.

The American Dietetic Association has given its "seal of approval" to the vegetarian diet affirming the diet can meet all known nutrient needs. The U.S. Department of Agriculture (USDA) and Department of Health and Human Services (HHS) has also endorsed the vegetarian diet. As HHS secretary Donna E. Shalala stated in the *Aspen Science News* (vol. 149, January 6, 1996), "These guidelines are the gold standard for nutrition and health. Three hundred thousand people in the United States die each year as a result of poor diet, we are sending the message loud and clear: Diet and exercise are twin engines that will carry you on the road to a longer, healthier life."

Special Features of This Book

In many of my recipes I have indicated brand names. This is not because I am being paid by these companies, it is because when I became a vegetarian I had to blindly try many different brands before finding ones that satisfied my taste buds. These are the brands I use in my recipes and I do not recommend substitutions (if at all possible) as there is a vast difference in quality and taste. Also look for helpful hints or variations at the end of many of the recipes. Some recipes also contain important nutritional information that can make a difference to your health and well being. I am not prescribing nor diagnosing, only reporting the most up-to-date nutritional information I have found available.

The Vegetarian Kitchen

In many ways, the vegetarian kitchen is like any other kitchen: good pots and pans, sharp knives, and helpful small appliances. A properly equipped kitchen will not only make your life easier, it will enable you to create culinary masterpieces in half the time. Good equipment is an investment just as your silver or other precious items are. I have learned the hard way that you need the right tool for the right job.

Because a lowfat diet is essential to good health, I have included hints on pan preparation as well as information on organic foods and some other kitchen staples. If you don't already have a vegetarian kitchen, don't clean out your refrigerator and pantry. Replace food as needed with the "alternative lifestyle" foods.

Pots and Pans

Without good heavy nonstick pans cooking is a chore. Thin ones will not hold up. With nonstick pans you want a finish that will last and not flake off into your food. Never use high heat when cooking with a nonstick surface. Listed below are some pans I have used and can recommend. Nonstick pans are a must for lowfat or fat-free recipes.

- All-clad (nonstick line)
- T-fal "Excellence" (my favorite is their wok)
- Haute Cuisine by Le Creuset (a nonstick line)

- Professional nonstick from Calphalon
- Scanpan
- Faberware "Millennium"

Food Processor and Blender

I believe these two pieces of equipment have made themselves just about indispensable in the kitchen. My first food processor was purchased at the Salvation Army for $5.00. When that one wore out I graduated to the Cusinart and found what a time saver it is. There are many good blenders on the market. I use the Waring Professional because I like the way it processes tofu.

Electric Coffee Grinder

Not a necessity but nice to have for grinding spices. Grind a piece of bread after use to keep the grinder clean and prevent mingling of flavors.

Griddle/Grill

I seem to find more and more uses for this piece of equipment. I have one made by Le Creuset that is flat on one side and ridged on the other. The ridged side is wonderful for cooking foods when you want a scored appearance as if you had cooked on a barbecue.

Knives

James Beard once said, "The most important tool in the kitchen, next to the knife is your hands." There is nothing more pleasurable than to have sharp knives. They will make preparation work much easier and faster. It is worth the investment to have good knives. They should last a lifetime. I was lucky enough to have been able to buy a full set of Solingen no-stain Friodur knives when visiting Germany years ago. They still are one of my valued possessions.

Pressure Cookers

I have used this handy piece of equipment in some recipes. Pressure cookers are enjoying a resurgence in popularity probably because they reduce the cooking time by as much as 50% while keeping most of the food's nutritional value. Some people say they won't use one because they are afraid that the pressure cooker will explode. My Futura pressure cooker by Hawkins is not supposed to explode because of the way it is constructed. Functional and pleasing to the eye, it is made of Satilon, which is stick-resistant—very important for our new Alternative Cooking. Pressure cookers cook food faster than any other means of heat. Beans that normally take over an hour can cook in 12 minutes. What a time saver!

Organic Foods

According to a recent report by the U.S. Department of Agriculture, 61% of 6,000 fruits and vegetables tested had measurable residues from *at least* one pesticide. This was *after washing, peeling, and coring* ready-to-eat foods! The apples contained up to 8 pesticides, peaches 7, and grapes and celery 6 different pesticides.

Most people are aware that they should be buying organic foods. Not only do they taste much better, and they are free of pesticides, fertilizers, and hormones that are dangerous to our bodies as well as our environment.

What is stopping a lot of people is the price. Yes, organic foods are a little more expensive. But, let's remember the old law of supply and demand. If more people buy organic foods the price will come down. With medical costs being what they are, can we really afford not to buy organic?

If organic food is not available please wash your vegetables in a *Veggie Bath* (recipe follows).

Veggie Bath

When not using organic foods, prepare and use the bath below:

1	bottle pure, unscented castile* soap
$1/8$	teaspoon red cayenne pepper

Add cayenne pepper to the bottle of castile soap and shake well. You can use this bath directly on the vegetables or add a few drops to a basin of water for soaking. Rinse food well with distilled water.

Wear rubber gloves when
using Veggie Bath if your
skin is sensitive.

Cooking Sprays

Granted, most cooking sprays do not contain chloroflurocarbons (CFCs), but they do contain carbon and hydrogen (hydrocarbons) which is a greenhouse gas and does contribute to the heat-

*Some drugstores carry pure castile soap. In health food stores look for Dr. Bronner's baby castile.

The Vegetarian Kitchen

ing of our planet. This heating is causing the polar ice caps to melt, raising the sea levels, and flooding low lying coastal areas. This is why I recommend non-aerosol sprays.

And think of all those spray cans that can't be recycled! Why not recycle a jam jar and make the following oil applicator: In a recycled jam jar, cut a slit in the lid large enough to accommodate a pastry brush. Fill with oil (I use safflower oil—it doesn't solidify in the refrigerator).

Pan Preparation (using oil)

1. Liberally spray a heavy nonstick pan with water. The water and its vapor help to keep the temperature of the oil at 212 degrees F.
2. Remove brush from your prepared oil jar removing most of the oil from the pastry brush and apply a thin coat of oil over the water-sprayed pan
3. Cook foods at low heat.

Keep oils in the refrigerator.
They can become rancid at
room temperature.

Pan Preparation (using no oil)

1. In a heavy nonstick pan heat 2 tablespoons water. Add 1 tablespoon of either liquid Aminos, low-sodium tamari, wine, or lemon juice.
2. Add food and sauté over low heat.

JUST FOR STARTERS

❧❧ ❧❧

One of my favorite ways of entertaining is a finger-food buffet. I prepare everything ahead of time and just re-heat before serving. This way I can spend most of my time enjoying my guests.

I take delight in serving nonfat, vegetarian, good-for-you foods. Only at the end of the evening when the compliments are flying do I divulge my secret. The nonvegetarians (usually the majority) say over and over again, "You mean (this or that) has no meat!" or "I don't believe this dish has no fat, how can you cook this without fat!" Our guests take their leave lighter in body and spirit.

I will never understand why some people, who normally eat well, feel that when entertaining they have to prepare dishes they normally wouldn't eat themselves; high in cholesterol and fat.

If you really want to make a guest happy, serve some of these starters and let everyone know how good the dishes are. Who knows—you might become a trend setter?

Recipes

Crudités

Baba Ganoosh

Zucchini Pâté

Bean Dip

Lentil Dip

Black Bean and
   Kombu Spread

Carrot Pâté

Neatballs

Cornish Pasties

Dolmas

French Bean Pâté

"Meatballs" in
   Dill Sauce

French Onion Toast

"Refried" Beans

Fruitopia

Guacamole Dip

Hummus

Melonballs

Moroccan Eggplant

Mushroom Nut Pâté

Onion Dip I

Onion Dip II

Stuffed Celery

Peanut Butter Dip

Samosas

Green Sauce

Seven-Layer Dip

Taco Bites

Barbecue Cups

Soys in a Shawl

"Cream Cheese" and
   Black Beans

Stuffed "Bacon"

Black Bean Hummus

Stuffed Mushrooms

Texas Caviar

Sweet and Sour
   "Meatballs"

Sweet Pea Dip

Tex-Mex Wontons

Chile con Queso

Crudités

Some suggestions to serve with dips:

Carrot sticks
Mushrooms
Cherry tomatoes
Radishes
Broccoli florets
Cauliflower florets
Zucchini slices
Cucumber slices
Brussels sprouts
Jicama strips
Celeriac
Baby ears of corn
Endive leaves

Pea pods
Asparagus
Celery sticks
Kohlrabi
Turnip slices
Apple slices
Beets
Sugar snap peas
Bell peppers
Scallions
Baby squash
Baby Carrots
Fennel bulb strips

Baba Ganoosh (Eggplant Dip)

1 large eggplant (1 pound)
¼ cup tahini
2 tablespoons fresh
    lemon juice
2 cloves garlic, pressed
    or minced
1 tablespoon liquid
    aminos
Minced fresh parsley
    for garnish

Preheat oven to 400 degrees F.

You will seldom see a Middle Eastern buffet without this delectable dish. Traditionally it is served with pita bread.

1. Pierce the eggplant 10 to 12 times with a fork and place in a baking dish. Cover loosely with foil and bake for about 40 minutes or until soft. Remove skin.
2. Finely chop eggplant and combine with remaining ingredients.
3. Garnish and serve at room temperature.

Makes 2 cups

Parsley has more iron than any other green vegetable. Parsley juice has been used as a treatment in the removal of small kidney and gallstones, ailments of the liver, and as a tonic for the blood vessels, capillaries, and arterioles.

30	Calories
1 g	Protein
3 g	Carbohydrates
2 g	Fat
62%	Calories from Fat
1 g	Fiber
47 mg	Sodium
0 mg	Cholesterol

Zucchini Pâté

4 medium zucchini, sliced
1 medium onion, sliced
1 clove garlic, pressed or
   minced
¼ pound fresh mushrooms,
   chopped
½ teaspoon dried basil
½ teaspoon curry powder
1 teaspoon liquid aminos
1 tablespoon fresh lemon
   juice
2 tablespoons fat-free,
   dairy-free mayonnaise
2 tablespoons grated
   Parmesan cheese
   alternative

For a smoky flavor, instead
of fresh mushrooms use 2
packages (10 grams each)
dried porcini mushrooms
reconstituted in warm water
for 15 minutes.

Zucchini is high in vitamin A and low in calories which makes this pâté good for dieters and health seekers.

1. Prepare a nonstick skillet by lightly coating surface with vegetable cooking spray or by using an oiled pastry brush. Sauté zucchini, onion, and garlic until soft. Stir frequently. Add mushrooms, basil, curry powder, and liquid aminos. Cook an additional 5 minutes. Add lemon juice, mayonnaise and cheese.
2. Place in food processor or blender and process until smooth.
3. Spoon into 1-quart pâté dish or serving bowl. Cover and chill overnight.
4. To serve, surround serving dish with crisp bread, fat-free crackers, pita or toast points.

Makes 3 cups

11	Calories
1 g	Protein
2 g	Carbohydrates
1 g	Fat
25%	Calories from Fat
0 g	Fiber
28 mg	Sodium
0 mg	Cholesterol

Bean Dip

1   can (16 ounces) fat-free refried beans

¼   cup shredded Cheddar soy cheese (lowfat or fat-free)

1   teaspoon minced dehydrated onions

¼   teaspoon garlic powder
Pinch of cayenne

This popular dip is quick and easy to make.

1. Combine all the ingredients in a small saucepan and heat just until cheese melts and ingredients are well blended.
2. Serve in a chafing dish or fondue pot over low flame with baked tortilla chips or corn chips.

Makes about 2 cups

Natural forces within us are the true healers of disease.
—HIPPOCRATES

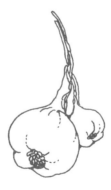

33	Calories
2 g	Protein
7 g	Carbohydrates
0 g	Fat
0%	Calories from Fat
2 g	Fiber
158 mg	Sodium
0 mg	Cholesterol

Lentil Dip

1	cup red lentils, rinsed
1	tablespoon low-sodium tamari sauce plus additional for seasoning
$1/2$	cup chopped onion
2	cloves garlic, pressed or minced
$1/8$	teaspoon ground ginger
$1/8$	teaspoon mace
$1/2$	teaspoon lemon juice

Peel ginger by scraping the skin with a teaspoon. The spoon will get into those hard to reach crevices.

Lentils have been eaten for thousand of years and are a very good source of protein, providing as much as many meats. This legume helps build the glands and blood, and is especially good for the heart.

1. Put lentils in a saucepan with enough water to cover. Bring to a boil, cover and simmer for 20 minutes or until soft.
2. In a small nonstick skillet add 1 tablespoon water and 1 tablespoon tamari. Add onion and garlic; simmer until soft. Drain cooked lentils, reserving the liquid.
3. In a food processor add the drained lentils, onion and garlic mixture, ginger, mace, and lemon juice. Process until smooth, adding some of the reserved liquid if necessary.
4. Add tamari to taste. Chill.

Makes 2 cups

41	Calories
3 g	Protein
7 g	Carbohydrates
1 g	Fat
3%	Calories from Fat
1 g	Fiber
44 mg	Sodium
0 mg	Cholesterol

Black Bean and Kombu Spread

୨⳽ ⳼ଓ

1	cup black beans, soaked overnight and then drained
1	strip (10 inches) dried kombu
1	bay leaf
1	large onion, chopped
1	carrot, chopped
2	celery stalks, chopped
	Distilled water
1	teaspoon miso (see "Glossary")
1	teaspoon tahini
1	teaspoon dark, grainy mustard
1	teaspoon balsamic vinegar
	Pinch of cayenne
3	scallions, sliced for garnish

The sea vegetable kombu is a nutritional powerhouse containing calcium, iron, magnesium, potassium, iodine, and vitamins A, C, and D.

1. In a medium saucepan place the beans, kombu, bay leaf, onion, carrot, and celery with enough water to cover. Bring to a boil, reduce heat, cover and simmer until beans are done and liquid is absorbed, approx. 1 ½ hours. Excess liquid can be absorbed by removing the lid and cooking for additional time.
2. Add miso, tahini, mustard, vinegar, and cayenne to the cooked bean mixture. Cook an additional 10 minutes over very low heat.
3. Blend to a smooth consistency in a food processor or mash with a potato masher.
4. Chill and garnish with scallions before serving. May be served with crackers, pita, rice cakes, toast wedges, or crisp bread.

Makes 1 ½ cups

72	Calories
4 g	Protein
13 g	Carbohydrates
1 g	Fat
8%	Calories from Fat
3 g	Fiber
52 mg	Sodium
0 mg	Cholesterol

The First Book of Vegetarian Cooking

Carrot Pâté

1 cup carrot pulp
1 clove garlic, pressed
½ teaspoon dill weed
2 tablespoons fat-free, dairy-free mayonnaise

After juicing carrots don't throw away the pulp, use it in this surprisingly tasty spread.

1. In a small bowl mix the carrot pulp, garlic, and dill. Add the mayonnaise and mix well.
2. Serve on crackers, pita, or toast points.

Makes 1 cup

10	Calories
0 g	Protein
2 g	Carbohydrates
1 g	Fat
3%	Calories from Fat
1 g	Fiber
53 mg	Sodium
0 mg	Cholesterol

Neatballs

1   package (5.3 ounces)
      Burger 'n' Loaf,
      original
3   tablespoons dehydrated
      minced onion
$\frac{1}{2}$ teaspoon dried oregano
$\frac{1}{4}$ teaspoon garlic powder
      Pinch of cayenne
1 $\frac{1}{3}$ cups cold distilled water

1. Combine the burger, onion, oregano, garlic powder, and cayenne. Mix in the water. Let the mixture rest 15 minutes.
2. Form into walnut-size balls (the mixture will be sticky). Brown on all sides in a sprayed nonstick skillet.

Makes 16 to 18 balls

Neatballs can be added to Barbecue Sauce, Pronto Plum Sauce, Pizza Sauce or Sweet and Sour Sauce. For recipes see "Sauces, Marinades, and Salad Dressings."

41	Calories
2 g	Protein
7 g	Carbohydrates
1 g	Fat
22%	Calories from Fat
0 g	Fiber
23 mg	Sodium
0 mg	Cholesterol

Cornish Pasties

2   pounds potatoes, peeled and quartered

1   package (5.3 ounces) Original Burger 'n' Loaf

1   extra large onion, chopped

1   tablespoon liquid aminos

2   sheets pie pastry dough (enough for two 9-inch pies)

Preheat oven to 350 degrees F.

My English husband's absolute favorite. He likes this adaptation better than the original which contains tons of fat and animal products.

1. Place potatoes in medium saucepan with water to cover. Cover pan and cook until potatoes are tender, about 20 minutes.
2. Prepare burger according to package directions, omitting the oil.
3. Prepare a nonstick skillet by lightly coating surface with vegetable cooking spray or by using an oiled pastry brush. Cook burger, breaking up with a wooden spoon until brown. Remove contents to large bowl.
4. Sauté onion until tender. Add onions and liquid aminos to bowl of burger.
5. Drain potatoes and coarsely chop. Add to bowl and combine well.
6. Using a floured biscuit cutter or drinking glass rim, cut out 3-inch circles. Place a rounded spoonful of filling into the center of each circle. Moisten edges of rounds with cold water. Fold in half pressing the seams together firmly and crimp with the tines of a fork.
7. Place on an oil-sprayed cookie sheet and bake for 15 minutes or until golden.

Makes 1 ½ dozen

162	Calories
7 g	Protein
17 g	Carbohydrates
8 g	Fat
44%	Calories from Fat
2 g	Fiber
261 mg	Sodium
0 mg	Cholesterol

Dolmas (Stuffed Grape Leaves)

༡ ༢

1	jar (8 ounces) grape leaves, in water
1	large onion, chopped
2	cloves garlic, pressed or minced
2	cups cooked basmati or brown rice
3	tablespoons sunflower seeds
¼	cup chopped fresh parsley
2	teaspoons dried mint
2	teaspoons dill weed
2	tablespoons fresh lemon juice
¼	cup dried currants, raisins can be substituted
1	tablespoon liquid aminos
1	cup orange juice
	Fresh parsley, mint, or dill sprigs for garnish

A Greek finger food enjoyed by all.

1. Remove grape leaves from jar and rinse in a large saucepan filled with warm water. Drain. Gently separate the leaves, selecting 30 to 35 leaves with no tears. Set aside rejected leaves. Remove stems from selected leaves and drain on paper towels. Pat dry.
2. Prepare a nonstick skillet by lightly coating surface with vegetable cooking spray or by using an oiled pastry brush. Sauté the onions and garlic until soft and starting to brown. Add remaining ingredients (excluding the orange juice and garnish). Set aside.
3. Place a steamer rack into a 10-inch domed skillet. Add water to bottom of pan. Line the rack with half of the rejected grape leaves. (Grape leaves should not be sitting in water).
4. Place one rounded tablespoon of the stuffing on each selected grape leaf (near the stem end), folding sides in and rolling up from the base, jelly-roll fashion.
5. Place dolmas, seam-side down on top of the leaves in the steamer. Pack them close together. Make a second layer if necessary.

The First Book of Vegetarian Cooking

6. Drizzle orange juice over dolmas and spray with non-aerosol olive oil cooking spray. Use remaining grape leaves as a covering layer.
7. Cover pan and steam dolmas over medium heat for 40 minutes, adding water as needed.
8. Serve warm, arranged on a platter of grape leaves garnished with herb sprigs.

Makes 30 to 35 dolmas

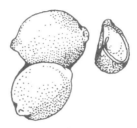

36	Calories
1 g	Protein
6 g	Carbohydrates
1 g	Fat
26%	Calories from Fat
1 g	Fiber
21 mg	Sodium
0 mg	Cholesterol

French Bean Pâté

1 cup TVP (textured vegetable protein)
1 tablespoon ketchup
1 cup boiling distilled water
3 large dried shiitake mushrooms
1 medium onion, chopped (about 1 cup)
2 cloves garlic, pressed or minced
1/2 teaspoon ground dried marjoram
1 teaspoon whole dried oregano leaves
2 cups cooked pinto beans *or* 1 can (15 ounces) pinto beans, drained
2 tablespoons mirin rice vinegar
1 tablespoon low-sodium tamari
1/2 teaspoon mace

Preheat oven to 350 degrees F.

A delicious pâté. No one will say, "Where's the meat?" Serve with French bread slices or toast points.

1. Combine TVP, ketchup, and water. Let stand 10 minutes. The water should be completely absorbed.
2. Soak dried mushrooms in enough warm water to cover for 15 minutes. Drain, reserving the liquid for soups, gravies, or sauces. Squeeze excess liquid from mushrooms. Remove stems. On a paper towel cut mushrooms into 1/4-inch slices.
3. Prepare a nonstick skillet by lightly coating surface with vegetable cooking spray or by using an oiled pastry brush and sauté onions and garlic until soft; add marjoram and oregano. Cook 1 more minute.
4. Combine beans, onion mixture, TVP, mirin, tamari, and mace in food processor. Process till smooth.
5. Lightly oil pâté dish or mold. Line bottom with sliced mushrooms, white-side up. Add pâté, cover with lid or foil and place into a pan of hot water and bake for 1 hour.

6. Remove from oven and cool slightly. The pâté must be weighted to become firm. Cut a piece of foil that will fit over the pâté. Lay the foil over a heavy piece of cardboard and cut to same shape. Lay the foil, followed by the cardboard, over the pâté. Place heavy items on top (some people use bricks). Refrigerate overnight.

7. At serving time, run knife around inside of mold and invert pâté onto serving dish.

Makes 3 cups

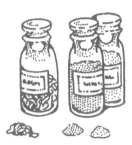

57	Calories
4 g	Protein
10 g	Carbohydrates
1 g	Fat
4%	Calories from Fat
2 g	Fiber
56 mg	Sodium
0 mg	Cholesterol

"Meatballs" in Dill Sauce

2 cups distilled water
2 tablespoons Vogue Instant Vege Base mix
2 tablespoons arrowroot
1 container (8 ounces) dairy-free cream cheese
2 tablespoons dill weed
1 recipe Neatballs (page 10)

This elegant buffet dish is neat because there's no meat. Your guests won't know the difference and your vegetarian friends will beg for the recipe.

1. In a small saucepan combine water, Vogue Instant Vege Base mix, and arrowroot. Simmer, stirring constantly until just thickened.
2. Remove from heat. Stir in sour cream and dill weed. Mix until well blended. Add prepared Neatballs.
3. Serve in a chafing dish or fondue pot over a low flame.

Makes 1 ½ dozen balls and 2 ½ cups sauce

72	Calories
7 g	Protein
5 g	Carbohydrates
3 g	Fat
41%	Calories from Fat
1 g	Fiber
191 mg	Sodium
0 mg	Cholesterol

French Onion Toast

1 loaf whole grain French
bread, cut into
$\frac{1}{2}$-inch slices
3 pounds onions (Vidalia
if in season), thinly
sliced
2 cloves garlic, pressed or
minced
1 teaspoon dried sage,
crumbled
1 teaspoon dried thyme,
crumbled
1 cup dry red wine
1 clove garlic, halved
1 tablespoon liquid
aminos
Fresh herb leaves (sage,
rosemary sprigs, etc.)
for garnish

Preheat oven to 350 degrees F.

If you like onions, you'll love this recipe. You can keep the onion mixture for up to a week in the refrigerator before serving.

1. Place bread slices on cookie sheet and bake until lightly browned and slightly crisp. Set aside.
2. In a large nonstick skillet or wok sprayed with water and lightly brushed with oil, sauté onion and pressed garlic over medium-low heat Add sage and thyme. Sauté for 15 minutes, stirring often. Spray with more water if needed.
3. Add wine and sauté an additional 15 minutes, stirring often. Most of the wine should be absorbed and the mixture moist.
4. Rub the cut side of the halved garlic on the browned bread slices. Spread the bread with onion mixture and garnish with herb leaves.

Makes 24 pieces

83	Calories
2 g	Protein
15 g	Carbohydrates
1 g	Fat
9%	Calories from Fat
1 g	Fiber
138 mg	Sodium
0 mg	Cholesterol

"Refried" Beans

꧁ ꧂

1 small onion, chopped
2 cloves garlic, pressed or
   minced
1 teaspoon chili powder
1 teaspoon ground cumin
1 teaspoon liquid aminos
   Pinch of cayenne
2 cups cooked pinto beans
   or 1 can (15 ounces),
   drained (reserve
   liquid)

A basic ingredient for several of the recipes in this book. If you or your guests like spicy foods, add minced jalapeño peppers to the skillet. This recipe can also be used as a dip accompanied by oven-baked tortilla chips.

1. Prepare a nonstick skillet by lightly coating surface with vegetable cooking spray or by using an oiled pastry brush. Sauté the onion and garlic until tender. Add chili powder, cumin, aminos, and cayenne and cook 1 or 2 minutes longer.
2. Add beans to pan and mash with potato masher. If necessary add liquid aminos and additional liquid.
3. Refrigerate until ready to serve.

Makes 2 cups

A CURE FOR ONION TEARS?

- *Burn a candle next to the chopping block.*
- *Hold a wooden match in your teeth.*
- *Keep the cut end of the onion away from you.*
- *Leave the root attached to the onion.*

63	Calories
4 g	Protein
12 g	Carbohydrates
1 g	Fat
4%	Calories from Fat
2 g	Fiber
17 mg	Sodium
0 mg	Cholesterol

Fruitopia

꿍 ꙩ

1 quart strawberries, stems removed and halved
1 bunch seedless grapes
1 fresh pineapple, cored, sliced and cut into bite-size pieces
2 kiwi fruits, peeled and sliced
1 mango, peeled and cut into bite-size pieces (if not in season, substitute 2 peaches)
1 cup walnut pieces
2 cups white wine or orange juice
1/2 cup crème de cassis (optional)

Pineapple contains bromelain, a protein digesting enzyme, which enhances digestion of all protein foods.

꿍 ꙩ

All nuts should be refrigerated to prevent them from becoming rancid.

꿍 ꙩ

In ancient Persia the walnut was so rare and highly valued it was used as currency.

1. Place fruit into a large serving bowl (a trifle dish looks lovely). Combine walnuts, wine, and crème de cassis and pour over fruit. Toss lightly.
2. Refrigerate for at least 1 hour before serving.

Makes 14 servings

151 Calories
2 g Protein
24 g Carbohydrates
5 g Fat
31% Calories from Fat
4 g Fiber
5 mg Sodium
0 mg Cholesterol

Guacamole Dip

1 large soft avocado (11 to 12 ounces), peeled
1 clove garlic, pressed or minced
2 teaspoons fresh lemon juice
1 can (4 ounces) green chiles, drained and minced
1 teaspoon low-sodium tamari sauce
1 tablespoon minced onion
   Pinch of cayenne

The avocado found its way to America from Persia. We now have over 400 varieties available. Avocados contain 14 minerals, natural sodium, and potassium. They are alkaline and contain no starch and very little sugar. Because of their high fat content, be careful if you are on a weight loss program.

1. In a small bowl mash the avocado with a fork. Add remaining ingredients and mix to blend.
2. Refrigerate until serving time. Serve with baked tortilla chips or corn chips.

Makes 1 ½ cups

Submerge the avocado pit into the dip to prevent the dip from darkening.

34	Calories
1 g	Protein
2 g	Carbohydrates
3 g	Fat
81%	Calories from Fat
1 g	Fiber
29 mg	Sodium
0 mg	Cholesterol

The First Book of Vegetarian Cooking

Hummus

1 cup cooked chickpeas
  (garbanzos)
¼ cup tahini
2 tablespoons chopped
  fresh parsley
1 clove garlic, pressed or
  minced
1 tablespoon fresh lemon
  juice
1 teaspoon liquid aminos

Serve with pieces of pita bread or vegetable sticks. Look for fat-free whole wheat pita bread at health food stores or Middle Eastern markets.

1. Purée all ingredients in a food processor or blender. If mixture is too thick, add a little bean liquid or distilled water as needed for desired consistency. Dip should be thick.
2. Refrigerate until serving time.

Makes about 1 ¼ cups

NIGHTSHADE FAMILY VEGETABLES

These vegetables are named after one member of their vast family, belladonna (deadly nightshade). The food plants of that family are what interest us. They are:

Tomatoes	*Eggplant*	*Potatoes*
Cayenne	*Chile peppers*	*Paprika*
Bell peppers	*Hot peppers*	*Pimento*
(Green, red, yellow	*(long, red and*	
and cherry)	*red cluster)*	

The nightshade family is high in alkaloids, which for certain people seem to remove calcium from bones and deposit it in the joints, kidneys, arteries, and other areas of the body where they don't want it.

Eating nightshade vegetables seems to aggravate arthritic pain in these people and eliminating these foods from their diets often makes aches and pains vanish completely!

32	Calories
1 g	Protein
3 g	Carbohydrates
2 g	Fat
51%	Calories from Fat
1 g	Fiber
15 mg	Sodium
0 mg	Cholesterol

Melonballs

1   large cantaloupe, halved and seeded
1   large honeydew melon, halved and seeded
1   package (6 ounces) vegetarian ham slices
     Bibb lettuce leaves

Most health food stores have a varied selection of vegetarian deli slices that taste very much like meat. These "ham-"wrapped melon balls are served in a fruit shell serving bowl.

1. With a melon-baller scoop pulp from melon halves. Reserve melon halves for serving bowls.
2. Cut ham into $1/2$-inch strips and wrap around the melon balls. Secure with a decorative toothpick.
3. For the serving bowl; make triangular notches around the reserved melon half. Arrange lettuce leaves inside the bowl and fill with wrapped melon.
4. Chill until ready to serve.

Vitamin-rich fruits have been associated with protection against cancer of the esophagus. Cantaloupe is rich in both vitamins A and C as well as potassium; one-half provides 825 milligrams potassium.

100	Calories
8 g	Protein
18 g	Carbohydrates
0 g	Fat
3%	Calories from Fat
2 g	Fiber
185 mg	Sodium
0 mg	Cholesterol

Moroccan Eggplant

1   large eggplant, peeled and cubed
1   medium zucchini, diced
2   cloves garlic, pressed or minced
1   large onion, chopped
1   can (14 ounces) Italian-style chopped tomatoes, do not drain
¼   cup sliced pimiento-stuffed olives
1   tablespoon capers
1   tablespoon red wine vinegar
1   teaspoon salt substitute
2   tablespoons chopped fresh cilantro leaves
¼   teaspoon dried basil leaves
   Pinch of cayenne
1   eggplant, halved with pulp removed, leaving ½ inch of shell (reserve shells for use as serving containers)
   Pita bread pieces or French bread slices

This recipe is one of my favorites when I'm called upon to bring an appetizer to a party. People always ask for the recipe. For a really impressive presentation, serve in hollowed eggplant halves.

1. Prepare a nonstick skillet by lightly coating surface with vegetable cooking spray or by using an oiled pastry brush. Cut the eggplant pulp into one-inch cubes and sauté until soft, about 3 to 4 minutes.
2. Add the remaining ingredients (except eggplant shell and pita pieces) to the eggplant and cook over medium heat until vegetables are soft and most of the liquid is absorbed, about 20 minutes. Stir occasionally.
3. Spoon into serving dish or eggplant halves. Surround with pita or French bread for scooping.

Makes about 4 cups

Brush lemon juice over inside of eggplant shells to prevent discoloration.

12	Calories
0 g	Protein
2 g	Carbohydrates
1 g	Fat
31%	Calories from Fat
0 g	Fiber
51 mg	Sodium
0 mg	Cholesterol

The Chinese have long used eggplant in treating diseases of the stomach, spleen, and large intestines. Eggplant adheres to cholesterol in the intestines, preventing it from being absorbed into the bloodstream, thereby helping to reduce cholesterol levels.

Mushroom Nut Pâté

೧೪ ೪ఌ

1   large onion, minced
5   cloves garlic, pressed or
       minced
1   pound fresh mush-
       rooms, chopped
¼   cup dry white wine
½   cup roasted and ground
       hazelnuts (30 nuts)
½   cup whole wheat bread
       crumbs
½   tablespoon liquid
       aminos
½   teaspoon salt
       substitute
¼   teaspoon dried thyme
¼   teaspoon dried sage
¼   teaspoon black pepper

Preheat oven to 350 degrees F.

Contrary to what has been written, mushrooms are not all grown in a sterile medium, therefore they should briefly be washed in Veggie Bath (see "Glossary"). Soaking mushrooms makes them soggy and ruins their texture.

1. Prepare a nonstick skillet by lightly coating surface with vegetable cooking spray or by using an oiled pastry brush. Sauté onion and garlic until soft; add mushrooms and wine. Cook over medium-high heat, stirring frequently, until liquid is almost evaporated. Stir in remaining ingredients. Allow mixture to cool.
2. Transfer to blender or food processor. Blend until smooth.
3. Pack pâté into a 2-cup pâté or casserole baking dish that has been sprayed with vegetable spray.
4. Bake 30 minutes or until top is set. Cool on wire rack. Refrigerate.

Makes 1 ½ cups

24	Calories
1 g	Protein
2 g	Carbohydrates
1 g	Fat
54%	Calories from Fat
1 g	Fiber
20 mg	Sodium
0 mg	Cholesterol

Onion Dip I

1   container (12 ounces)
      Sour Supreme
      (nondairy sour cream)
      or
1 ½ cups Dairyless Sour
      Cream (page 361)
1   package (1 ¾ ounces)
      Mayacama's French
      Onion Soup Mix or
      Spice Hunter's Five
      Onion and Herb
      Dip Mix

Combine both ingredients and refrigerate at least one hour.

Makes about 1 ½ cups

36	Calories
1 g	Protein
2 g	Carbohydrates
3 g	Fat
72%	Calories from Fat
1 g	Fiber
85 mg	Sodium
0 mg	Cholesterol

Onion Dip II

1/4 cup dehydrated
    chopped onions
2 tablespoons liquid
    aminos
1 package (10.5 ounces)
    extra-firm, lite silken
    tofu, drained
2 tablespoons lemon juice
2 teaspoons tahini
1/4 teaspoon salt substitute
1/2 teaspoon garlic powder
1/2 teaspoon onion powder
1 teaspoon Vogue Instant
    Vege Base
1 teaspoon honey
1 teaspoon dried parsley
    flakes

Here's another version that takes a little longer to make but saves some fat calories.

1. In a saucer, soak the onions with the liquid aminos for about 15 minutes.
2. In a blender or food processor, purée the tofu until smooth and creamy. Add the lemon juice, tahini, and salt substitute. Process to blend.
3. Transfer tofu mixture to a bowl and add remaining ingredients. Stir well.
4. Refrigerate for several hours. Stir before serving.

Makes about 1 1/2 cups

13	Calories
1 g	Protein
1 g	Carbohydrates
1 g	Fat
27%	Calories from Fat
0 g	Fiber
62 mg	Sodium
0 mg	Cholesterol

The First Book of Vegetarian Cooking

Stuffed Celery

1 container (8 ounces) dairy-free cream cheese
2 tablespoons onion, minced
¼ teaspoon garlic powder
½ cup chopped brazil nuts
Dash of Tabasco
Salt substitute
1 package celery stalks

1. Combine cream cheese, onion, garlic powder, nuts, Tabasco, and salt substitute to taste. Fill celery stalks.
2. Refrigerate 1 hour before serving.

Makes 1 ½ cups filling

50	Calories
1 g	Protein
1 g	Carbohydrates
5 g	Fat
90%	Calories from Fat
1 g	Fiber
29 mg	Sodium
0 mg	Cholesterol

Peanut Butter Dip

~~~ ✥ ✥ ~~~

3   small jalapeño peppers*,
      seeded and chopped
3   cloves garlic, pressed or
      minced
1   teaspoon liquid aminos
1   cup reduced-fat natural
      peanut butter
1   cup distilled water

If you like peanut butter you'll love this dip.

1. Purée all ingredients in food processor until smooth and creamy. Add more water if needed.
2. Refrigerate and serve with vegetables.

Makes about 2 cups

✥ ✥

Pour off visible oil
from nut butters.

✥ ✥

Chile peppers are rich in the anticancer, antioxidant carotenoids including beta-carotene.

---

*Wear rubber gloves when handling hot peppers.

49	Calories
2 g	Protein
2 g	Carbohydrates
4 g	Fat
73%	Calories from Fat
1 g	Fiber
9 mg	Sodium
0 mg	Cholesterol

The First Book of Vegetarian Cooking

Samosas

2   tablespoons low-sodium
        tamari
½   cup minced onion
2   cloves garlic, pressed or
        minced
1   teaspoon fresh minced
        ginger
1   jalapeño pepper*,
        seeded and minced
1   teaspoon curry powder
½   teaspoon cumin
        Pinch of cayenne
1   teaspoon lemon juice
3   medium potatoes
        (1 pound), cooked
        and mashed
⅓   cup frozen peas, thawed
1   package (2 dozen)
        wonton wrappers,
        cut into 48 (3 × 3-
        inch) pieces

Preheat oven to 350 degrees F.

In India, these pyramid-shaped snacks are sold from street pushcarts and roadside vendors.

1. In a nonstick skillet add 2 tablespoons water with 2 tablespoons tamari. Bring to a simmer and add onion, garlic, ginger, jalapeño pepper, curry powder, cumin, cayenne, and lemon juice and cook over medium-low heat until tender. Add additional water if too dry. Stir in potatoes and peas. Mix well.
2. Into each wonton square place a teaspoonful of filling. Moisten edges with water and fold over to form triangles. Pinch edges together with fork tines. Place samosas on cookie sheet and bake for 12 to 14 minutes or until golden. Serve with Green Sauce (recipe follows).

Makes 40 samosas

*Wear rubber gloves when handling hot peppers.

29	Calories
1 g	Protein
6 g	Carbohydrates
1 g	Fat
1%	Calories from Fat
0 g	Fiber
10 mg	Sodium
0 mg	Cholesterol

Green Sauce

2   cloves garlic, pressed or minced
2   teaspoons minced ginger
2   cans (4 ounces each) green chiles

They say if a person is angry when planting chili peppers, the peppers will mature into very hot peppers, but if he is happy they will be mild. I guess this explains why a chili varies so in the degree of hotness.

Purée all ingredients in food processor or blender.

Makes 1 cup

In India, the highly successful Ayurvedic system of medicine recommends eating ginger in the treatment of arthritis as well as many other aliments. Dutch doctors have found it beneficial in treating arthritic pain because ginger has the ability to increase blood circulation, carrying inflammatory substances from the affected area.

If you want to remove some of the hotness from dried or fresh chili peppers, remove seeds and membranes and soak in water with vinegar for 30 minutes.

1	Calorie
0 g	Protein
0 g	Carbohydrates
1 g	Fat
4%	Calories from Fat
0 g	Fiber
3 mg	Sodium
0 mg	Cholesterol

The First Book of Vegetarian Cooking

Seven–Layer Dip

1 ½ cups "refried" beans *or*
    one can (16 ounces)
    fat-free refried beans
1   large ripe avocado,
    peeled, seeded, and
    cubed
1   tablespoon lemon juice
2   cups chopped romaine
    lettuce
1   can (4 ounces) green
    chiles, chopped and
    drained
1   can (4 ¼ ounces)
    chopped black olives,
    drained
2   cups salsa, drained
1   cup shredded fat-free
    Cheddar soy cheese

One of my absolute favorites. I like hot foods so I sprinkle cayenne pepper between layers. Serve surrounded by baked tortilla chips.

1. Spread refried beans on a platter forming a 10-inch circle.
2. Mash avocado with lemon juice until smooth. Spoon onto the beans, spreading out to cover first layer.
3. Add layers of chopped lettuce, green chiles, black olives, and salsa. Top with shredded cheese.
4. Cover and chill for several hours.

Makes 5 cups

46	Calories
2 g	Protein
7 g	Carbohydrates
2 g	Fat
33%	Calories from Fat
1 g	Fiber
224 mg	Sodium
0 mg	Cholesterol

Taco Bites

1 large package round
    (2-inch) tortilla chips
2 cups refried beans or
    1 can (16 ounces)
    fat-free refried beans
½ teaspoon cumin
1 teaspoon chili powder
¼ teaspoon onion powder
¼ teaspoon garlic powder
8 ounces shredded lite
    Cheddar soy cheese
1 cup salsa, drained
    Avocado slices for
        garnish

Preheat broiler.

What could be better? Individual taco finger food.

1. Arrange chips on cookie sheet. Combine beans with seasonings and spread on tortilla chips. Top with cheese.
2. Heat under broiler until cheese melts.
3. Top with salsa and avocado slices.

Makes 30 to 40

Fiber is to your intestines and digestive tract as a toothbrush is to your teeth. Experts say 20 to 30 grams of dietary fiber a day may reduce the risk of developing some cancers.

106	Calories
5 g	Protein
15 g	Carbohydrates
3 g	Fat
28%	Calories from Fat
2 g	Fiber
328 mg	Sodium
0 mg	Cholesterol

Barbecue Cups

1 package (5.3 ounces) Original Burger 'n' Loaf
1 cup naturally sweetened barbecue sauce
2 tablespoons dehydrated minced onions
3 tablespoons date sugar
24 slices whole grain bread (soft style), crusts removed
¾ cup shredded fat-free Cheddar soy cheese

Preheat oven to 400 degrees F.

Replace bread with whole grain flaky biscuit dough, pressing the dough up the sides of the muffin tins.

I always have a platter or two of these tasty appetizers on my buffet table. I remember one such evening, we had a newly arrived family from China among our guests. In halting English, the mother apologized and explained that her son didn't care for American food and I should not take this personally. Later in the evening I spotted our little Chinese guest devouring a plate full of, you guessed it, Barbecue Cups.

1. Prepare burger according to package directions, omitting the oil.
2. Prepare a nonstick skillet by lightly coating surface with vegetable cooking spray or by using an oiled pastry brush. Brown the burger, stirring, breaking it up with a large wooden spoon.
3. To the skillet add barbecue sauce, onions, and sugar. Stir to combine and cook for 1 minute. Remove from heat.
4. In two 12-cup oiled or sprayed muffin tins, press bread into each cup making a container for the barbecue.
5. Spoon filling into the cups and top with cheese.
6. Bake 10 to 12 minutes or until cheese is melted.

Makes 2 dozen

116	Calories
6 g	Protein
22 g	Carbohydrates
2 g	Fat
14%	Calories from Fat
3 g	Fiber
272 mg	Sodium
0 mg	Cholesterol

Soys in a Shawl or No Pigs in These Blankets

~ ~

1   package (9 pack) Yves Veggie Tofu Wieners

1   package (16 ounces) phyllo pastry, whole wheat (if available), defrosted according to package directions

1/4   cup dark and grainy mustard

Preheat oven to 375 degrees F.

~ ~

Before cutting hot dog into 1 1/2 -inch pieces, make a slit lengthwise and stuff with lite soy cheese.

~ ~

Another finger food that will fool your meat-eating guests.

1. Cut each wiener into three 1 1/2-inch pieces.
2. Unfold defrosted phyllo dough (14 × 18-inch pile) and cut through layers making three 1 × 14-inch strips. Wrap unused portion and return to freezer.
3. Cut the three phyllo strips in half, making 6 stacks of 1 × 7-inch piles. Keep piles covered with a damp dish towel to prevent drying out.
4. From one of the piles take three layers of phyllo dough and place on a sheet of wax paper and spray with vegetable spray. Turn over and brush unsprayed side with mustard. Place wiener at base of sheet and roll up jelly-roll fashion. Moisten edges with water and press to seal.
5. Repeat using remaining wieners. Place rolls on baking sheet and bake for 15 minutes, turning over after 10 minutes.

Makes 27

43	Calories
5 g	Protein
4 g	Carbohydrates
1 g	Fat
18%	Calories from Fat
0 g	Fiber
138 mg	Sodium
0 mg	Cholesterol

The First Book of Vegetarian Cooking

"Cream Cheese" and Black Beans

1   cup dairy-free cream
       cheese
1   cup cooked black beans,
       drained and mashed
½   teaspoon oregano
½   teaspoon chili powder
1   tablespoon dehydrated
       chopped onion
1   teaspoon liquid aminos
1   tablespoon vegetarian
       Worcestershire sauce

This is a luscious spread enjoyed by all. Serve with pita bread, veggies, tortilla or pita chips.

1. Combine all ingredients, blending well and refrigerate for at least 1 hour.

Makes 2 cups

47   Calories
4 g   Protein
3 g   Carbohydrates
2 g   Fat
46%   Calories from Fat
0 g   Fiber
105 mg   Sodium
0 mg   Cholesterol

Stuffed "Bacon"

2 dozen pitted dates
1 dozen slices vegetarian
   bacon (Stripples),
   cut in half
   Non-aerosol vegetable
   spray

Preheat oven to 400 degrees F.

Don't let this combination fool you, these are really most unusual and delicious.

1. Wrap each date with half of a bacon strip and secure with a toothpick. Spray with non-aerosol vegetable spray.
2. Place on a sprayed cookie sheet and bake for five minutes or until bacon is browned and crisp.

Makes 2 dozen

34	Calories
1 g	Protein
6 g	Carbohydrates
1 g	Fat
37%	Calories from Fat
1 g	Fiber
59 mg	Sodium
0 mg	Cholesterol

The First Book of Vegetarian Cooking

Black Bean Hummus

2 cups cooked black beans, drained or 1 can (15 ounces), drained (reserve liquid)
¼ cup tahini
1 tablespoon low-sodium tamari
1 tablespoon balsamic vinegar
1 clove garlic, pressed or minced
½ teaspoon ground cumin
Pinch of cayenne

Another quick and easy dip. Serve with pita bread or vegetables.

1. Place all ingredients in food processor and blend until smooth, adding a tablespoon or two of the reserved bean liquid or water if needed. The consistency should not be soupy.
2. Refrigerate until ready to serve.

Makes about 1 ½ cups

Use leftover bean liquid in soup to add extra flavor and nutrition.

38	Calories
2 g	Protein
4 g	Carbohydrates
1 g	Fat
34%	Calories from Fat
1 g	Fiber
119 mg	Sodium
0 mg	Cholesterol

Stuffed Mushrooms

❧ ❧

½ pound (about 10)
    medium mushrooms,
    stems removed
1 teaspoon liquid aminos
1 clove garlic, pressed or
    minced
3 tablespoons shredded
    lite Cheddar soy
    cheese
2 tablespoons dry white
    wine
⅓ cup cracker crumbs

Preheat broiler.

❧ ❧

For stuffed tomatoes,
substitute cherry tomatoes
for mushrooms.
❧ ❧

An old reliable finger food with a meatless twist.

1. Brush tops of mushrooms with liquid aminos. Set aside.
2. Chop mushroom stems and combine with remaining ingredients. Mound filling into mushroom cavities, pressing in lightly.
3. Place mushrooms on cookie sheet and broil 6-inches below broiler element until brown and bubbly.

Makes 10 mushrooms

26	Calories
1 g	Protein
4 g	Carbohydrates
1 g	Fat
14%	Calories from Fat
0 g	Fiber
93 mg	Sodium
1 mg	Cholesterol

The First Book of Vegetarian Cooking

Texas Caviar

❧ ❧

1   cup cooked black-eyed
      peas or 1 can
      (15 ounces), drained
1   cup chopped onion
1   cup chopped bell pepper
½   cup chopped scallions
1   jar (4 ounces) pimentos,
      minced
3   cloves garlic, pressed or
      minced
1   tablespoon minced
      jalapeño pepper*
¼   cup fat-free Italian
      dressing
1   tablespoon liquid
      aminos

❧ ❧

In place of black-eyed peas
you can substitute kidney,
pinto, or black beans.
❧ ❧

Serve with baked tortilla chips, pita chips, or wedges of pocket bread.

Combine all ingredients in a glass bowl. Cover and marinate overnight in the refrigerator.

Makes 4 cups

*I keep a pair of disposable surgical gloves in my kitchen to wear when handling hot peppers.

14 Calories
1 g Protein
3 g Carbohydrates
1 g Fat
4% Calories from Fat
1 g Fiber
41 mg Sodium
0 mg Cholesterol

Sweet and Sour "Meatballs"

1	recipe Neatballs (page 10)
1	cup distilled water
½	cup dried unsulphured apricots, chopped
¼	cup honey
¼	cup apple cider vinegar
2	teaspoons lemon juice
½	teaspoon ground ginger

When I prepare Neatballs, I make an extra batch for the freezer shaped into patties. I love burgers and this way they are always convenient. Make sure to place wax paper between layers.

A new twist on an old-time favorite. These are made with beta-carotene-rich apricots and are naturally cholesterol-free because only animal products contain cholesterol.

1. Prepare the Neatballs and set aside.
2. In a saucepan combine the remaining ingredients. Simmer for 5 minutes. Cool slightly and pour into blender or food processor. Process until smooth. Return to saucepan.
3. Add Neatballs to sauce and toss to coat. Simmer until heated through, about 5 minutes.

Makes 1 cup sauce for 16 to 18 Neatballs

60	Calories
5 g	Protein
10 g	Carbohydrates
1 g	Fat
16%	Calories from Fat
2 g	Fiber
97 mg	Sodium
0 mg	Cholesterol

The First Book of Vegetarian Cooking

Sweet Pea Dip

2   cups frozen sweet peas,
        cooked and drained
$1/4$ cup chopped onion
$1\,1/2$ tablespoons fresh lime
        juice
$1/2$ teaspoon chili powder
$1\,1/2$ teaspoons liquid aminos
2   large cloves garlic,
        pressed
$1/8$ teaspoon cayenne

If the kids or hubby won't eat their peas; serve this dip with baked tortilla chips and no one will be the wiser.

1. Combine all the ingredients in food processor or blender until smooth.
2. Chill in refrigerator for 2 hours to allow flavors to mingle.

Makes 2 cups

The pea, alkaline in nature, is a good source of vitamins A, B, and C. Peas have been used successfully, puréed, to give relief to ulcer pains because they consume stomach acids.

19	Calories
1 g	Protein
4 g	Carbohydrates
0 g	Fat
4%	Calories from Fat
1 g	Fiber
40 mg	Sodium
0 mg	Cholesterol

Tex–Mex Wontons

❧ ❧

1 cup chopped onion
1/2 cup minced bell pepper
2 cloves garlic, pressed or minced
2 teaspoons chili powder
1/2 teaspoon ground cumin
1 1/2 cups refried beans *or* 1 can (16 ounces) fat-free
1 tablespoon fruit-sweetened ketchup
Pinch of cayenne
1 package (2 dozen) wonton wrappers, cut into 48 (3 × 3-inch) pieces

Preheat oven to 350 degrees F.

These little morsels are delicious. Serve warm with salsa for dipping.

1. Prepare a nonstick skillet by lightly coating surface with vegetable cooking spray or by using an oiled pastry brush. Sauté onion, bell pepper, and garlic until soft. Stir in chili powder and cumin and cook for an additional 2 minutes. Add beans, ketchup, and cayenne.

2. Position wonton wrapper with the point facing you. Place 1 teaspoon of filling into center of wonton. Fold up bottom point and tuck under filling. Fold sides over, tucking under point forming envelope. Roll up toward remaining corner. Moisten point with water and press to seal. Repeat using remaining wontons and filling. Spray with non-aerosol vegetable spray.

3. Bake on cookie sheet, seam-side down, until golden, 15 to 20 minutes. Turn over after 10 minutes.

Makes 48 pieces

41	Calories
2 g	Protein
9 g	Carbohydrates
1 g	Fat
5%	Calories from Fat
1 g	Fiber
60 mg	Sodium
5 mg	Cholesterol

The First Book of Vegetarian Cooking

Chile con Queso

1   package (12 ounces)
Cheddar Soya Kaas,
cubed (for more
spice use jalapeño
style)
1   can (4 ounces) green
chiles, drained and
minced
1   medium tomato, diced
and drained (reserve
juice)
2   green onions, sliced
¼   teaspoon garlic powder
¼   teaspoon onion powder

Serve this dip in a chafing dish or fondue pot accompanied by baked tortilla chips.

1. Combine all ingredients in medium saucepan and cook until cheese melts and ingredients are blended.
2. Thin to desired consistency with the reserved tomato juice, mixing in a little at a time.

Makes 2 cups

31	Calories
2 g	Protein
1 g	Carbohydrates
2 g	Fat
59%	Calories from Fat
0 g	Fiber
96 mg	Sodium
0 mg	Cholesterol

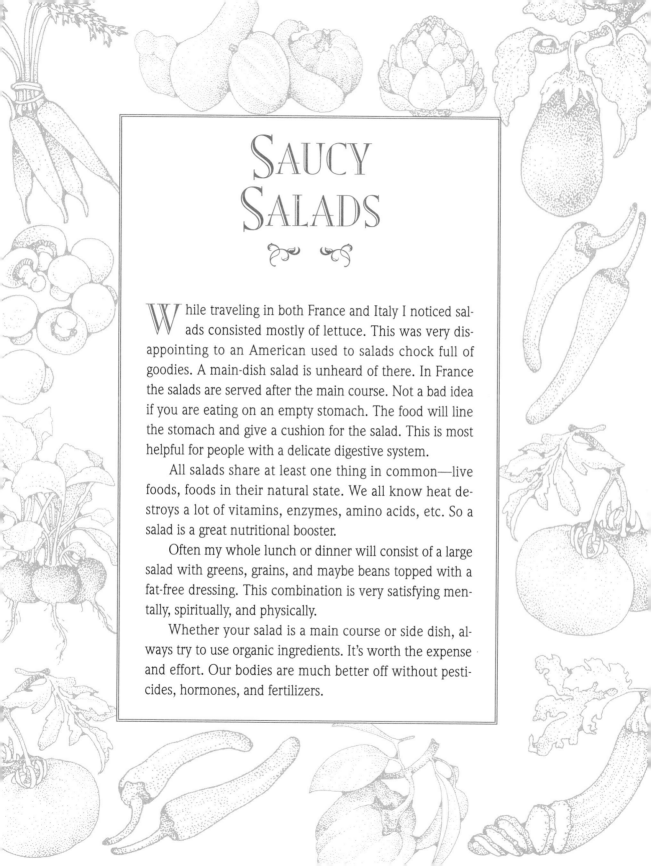

Saucy
Salads

While traveling in both France and Italy I noticed salads consisted mostly of lettuce. This was very disappointing to an American used to salads chock full of goodies. A main-dish salad is unheard of there. In France the salads are served after the main course. Not a bad idea if you are eating on an empty stomach. The food will line the stomach and give a cushion for the salad. This is most helpful for people with a delicate digestive system.

All salads share at least one thing in common—live foods, foods in their natural state. We all know heat destroys a lot of vitamins, enzymes, amino acids, etc. So a salad is a great nutritional booster.

Often my whole lunch or dinner will consist of a large salad with greens, grains, and maybe beans topped with a fat-free dressing. This combination is very satisfying mentally, spiritually, and physically.

Whether your salad is a main course or side dish, always try to use organic ingredients. It's worth the expense and effort. Our bodies are much better off without pesticides, hormones, and fertilizers.

Recipes

Bean Sprout Salad

Caesar Salad

Waldorf Salad

Carrot Salad

Tostada Salad

"Chicken" Salad Spread

Thai Salad with
   Peanut Sauce

Coleslaw

Tomato Salad on
   Garlic Toast

Confetti Slaw

Tabbouleh

Corn Salad

Eggplant Salad

Couscous Salad

"Egg" Salad

Melon Delight

Fruit Salad

Jicama Salad

Marinated Bananas
   and Papaya

Quinoa Salad

Sweet and Sour
   Spinach Salad

Potato Salad

Sweet Potato Salad

Thai Rice Salad

Bulgur Salad

"Tuna" Salad

Bean Sprout Salad

1	pound bean sprouts
1/2	cup pure apple cider vinegar
1/4	cup honey
1	tablespoon low-sodium tamari
1/8	teaspoon powdered barley malt sweetener (Dr. Bronner's)

For variation many other live (uncooked) foods can be added: onions, scallions, bell peppers, string beans, water chestnuts, etc.

I first tasted this salad while staying for a couple of months in Germany. I found eating out and being a vegetarian very difficult there, so I was delighted when I found a Chinese restaurant where they served this wonderful salad.

1. Place sprouts into a glass serving bowl.
2. In a small bowl, whisk vinegar, honey, sweetener, and tamari. Pour dressing over sprouts and toss to coat.
3. Cover and refrigerate for 3 to 4 hours. Drain and serve.

Makes 2 cups

53	Calories
4 g	Protein
12 g	Carbohydrates
1 g	Fat
4%	Calories from Fat
1 g	Fiber
49 mg	Sodium
0 mg	Cholesterol

Caesar Salad

❧ ❦

Dressing

1   clove garlic, pressed
¼   cup fat-free mayonnaise
¼   cup fat-free Italian
      dressing
      Freshly cracked pepper

Salad

1   head romaine lettuce,
      broken into bite-size
      pieces
2   tablespoon soy grated
      Parmesan cheese
2   tablespoon vegetarian
      bacon bits*
⅓   cup croutons

❧ ❦

If you are out of croutons, toast whole grain bread and cut into cubes. In a pinch use cubed stuffing mix.

❧ ❦

I receive raves on this salad from nonvegetarians as well as vegetarians. The ingredients should be well chilled.

1. Whisk dressing ingredients together and toss with romaine. The leaves should be just coated.
2. Add cheese, bacon bits, and croutons. Toss again.

Makes 4 servings

Think your body well.

    —ANONYMOUS

*Check labels to make sure there are no artificial dyes or additives.

82	Calories
5 g	Protein
14 g	Carbohydrates
2 g	Fat
18%	Calories from Fat
2 g	Fiber
549 mg	Sodium
0 mg	Cholesterol

The First Book of Vegetarian Cooking

Waldorf Salad

3   Red Delicious apples,
     cored and coarsely
     chopped
     Distilled water
     Juice of 1 lemon
½   cup seedless grapes,
     halved
½   cup chopped celery
½   cup chopped walnuts
½   cup chopped apricots
     (unsulfured)
¼   cup dairy-free, fat-free
     mayonnaise
     Eden Shake for garnish
     (optional)

I brought a large bowl of this salad to a Thanksgiving dinner party. It was a resounding hit.

1. Prepare a lemon-water bath by covering apples with water and adding the lemon juice. Set aside while chopping celery, walnuts, and apricots. Drain apples and rinse.
2. Combine ingredients tossing to coat. Garnish.

Makes 6 servings

A good cook is like a sorceress who dispenses happiness.

—ELSA SCHIAPARELLI

156	Calories
2 g	Protein
25 g	Carbohydrates
7 g	Fat
38%	Calories from Fat
3 g	Fiber
139 mg	Sodium
0 mg	Cholesterol

Carrot Salad

1/4 cup raisins
1 cup boiling distilled
   water
4 carrots (12 ounces),
   shredded
1/8 teaspoon powdered
   barley malt sweet-
   ener (Dr. Bronner's)
1/4 cup dairy-free, fat-free
   mayonnaise
1 can (8 ounces) crushed
   pineapple in its own
   juice, drained well
Pinch of cinnamon

A new twist to an old favorite.

1. Place raisins in boiling water. Set aside.
2. In a medium bowl place carrots and sweetener; toss to mix.
3. Rinse raisins with cold water and drain well; fold into carrot mixture.
4. Stir in mayonnaise, pineapple, and cinnamon.

Makes 4 servings

Clean the air we live in. Our homes can be filled with formaldehyde and many other undesirable chemicals that can effect our health. Plants are wonderful air cleansers. According to recent tests, the best plants for cleaning air are: Peace lily, Lady palm, Areca palm, and the Ficus plant. The study recommends 2 to 3 good-size plants per 100-square-foot room.

105	Calories
1 g	Protein
29 g	Carbohydrates
1 g	Fat
2%	Calories from Fat
3 g	Fiber
222 mg	Sodium
0 mg	Cholesterol

Tostada Salad

2   large fat-free whole
      wheat tortillas
8   ounces fat-free refried
      beans
¼   cup chopped onion
2   cups shredded romaine
      lettuce
1   tomato, diced
      Salsa for garnish

Preheat oven to 400 degrees F.

I love having this salad when eating out. This recipe will save some fat calories over the restaurant version.

1. Place tortillas over small ovenproof bowls that have been sprayed with vegetable oil.
2. Bake tortillas in oven for about 10 minutes or until they are crisp and hold their shape.
3. Heat beans and spread over bottom of tortillas bowls. Top with onion, lettuce, tomato, and salsa.

Makes 2 servings

209	Calories
11 g	Protein
46 g	Carbohydrates
1 g	Fat
3%	Calories from Fat
17g	Fiber
760 mg	Sodium
0 mg	Cholesterol

"Chicken" Salad Spread

6   ounces Meat of Wheat, chicken style
1   cup chopped celery
2   tablespoons minced fresh parsley
3   scallions, minced
¼   cup chopped walnuts
½   teaspoon celery seed
⅓   cup fat-free, dairy-free mayonnaise
1   teaspoon vegetarian Worcestershire sauce

Use this recipe as you would use any chicken salad recipe. It is good as a veggie stuffing, mini sandwich, or accompanied by crackers, pita bread, or toast points.

1. Finely chop Meat of Wheat and mix in remaining ingredients.
2. Chill and serve.

Makes 2 cups

65	Calories
6 g	Protein
4 g	Carbohydrates
3 g	Fat
38%	Calories from Fat
1 g	Fiber
246 mg	Sodium
0 mg	Cholesterol

Thai Salad with Peanut Sauce

Peanut Sauce

¼	cup reduced-fat natural chunky peanut butter*
2	tablespoons lite rice milk
1	teaspoon reduced-sodium tamari sauce
2	tablespoons frozen orange juice concentrate
1	teaspoon fresh lime juice
1	teaspoon honey
2	scallions (1 tablespoon), thinly sliced
½	teaspoon freshly grated ginger
⅛	teaspoon cayenne
	Dash of coconut extract (scant ⅛ teaspoon)

Salad

1	head romaine lettuce, torn into bite-size pieces
2	tomatoes, cut into eighths
1	English cucumber, sliced

Whenever we go to our neighborhood Thai restaurant I always start with this delicious salad. You will have about half the peanut sauce leftover. Why not use it for Pad Thai (page 187)?

1. In a bowl, whisk peanut butter and milk. Add remaining sauce ingredients; mix well and refrigerate.
2. Arrange lettuce, tomato wedges, and cucumber on plates and top with peanut sauce.

Makes 4 servings

*Always pour off the oil floating on top of nut butters. You don't need the extra fat.

98	Calories
5 g	Protein
12 g	Carbohydrates
5 g	Fat
42%	Calories from Fat
4 g	Fiber
82 mg	Sodium
0 mg	Cholesterol

Coleslaw

1 cup dairyless sour cream
1 small head of cabbage
   (about 1 pound),
   shredded
2 carrots, shredded
¼ bell pepper, minced
¼ onion, minced
½ teaspoon powdered bar-
   ley malt sweetener
   (Dr. Bronner's)
¼ teaspoon salt substitute
3 tablespoons apple cider
   vinegar
   Eden Shake's Sesame
   and Sea vegetable
   seasoning for garnish

Coleslaw is always a popular dish. Health food stores carry dairyless sour cream, or try the recipe on page 361.

Combine all ingredients except seasoning, which should be sprinkled on top, and refrigerate.

Makes 5 cups

Cabbage as well as broccoli and cauliflower contains a phytochemical compound that boosts the production of anticancer enzymes enabling them to destroy cancer-causing substances.

67	Calories
1 g	Protein
7 g	Carbohydrates
5 g	Fat
62%	Calories from Fat
2 g	Fiber
36 mg	Sodium
0 mg	Cholesterol

Tomato Salad on Garlic Toast

2   medium tomatoes,
        chopped (2 cups)
1   large bell pepper,
        chopped (1 cup)
1   medium onion, chopped
        (1 cup)
2   tablespoons chopped
        fresh basil
2   cloves garlic, pressed
1   teaspoon dried oregano
        leaves
1   tablespoon balsamic
        vinegar
1   teaspoon liquid aminos
2   teaspoons fresh lemon
        juice
1   loaf whole grain French
        bread, cut into
        ¼-inch slices
1   clove garlic, halved

Preheat broiler.

Serve this salad in small individual dishes with toasted French bread, spooning the salad onto the toast. Make this dish when tomatoes are vine-ripened and at their peak in flavor.

1. In a large mixing bowl, combine all the ingredients (excluding bread and halved garlic).
2. Cover and refrigerate for 1 hour.
3. Place bread slices on cookie sheet and toast under broiler until brown. Rub cut side of garlic over bread.
4. Serve toast and tomato salad in individual dishes or place in a large bowl surrounded by toast where guests can help themselves.

Makes 6 to 8 individual servings

186	Calories
6 g	Protein
34 g	Carbohydrates
2 g	Fat
9%	Calories from Fat
2 g	Fiber
360 mg	Sodium
0 mg	Cholesterol

Confetti Slaw

꩜ ꩜

1   daikon radish (12 ounces), shredded
1   garden beet (4 ounces), shredded
5   carrots (10 ounces), shredded
½   teaspoon ground fennel seeds
¼   teaspoon powdered barley malt sweetener (Dr. Bronner's)
    Fat-free Italian dressing (just enough to moisten)

This slaw is chock full of vitamins and nutrients. I keep a bowl in my refrigerator for snacking, adding dressing when serving. The beet has been grown since the third century B.C., when it was only used for medicinal purposes. The radish, a member of the mustard family, dates back to China and prehistoric times. Carrots come to us from Europe and are ancient also.

Combine all the ingredients and chill.

Makes 6 servings

꩜ ꩜

A piece of daikon radish is good for removing stains from silk. I keep a piece in my freezer.

꩜ ꩜

Do not throw away the beet greens. They contain more vitamins and minerals per gram than any other food according to nutritional testing. Carrots and beets are high in vitamin A, aiding eyesight. Radishes are a good diuretic and, along with beets, are beneficial in ailments of the gallbladder and liver.

59	Calories
1 g	Protein
15 g	Carbohydrates
2 g	Fat
3%	Calories from Fat
2 g	Fiber
192 mg	Sodium
0 mg	Cholesterol

Tabbouleh

1 ¼ cups vegetable broth *or*
    1 ¼ cups water
    mixed with 2 table-
    spoons Vogue Instant
    Vege Base
1 cup couscous, uncooked
1 large tomato, diced
6 scallions, sliced
¼ cup chopped fresh
    parsley
¼ cup chopped fresh mint
3 tablespoons fresh lemon
    juice (about 1 lemon)

Serve on romaine lettuce leaves.

1. Bring vegetable broth to a boil and add couscous. Cover and remove from heat. Uncover after 5 minutes and fluff with a fork. Cool.
2. Combine couscous with the remaining ingredients. Cover and chill for several hours.

Makes 4 ½ cups

Scallions, along with garlic and onions, contain a compound called al-lium which blocks carcinogens that have been linked to colon, stomach, lung, and liver cancers.

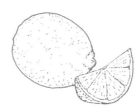

89	Calories
3 g	Protein
18 g	Carbohydrates
1 g	Fat
4%	Calories from Fat
1 g	Fiber
76 mg	Sodium
0 mg	Cholesterol

Corn Salad

꽃

8	cups of greens, torn into bite-size pieces
1	cup grated carrot (2 large)
1	European cucumber, sliced
1/2	cup sliced celery
1/2	cup diced green bell pepper
1/2	cup diced red bell pepper
1 1/2	cups cooked corn kernels
2	cups cooked black beans, drained *or* 1 can (15 ounces), drained
1/2	cup fat-free Italian dressing
1/4	cup minced fresh parsley
1/4	cup salsa
1/3	cup minced scallions Bunch of alfalfa sprouts

1. Layer ingredients in a large salad bowl in the following order: greens, carrots, cucumber, celery, peppers, corn, and beans.
2. Drizzle with non-fat Italian dressing and garnish with the parsley, salsa, scallions, and sprouts.

Makes 6 servings

176	Calories
9 g	Protein
36 g	Carbohydrates
1 g	Fat
6%	Calories from Fat
6 g	Fiber
385 mg	Sodium
0 mg	Cholesterol

꽃

Kidney or pinto beans can be substituted for black beans.

꽃

Eggplant Salad

1   tablespoon low-sodium tamari sauce
2   tablespoons balsamic vinegar
1   tablespoon honey
1   eggplant (about 1 pound), peeled
2   tablespoons fresh lemon juice
1   teaspoon extra-virgin olive oil
½   cup minced fresh mint leaves
½   cup minced fresh flat-leaf parsley
1   onion, chopped
1   green bell pepper, chopped
1   red bell pepper, chopped
1   large tomato, seeded and diced
2   cloves garlic, pressed or minced
1   head lettuce*
1   tablespoon grated Parmesan substitute for garnish

Centuries ago the eggplant was imported from India by Arab merchant caravans and to the United States by Thomas Jefferson. It has been used successfully for abdominal pains and lowering cholesterol.

1. Whisk tamari, vinegar, and honey together. Cut eggplant crosswise into ½-inch slices and brush vinegar mixture onto all sides. Reserve leftover liquid.
2. Prepare a nonstick skillet by lightly coating surface with vegetable cooking spray or by using an oiled pastry brush. Brown eggplant slices on both sides until tender. Cool and cut into ½-inch cubes.
3. Whisk, lemon juice, olive oil, and 2 tablespoon of the reserved vinegar mixture together.
4. In a large bowl, toss all the ingredients except the lettuce and cheese. Serve on lettuce leaves and sprinkle with the Parmesan substitute.

Makes 4 to 6 servings

*The greener the leaves the more vitamins, minerals, and antioxidants they contain. Iceberg lettuce contains the least of all the lettuces.

89	Calories
3 g	Protein
17 g	Carbohydrates
2 g	Fat
15%	Calories from Fat
3 g	Fiber
152 mg	Sodium
0 mg	Cholesterol

Couscous Salad

꙲ ꙮ

1 ½ plus ⅓ cups distilled water
1 teaspoon Vogue Instant Vege Base
1 cup couscous
¼ cup tahini*
2 tablespoons liquid aminos
1 tablespoon fresh lemon juice
½ cup thinly sliced scallions
2 stalks chopped celery (½ cup)
1 large shredded carrot (½ cup)
½ cup cooked peas
½ cup minced fresh parsley

1. Bring 1 ½ cups of the water to a boil; add Vogue Instant Vege Base and couscous. Remove from heat, stir, and cover for 5 minutes. Fluff couscous with fork; transfer to large bowl.
2. In a small bowl whisk tahini, liquid aminos, lemon juice, and ⅓ cup water until well blended and creamy. Pour over warm couscous and mix well.
3. Stir in scallions, celery, carrots, peas, and parsley, mixing well.
4. Cover and refrigerate. This can be served on a bed of greens or used as a stuffing for cherry tomatoes, etc.

Makes 6 to 8 servings

*Pour off visible oil from nut butters.

꙲ ꙮ

Be kind to our environment; recycle, recycle!! Next time you do your nails, instead of using purchased cotton balls why not use the cotton that comes packed in supplements. Every little bit helps.

꙲ ꙮ

154	Calories
6 g	Protein
24 g	Carbohydrates
4 g	Fat
25%	Calories from Fat
2 g	Fiber
210 mg	Sodium
0 mg	Cholesterol

"Egg" Salad

~ ~

1   package (10.5 ounces) firm lite silken tofu, wrapped in a clean kitchen towel for 30 minutes

2   stalks celery, chopped

3   scallions, chopped (include 1 inch of green stalk)

1   teaspoon apple cider vinegar

1   teaspoon honey

2   teaspoons dark and grainy mustard

2   tablespoons fat-free, dairy-free mayonnaise

$1/2$ teaspoon turmeric

1   tablespoon minced fresh parsley

$1/2$ teaspoon powdered dulse

$1/2$ teaspoon lemon juice

    Pinch of cayenne

A wonderful substitute for eggs that is cholesterol-free. Tofu is loaded with beneficial protein.

1. In a small bowl, crumble tofu with a fork. Mix in celery and scallions. Set aside.
2. In another bowl, mix vinegar and honey together. Stir in remaining ingredients. Add to tofu mixture and toss to coat.
3. Refrigerate 1 hour before serving.

Makes 1 $1/2$ cups

40	Calories
4 g	Protein
4 g	Carbohydrates
1 g	Fat
26%	Calories from Fat
0 g	Fiber
113 mg	Sodium
0 mg	Cholesterol

~ ~

Wrapping tofu helps to make a firmer texture.

~ ~

Melon Delight

2   cantaloupes, halved and
     seeded
1   bunch seedless red
     grapes, halved
3   tablespoons balsamic
     vinegar
    Eden Shake (a sesame
     seed blend) for
     garnish

A cantaloupe is ripe when it
has a sweet, delicate odor and
yields to gentle pressure on
the base.

My most memorable New Year's Eve was spent on a cruise up the Nile River. Close to midnight the waiters brought out a huge table of grapes and the band began to play. It seems that at the stroke of twelve you eat 12 grapes to bring good luck for the 12 months ahead. I don't know if this custom was for the Spanish tour aboard our ship or a local custom, all I know is I couldn't eat the grapes. We were warned not to eat anything that was not peeled.

1. Form the melons into balls with a melon-baller.
2. In a bowl, toss the halved grapes and the melon balls with the balsamic vinegar. Chill until serving time.
3. At serving time, spoon into eight chilled wine glasses and garnish with a pinch of Eden Shake.

Makes 8 servings

The cantaloupe, a sought-after delicacy of the ancient Romans, has been cultivated for thousands of years. Low in calories, it is an excellent aid in elimination and is rejuvenating to the body.

89	Calories
2 g	Protein
21 g	Carbohydrates
1 g	Fat
7%	Calories from Fat
1 g	Fiber
16 mg	Sodium
0 mg	Cholesterol

The First Book of Vegetarian Cooking

Fruit Salad

6   cups watermelon, seeded and cubed
2   cups julienned jicama
½   cup minced scallions
2   tablespoons grated fresh ginger
¼   cup rice wine
2   tablespoons balsamic white vinegar
    Couple dashes of Tabasco

Tabasco originated on Avery Island, Louisiana, the site of America's first salt mine. The sauce was named after the Tabasco River in Mexico because the founder, Edmund McIhenny, liked the sound of the name. All this might not have come to pass if it hadn't been for the Civil War, when Union troops captured the island. The salt mines were owned by Mrs. McIhenny's family and the union troops took over their salt mining business on the island because they needed the salt to preserve meat for their troops.

The family escaped to Texas, returning only after the war was over. On their return, they found the plantation and mansion in ruin. The only possession remaining was a crop of capsicum hot peppers. The rest they say, my friends, is history.

1. Lightly toss all ingredients to blend. Place in serving bowl and refrigerate.
2. Serve on lettuce-lined salad plates.

59	Calories
1 g	Protein
14 g	Carbohydrates
1 g	Fat
9%	Calories from Fat
1 g	Fiber
8 mg	Sodium
0 mg	Cholesterol

Jicama Salad

୧୬ ୧୬

½ jicama (8 ounces),
    peeled and cut into
    ¼ × 2-inch pieces
1 English cucumber, sliced
    into ⅛-inch slices
1 orange, peeled,
    sectioned, and
    cut in half
1½ teaspoons unsweetened
    coconut

Dressing
2 tablespoons fresh lime
    juice
½ teaspoon chili powder
2 teaspoons honey
⅛ teaspoon powdered
    barley malt sweet-
    ener (Dr. Bronner's)

Jicama (pronounced HEE-kah-mah) is sometimes called the Mexican potato. It is a favorite food with dieters because of its low caloric content and crunchy, nutty flavor. Cooked, it is similar to the water chestnut retaining its crisp texture.

1. In a medium bowl, combine jicama, cucumber, orange, and coconut.
2. Prepare dressing mixing ingredients together with fork; and pour over jicama mixture.
3. Cover and chill in refrigerator for 2 hours to let flavors mingle.

Makes 4 to 6 servings

PAPAYA

This powerhouse fruit is low in calories and high in vitamins A, C, and E, potassium, calcium, phosphorus, and iron. It contains the enzyme papain, a veritable tonic to the stomach. The papaya takes top honors for vitamins, minerals, and fiber content.

Don't overlook their life force, the seeds. Peppery in taste, they make a healthful and tasty addition to salad dressings when ground or try them pickled and use them as you would use capers.

If you live in a tropical climate, try growing this horticultural wonder. A single seed can grow to a 20 foot fruit-bearing tree in less than 18 months.

43	Calories
1 g	Protein
10 g	Carbohydrates
1 g	Fat
11%	Calories from Fat
1 g	Fiber
5 mg	Sodium
0 mg	Cholesterol

The First Book of Vegetarian Cooking

Marinated Bananas and Papaya

1 small honeydew melon
2 small papayas, halved and seeded (reserve seeds)
4 bananas, cut into ¼-inch diagonal slices

Dressing
½ teaspoon papaya seeds
2 teaspoons honey
2 tablespoons fresh lemon juice
¼ cup orange juice
½ teaspoon vanilla
¼ teaspoon ground cinnamon
2 tablespoons shredded unsweetened coconut for garnish

1. With the small scoop of a melon-baller, form balls out of the melon and papaya. Place in a bowl with the bananas.
2. In a blender or food processor, purée the papaya seeds, honey, lemon and orange juice, vanilla, and cinnamon. The papaya seeds should look like coarse black pepper. Pour over fruits and toss to coat.
3. Marinate in the refrigerator for at least an hour. At serving time garnish with coconut.

Makes 8 servings

If you are taking diuretics or high blood pressure medication, you can benefit from the high potassium content in bananas. If you take antacids, try reaching for a banana instead.

Bananas are ripe and digestible when there is no green visible and the skin is yellow with small brown flecks.

Papayas are ripe when green with overtones of yellow and orange and they yield to slight pressure. The stem end will smell sweet.

142	Calories
2 g	Protein
34 g	Carbohydrates
1 g	Fat
9%	Calories from Fat
2 g	Fiber
16 mg	Sodium
0 mg	Cholesterol

Quinoa Salad

1 cup quinoa
2 cups plus 1 tablespoon distilled water
2 cups chopped English cucumber
2 tomatoes, diced
½ cup minced fresh parsley
1 cup chopped celery
½ cup chopped carrots
½ cup thinly sliced scallions
2 cloves garlic, pressed or minced
½ cup lemon juice
1 tablespoon extra-virgin olive oil
1 teaspoon liquid aminos

On a recent trip to Peru we were fed quinoa every way imaginable (soup being their favorite) except as a salad. Quinoa (pronounced KEEN-wa) is the best source of vegetable protein and can be substituted in any rice recipe. This ancient grain has a nutty, mild taste when cooked but must always be rinsed well to avoid a bitter taste.

1. Place quinoa in a strainer and rinse well. Transfer to a medium saucepan and add 2 cups of the water. Bring to a boil, reduce heat, cover and simmer for 10 to 15 minutes or until the water is absorbed. Cool.
2. Place into a large bowl and add cucumber, tomatoes, parsley, celery, carrots, scallions, and garlic.
3. In a small bowl, whisk lemon juice, olive oil, 1 tablespoon water, and liquid aminos. Pour over salad and mix well.
4. Chill 1 hour before serving

Makes 6 to 8 servings

118	Calories
4 g	Protein
20 g	Carbohydrates
3 g	Fat
24%	Calories from Fat
2 g	Fiber
52 mg	Sodium
0 mg	Cholesterol

The First Book of Vegetarian Cooking

Sweet and Sour Spinach Salad

Dressing

2	tablespoons orange juice
1	tablespoon honey
¼	cup natural apple cider vinegar
2	tablespoons Dijon mustard
1	teaspoon low-sodium tamari

Salad

5	cups spinach, broken into bite-size pieces
1	cup mandarin oranges, drained
½	cup sliced water chestnuts *or* jicama

Chill spinach, oranges, and water chestnuts before preparing salad.

1. Whisk dressing ingredients together.
2. Toss spinach with oranges, water chestnuts, and dressing.

Makes 4 servings

There is no love sincerer than the love of food.

—GEORGE BERNARD SHAW, VEGETARIAN

98	Calories
3 g	Protein
21 g	Carbohydrates
1 g	Fat
12%	Calories from Fat
2 g	Fiber
317 mg	Sodium
0 mg	Cholesterol

Potato Salad

❧ ❧

3   pounds potatoes, peeled and cut into quarters
3   stalks celery
1   medium onion (about 10 ounces)
½   bell pepper
½   cup dairy-free, fat-free mayonnaise
¼   cup fat-free Italian dressing
½   teaspoon salt-free, all-purpose Parsley Patch (or salt substitute)

❧ ❧

If you plan to use salad the next day, store in a container with a cover, placing a thick paper towel over the top to absorb excess moisture before sealing.

Sometimes I add slivered almonds and leftover Tangy Green beans (page 148).

❧ ❧

This is a simple, easy-to-make potato salad and the best I have ever tasted. I guess you would call it a family secret recipe; the secret being to make the salad with warm potatoes. Warm potatoes absorb the delicious flavors of all the other ingredients.

1. In large saucepan place potatoes and enough water to almost cover. Bring to boil, cover, reduce heat and simmer until done, about 20 minutes.
2. While potatoes are cooking, mince celery, onion, and bell pepper.
3. Drain potatoes (reserving liquid for soups and gravies) and while still hot chop coarsely.
4. Add remaining ingredients to warm potatoes. Toss to coat.
5. Best served same day.

Makes 6 servings

209	Calories
4 g	Protein
49 g	Carbohydrates
1 g	Fat
1%	Calories from Fat
4 g	Fiber
608 mg	Sodium
0 mg	Cholesterol

Sweet Potato Salad

❧ ⧯

1 pound sweet potatoes,
   baked, peeled, and
   cooled, cut into
   ¼-inch slices
½ pound onions, baked in
   skins, cooled, peeled,
   and roughly chopped
½ pound Jerusalem arti-
   chokes (sunchokes),
   peeled, and roughly
   chopped
¼ cup fresh peas or frozen,
   defrosted
⅛ cup dairy-free, fat-free
   mayonnaise
1 teaspoon liquid aminos
   Freshly ground pepper
   Lettuce leaves

❧ ⧯

If artichokes are out of season,
jicama may be substituted.

❧ ⧯

The Jerusalem artichoke or sunchoke is a tuberous member of the sunflower family that is often mistaken for gingerroot as they are close in appearance. It lends itself well to salads with a nutty, sweet taste and crunchy texture and is a delicious source of iron.

Toss all ingredients except lettuce to combine. Serve on a bed of lettuce.

Makes 4 servings

134	Calories
3 g	Protein
30 g	Carbohydrates
1 g	Fat
2%	Calories from Fat
4 g	Fiber
166 mg	Sodium
0 mg	Cholesterol

Thai Rice Salad

Dressing

¼ cup lite coconut milk (Thai Kitchen*), shake can well
¼ cup fresh orange juice
2 teaspoons fresh lime juice
1 teaspoon powdered orange peel
1 teaspoon minced jalapeño pepper
2 teaspoons honey
1 teaspoon liquid aminos
½ teaspoon fresh grated ginger

Salad

1 cup brown basmati rice, cooked and cooled
¼ cup chopped red bell pepper
¼ cup chopped green bell pepper
¼ cup thinly sliced scallions
4 large lettuce leaves

1. Whisk dressing ingredients together.
2. Add to rice. Stir in peppers and scallions.
3. Refrigerate 1 hour to allow flavors to mingle. Spoon onto lettuce leaves at serving time.

Makes 4 servings

Happiness is contagious.

—ANONYMOUS

*I find mine at my local Kash & Karry supermarket.

199	Calories
5 g	Protein
41 g	Carbohydrates
2 g	Fat
7%	Calories from Fat
3 g	Fiber
65 mg	Sodium
0 mg	Cholesterol

Bulgur Salad

2 cups bulgur
3 cups boiling distilled
    water
2 zucchini, chopped
5 scallions, sliced
$^1/_2$ cup red wine vinegar
1 bell pepper (red or
    yellow), chopped
$^1/_4$ cup raisins
    Pinch of cayenne
    Pinch of ground cloves
    Pinch of mace
    Pinch of ginger
$^1/_4$ teaspoon ground
    cardamom
$^1/_4$ teaspoon ground
    coriander

Bulgur, a staple of the Middle East, are wheat kernels that have been steamed, dried, and crushed. It has a tender, chewy texture and is very nutritious. Serve on romaine lettuce leaves.

1. Place bulgur in large bowl and stir in boiling water. Cover and let rest for 30 minutes.
2. Stir in remaining ingredients and chill for 30 minutes.

Makes about 4 cups

Sweet green pepper (1 medium) contains 95 milligrams of vitamin C compared to 6 ounces of orange juice that contains only 78. The sweet red pepper (1 medium) contains a whopping 141 milligrams.

145	Calories
5 g	Protein
33 g	Carbohydrates
1 g	Fat
4%	Calories from Fat
5 g	Fiber
11 mg	Sodium
0 mg	Cholesterol

"Tuna" Salad

❧ ❦

1	package (10.5 ounces) firm lite silken tofu, that has been frozen*, thawed
2	stalks celery, chopped
3	scallions, minced
½	teaspoon kelp or dulse powder
½	teaspoon celery seed
⅓	cup fat-free, dairy-free mayonnaise
1	tablespoon nori flakes
3	tablespoons chopped pecans

Makes great sandwiches or a stuffing for tomatoes.

1. Drain tofu and remove from package. Wrap in a double thickness of paper towels. Squeeze out all the moisture. Change towels as needed.
2. Crumble tofu in a small bowl. Add remaining ingredients and combine.

Makes about 1 ½ cups

Let food be your medicine.
—HIPPOCRATES

*Freezing tofu firms-up the texture.

62	Calories
4 g	Protein
5 g	Carbohydrates
3 g	Fat
45%	Calories from Fat
1 g	Fiber
198 mg	Sodium
0 mg	Cholesterol

The First Book of Vegetarian Cooking

"Heart"y Soups

The Wide, Wide World of Soups

I love to make big pots of soup and feast on them all week. They're so comforting and homey, not to mention convenient. Some soups alone can actually provide all the nutrients needed for optimum health.

Some of the soups in this chapter can stand alone as an entrée while others make a good first course or luncheon dish.

For garnishes   Try soy bacon bits, croutons, tortilla strips, soy Parmesan cheese, chopped green onions, grated carrots, chopped peppers, nondairy sour cream or yogurt, fresh minced parsley or other herbs.

For thicker, creamier soups   Try puréeing a portion of the soup in the blender or food processor and adding it back into the pot. *Or* add instant potatoes that have been reconstituted with a little of the hot soup.

In a hurry   Try canned beans in soups. Drain and rinse if they are not organic.

Recipes

❧ ❧

African Stew	Leek Soup
Tomato Soup	Gumbo
Caldo Verde	Kale Soup
Lentil Stew	Lima-Barley Soup
Chilled Cucumber Soup	Green Matrix Soup
Onion Soup	Longevity Soup
Corn Reef Chowder	Minestrone
"Cream" of Avocado Soup	Mushroom Bisque
Miso Soup	Sea Vegetable Stock
"Cream" of Pumpkin Soup	"Cream" of Mushroom Soup
Free Soup	Vegetable Broth
Gazpacho	

❧ ❧

African Stew

꿍 꿍

1   large onion, chopped
2   cloves garlic, pressed or minced
1   tube (14 ounces) Gimme Lean*, beef taste
1 1/2   tablespoons Vogue Instant Vege Base
1 1/2   cups distilled water
1/4   cup natural peanut butter
1/4   cup salt-free tomato paste
1/8   teaspoon cayenne
2 1/2   cups cooked butternut squash
2   cups cooked brown rice

1. Prepare a nonstick Dutch oven or soup pot by lightly coating surface with vegetable cooking spray or by using an oiled pastry brush. Sauté onion and garlic until onion is soft. Add beef and cook, breaking up into pieces with the edge of a wooden spoon.
2. Mix Vogue Instant Vege Base with the water to make a broth. Add the broth, peanut butter, tomato paste, and cayenne to the beef mixture. Blend well.
3. Add squash and simmer covered for 5 minutes. Uncover and simmer an additional 5 minutes.
4. Serve over the cooked rice.

Makes 6 servings

*Available at most health food stores.

256	Calories
16 g	Protein
35 g	Carbohydrates
6 g	Fat
22%	Calories from Fat
5 g	Fiber
481 mg	Sodium
0 mg	Cholesterol

Tomato Soup

4   pounds tomatoes, cored
         and quartered
2   cups distilled water
3   teaspoons dried
         rosemary
1 ½   teaspoons dried thyme
1   bay leaf
2   cloves garlic, pressed
1   tablespoon liquid
         aminos
2   tablespoons Parmesan
         cheese substitute

1. In a large saucepan combine the tomatoes, water, rosemary, thyme, bay leaf, and garlic. Bring to a boil, reduce heat and simmer for 1 hour.
2. Press soup through a sieve. Return to pan and add liquid aminos.
3. Serve in individual soup cups topped with the Parmesan substitute.

Makes 6 cups

64	Calories
3 g	Protein
13 g	Carbohydrates
1 g	Fat
15%	Calories from Fat
4 g	Fiber
150 mg	Sodium
0 mg	Cholesterol

Caldo Verde (Green Soup)

꒱꒱ ꒱꒱

1   pound kale or collard greens

1   extra large onion, peeled and thinly sliced

3   cloves garlic, pressed

1 ½   cups Great Northern beans, soaked overnight and drained

2   cups shredded potatoes (1 large potato)

¼   cup Vogue Instant Vege Base

4   ounces Heartline Lite, Canadian bacon style, chopped

10   cups distilled water

¼   cup liquid aminos

A slimmed-down version of this Portuguese favorite.

1. Remove the ribs of the kale or collards leaving just the leaves*. Take a few leaves at a time and roll them like a cigar. Slice into very thin strips. Soak in bowl of cold water for 1 hour. Drain.
2. Prepare a nonstick Dutch oven or soup pot by lightly coating surface with vegetable cooking spray or by using an oiled pastry brush. Add onion and garlic and sauté until soft.
3. Add remaining ingredients (add liquid aminos at serving time). Simmer, covered for 1 hour or until beans are soft.

Makes 10 servings

*Save the ribs of the kale or collards for soups.

166	Calories
10 g	Protein
29 g	Carbohydrates
2 g	Fat
9%	Calories from Fat
13 g	Fiber
440 mg	Sodium
0 mg	Cholesterol

Lentil Stew

2 large onions, chopped
3 cloves garlic, minced
1 large jalapeño pepper,
    minced
8 cups distilled water
2 large carrots, diced
1 pound potatoes, diced
9 ounces lentils, rinsed
½ cup couscous
½ teaspoon cumin seed
1 bay leaf
2 heaping tablespoons
    Vogue Instant Vege
    Base
    Pinch of cayenne
¼ cup liquid aminos

Couscous is a staple in North African cuisine. It is granular semolina that is considered a pasta.

1. Place all ingredients except liquid aminos in a 4-quart kettle and bring to a simmer. Cover and cook for 30 minutes, or until lentils are tender.
2. Add liquid aminos at serving time.

Makes 6 servings

313	Calories
17 g	Protein
60 g	Carbohydrates
1 g	Fat
3%	Calories from Fat
8 g	Fiber
572 mg	Sodium
0 mg	Cholesterol

The First Book of Vegetarian Cooking

Chilled Cucumber Soup

2 tablespoons liquid aminos
½ cup sliced scallions plus additional for garnish
3 large English cucumbers, thinly sliced
2 cups peeled and cubed potatoes
6 cups distilled water
¼ cup Vogue Instant Vege Base
¼ teaspoon dried tarragon
½ teaspoon dried dill weed
½ cup dairy-free sour cream

The cucumber is thought originally to have reached us from India. They have been grown for thousands of years and were used by the ancient Egyptians, Greeks, and Romans. Cucumbers are one of the very few vegetables mentioned in the Bible.

1. In a Dutch oven or soup pot, heat 2 tablespoons water with 2 tablespoons liquid aminos. Add ½ cup scallions and sauté until tender. Add cucumbers and potatoes and sauté for an additional 3 minutes.
2. Add water, Vege Base, tarragon, and dill. Cover and simmer for 20 minutes or until potatoes are tender.
3. Refrigerate soup until cold.
4. Just before serving, whisk in the sour cream and garnish with scallions.

Makes 6 servings

Cucumbers are cooling, good for the digestion, alkaline in nature, and low in calories.

111	Calories
2 g	Protein
17 g	Carbohydrates
5 g	Fat
38%	Calories from Fat
2 g	Fiber
241 mg	Sodium
0 mg	Cholesterol

Onion Soup

2	tablespoons low-sodium tamari
3	large onions, sliced
3	cloves garlic, pressed
4	onion bouillon cubes, crumbled
1	tablespoon dried basil
8	cups distilled water
2	slices toast, quartered
2	tablespoons Parmesan cheese substitute
2	slices Swiss soy cheese, quartered

Preheat the broiler.

This soup can be made several days ahead of time and finished just before serving.

1. To a nonstick Dutch oven or large saucepan add 2 tablespoons water with 2 tablespoons tamari. Add onions and garlic and sauté until soft.
2. Add remaining ingredients, cover, and cook for 20 minutes.
3. Place a toast quarter into each flameproof soup cup. Add soup and top with cheeses. Place under broiler until cheese is melted, about 5 minutes.

Makes 8 cups

57	Calories
3 g	Protein
9 g	Carbohydrates
1 g	Fat
17%	Calories from Fat
1 g	Fiber
70 mg	Sodium
0 mg	Cholesterol

The First Book of Vegetarian Cooking

Corn Reef Chowder

1   large onion, chopped
3   stalks celery, chopped
1   medium red bell pepper,
      chopped
2   cloves garlic, pressed or
      minced
1   tablespoon potato starch
4   cups distilled water
1   large potato (1 pound),
      peeled and diced
1   teaspoon salt substitute
1   bay leaf
½   teaspoon dry thyme
      leaves
2   tablespoons Vogue
      Instant Vege Base
    Pinch of cayenne
3   cups corn kernels
⅓   cup Darifree powder,
      whisked with ⅓ cup
      warm distilled water
½   cup chopped dulse

Dulse is a sea vegetable that is mild in flavor and high in nutrition. It contains protein, iron, chlorophyll, enzymes, and vitamins A and B.

1. Prepare a nonstick Dutch oven or soup pot by lightly coating surface with vegetable cooking spray or by using an oiled pastry brush. Sauté the onion, celery, pepper, and garlic until soft. Stir in the potato starch and cook for a few seconds.
2. Add 1 cup of the water and bring to a boil. Reduce heat and cook for 1 minute. Add potatoes, remaining 3 cups water, and all the seasonings. Bring to a boil. Reduce heat and cook for 15 minutes or until potatoes are done.
3. Add corn and cook an additional 5 minutes. Stir in Darifree mixture and the dulse. Combine well and serve.

Makes 4 to 6 servings

207	Calories
6 g	Protein
47 g	Carbohydrates
2 g	Fat
6%	Calories from Fat
4 g	Fiber
851 mg	Sodium
0 mg	Cholesterol

"Cream" of Avocado Soup

❧ ❧

2	tablespoons liquid aminos
1/2	cup chopped onion
1	clove garlic, pressed
2	large avocados, pitted and halved
1/4	cup lemon juice
3	tablespoons cream sherry
2	tablespoons Vogue Instant Vege Base dissolved in 1/2 cup hot distilled water
2	cups distilled water
	Pinch of cayenne
2	tablespoons chopped fresh cilantro
2	cups lite soy milk

A refreshing chilled soup for those hot summer gatherings.

1. In a skillet, add 1 tablespoon water and 1 tablespoon liquid aminos. Sauté onion and garlic until soft. Set aside to cool.
2. Scoop avocado into food processor or blender and add lemon juice, onion mixture, sherry, broth, water, cayenne, and cilantro. Purée until smooth.
3. Pour contents into soup tureen or serving bowl and add soy milk and remaining 1 tablespoon of liquid aminos.
4. Chill and serve.

Makes 6 to 8 servings

Avocados are rich in protein and contain 14 minerals as well as vitamins A, D, and E. An excellent food for a healthy heart.

117	Calories
3 g	Protein
7 g	Carbohydrates
9 g	Fat
69%	Calories from Fat
2 g	Fiber
259 mg	Sodium
0 mg	Cholesterol

Miso Soup

5   cups distilled water
1   strip (7 inches) dried
        kombu (see "Glos-
        sary"), rinsed
4   small yellow onions
        ($1/2$ pound), peeled
        and thinly sliced
1   clove garlic, pressed
$1/4$ cup barley miso
1   tablespoon low-sodium
        tamari
1   teaspoon Mirin
        (see "Glossary")

I don't think a vegetarian cookbook would be complete without some sort of miso soup recipe, so here is mine with the addition of onions. If you have not tasted this mild, light soup before, you're in for a healthful treat. Quick and easy to make.

1. In large saucepan, bring water and kombu to a boil. Reduce heat and simmer for 5 minutes. Remove kombu and reserve for use in beans or soup.
2. Add onions and simmer until soft, about 5 minutes.
3. Add remaining ingredients and simmer for 2 minutes.

Makes 6 servings

Miso is a fermented food made by combining soybeans with rice, barley, wheat, or white rice and adding a bacterial agent called koju, has been used by the Japanese for centuries. They have found that miso strengthens weak intestines, aids digestion, and discharges toxins from the body. It is high in protein, calcium, iron, and the B vitamins. Miso is a vegetarian source of vitamin B_{12}.

38	Calories
2 g	Protein
6 g	Carbohydrates
1 g	Fat
14%	Calories from Fat
2 g	Fiber
664 mg	Sodium
0 mg	Cholesterol

"Cream" of Pumpkin Soup

6　cups distilled water
¼　cup Vogue Instant
　　　Vege Base
2　pounds pumpkin,
　　　peeled and cubed
1 ½　cups chopped onion
1　tablespoon arrowroot
1　cup soy or rice milk
2　tablespoons liquid
　　　aminos

A great soup for Thanksgiving. For an elegant presentation serve in a hollowed-out pumpkin with a large dollop of dairy-free yogurt.

1. In a Dutch oven or soup pot bring water to a boil. Add vege base, pumpkin, and onion. Cook for 20 minutes or until pumpkin is soft.
2. In a blender or food processor purée soup in batches.
3. Return soup to pan. Dissolve arrowroot in milk and add to the soup. Bring to a simmer and serve. Stir in aminos when ready to serve.

Makes 6 to 8 servings

Pumpkin is native to the Americas and is very rich in potassium. It is alkaline and a good source of vitamins B, C, and beta-carotene.

65	Calories
3 g	Protein
12 g	Carbohydrates
1 g	Fat
19%	Calories from Fat
2 g	Fiber
333 mg	Sodium
0 mg	Cholesterol

Free Soup (Vegetable Soup)

≈ ≈

1   bunch celery, sliced
2   large onions, chopped
4   cloves garlic, minced
½   bell pepper, diced
2   pounds carrots, cut into
       1-inch pieces
6   cups distilled water
1   can (16 ounces) salt-
       free, peeled tomatoes
¼   cup Vogue Instant
       Vege Base
¼   teaspoon cayenne
1   bay leaf
1   medium potato, peeled
       and cubed
1   pound mushrooms,
       sliced (about 4 cups)
8   fresh basil leaves,
       minced
2   tablespoons minced
       fresh parsley
¼   cup liquid aminos

When I was lecturing for an international weight-loss program, I came up with this "free soup" for our clients to eat to their heart's content. It is low calorie and nutritious.

1. Prepare a nonstick Dutch oven or soup pot by lightly coating surface with vegetable cooking spray or by using an oiled pastry brush. Sauté celery, onions, garlic, and bell pepper until tender.
2. Add carrots, water, tomatoes, Vege Base, cayenne, and bay leaf. Simmer for 10 minutes.
3. Add potatoes and mushrooms and cook an additional 5 minutes. Add basil and parsley and continue to cook 10 more minutes.
4. At serving time add the liquid aminos.

Makes 10 servings

≈ ≈

For a heartier soup, cooked rice or beans can be added. This dish also can be served over a baked potato.

≈ ≈

113	Calories
4 g	Protein
24 g	Carbohydrates
1 g	Fat
6%	Calories from Fat
6 g	Fiber
365 mg	Sodium
0 mg	Cholesterol

Gazpacho

1   medium English cucumber (or a regular cucumber, seeded), minced
1   medium bell pepper, minced
1   medium tomato, minced
½   small onion, minced
1 ¼ cups organic, salt-free tomato juice
⅔   cup spicy vegetable juice
    Pinch of cayenne

A chilled soup or a very refreshing first course.

Combine all the ingredients and chill.

Makes 4 to 6 servings

This soup can be made in a food processor. Make sure you do not purée the vegetables, they should still have definition and a crunchy texture.

33	Calories
1 g	Protein
8 g	Carbohydrates
1 g	Fat
7%	Calories from Fat
1 g	Fiber
105 mg	Sodium
0 mg	Cholesterol

Leek Soup

3 tablespoons liquid aminos
1 large onion, sliced
2 stalks celery, sliced
2 medium leeks, sliced
1 teaspoon dried ground thyme
1 teaspoon dried rosemary
2 large potatoes, diced
5 to 6 cups distilled water
⅓ cup Vogue Instant Vege Base

The leaves of leeks often contain sand, so they need to be well rinsed before cooking. Sliced leeks can be put into a colander and flushed with water.

The leek can be traced to Asia, going back to prehistoric times. It has long been a favorite in soups due to its delicate onion flavor.

1. In a Dutch oven or large nonstick saucepan, place 2 tablespoons water and 2 tablespoons liquid aminos. Add onion, celery, and leeks. Sauté until tender. Add thyme and rosemary and cook an additional 1 to 2 minutes.
2. Add potatoes, water, and Vogue Instant Vege Base. Cover and cook for 20 minutes. Cool slightly. Purée in batches in blender or food processor. Add remaining aminos when ready to serve.

Makes 10 cups

Leeks are very low in calories, 16 per ½ cup, and considered therapeutic for throat disorders and are good for the liver and respiratory system.

41	Calories
1 g	Protein
9 g	Carbohydrates
1 g	Fat
13%	Calories from Fat
1 g	Fiber
310 mg	Sodium
0 mg	Cholesterol

Gumbo

1   large onion, chopped
        (at least 2 cups)
1   cup chopped celery
1   bell pepper, chopped
4   cloves garlic, minced
3   shallots, minced
1   package (10 ounces)
        frozen chopped
        spinach
1   package (10 ounces)
        frozen chopped
        mustard greens
1   package (10 ounces)
        frozen chopped
        collard greens
1   package (10 ounces)
        frozen chopped
        turnip greens
1/2 cabbage, shredded
2   quarts distilled water
1   vegetable stock cube
2   bay leaves
1   teaspoon dried basil
1   teaspoon dried thyme
1/8 teaspoon dried allspice
1/8 teaspoon dried
        powdered cloves
2   tablespoons dried
        parsley
1/4 teaspoon Tabasco
4   cups rice, cooked
    Filé powder for garnish
        (optional)

*This recipe is based on the New Orleans gumbo called Gumbo Z' Herbs. Legend has it for every green vegetable put into the gumbo, a new friend will be made in the coming year. A true friend is wonderful, and we can always use another. So feel free to add more greens. ***

1. Prepare a nonstick Dutch oven or soup pot by lightly coating surface with vegetable cooking spray or by using an oiled pastry brush. Sauté the onion, celery, bell pepper, garlic, and shallots until soft.
2. Add remaining ingredients, omitting the rice and filé powder, and cook for 20 minutes. Remove two cups of soup and purée in blender or food processor. Return to pot and simmer for 5 minutes more.
3. Serve over rice with a pinch of filé powder.

Serves 8

*For convenience I have used frozen greens. Substitute fresh greens and herbs if time permits and if they are available.

81	Calories
5 g	Protein
17 g	Carbohydrates
1 g	Fat
8%	Calories from Fat
5 g	Fiber
95 mg	Sodium
0 mg	Cholesterol

The First Book of Vegetarian Cooking

Kale Soup

1 medium onion, chopped
½ pound kale leaves, washed and sliced thinly
1 large carrot, shredded
6 cups distilled water
¼ cup Vogue Instant Vege Base
2 teaspoons lemon juice
Pinch of cayenne
1 teaspoon dulse or salt substitute

Kale is high in calcium and iron. A ½ cup serving has as much vitamin C as an orange and four times as much beta-carotene as broccoli.

Kale and collards are the oldest known members of the cabbage family and have been enjoyed by mankind for over 4,000 years.

1. Prepare a nonstick skillet by lightly coating surface with vegetable cooking spray or by using an oiled pastry brush. Sauté onion for 3 to 4 minutes. Add kale and carrot. Sauté for 4 minutes more.
2. Stir in remaining ingredients. Bring to a boil over high heat. Remove from heat and serve.

Makes 4 to 6 servings

33 Calories
1 g Protein
7 g Carbohydrates
1 g Fat
21% Calories from Fat
1 g Fiber
189 mg Sodium
0 mg Cholesterol

Lima–Barley Soup

½ cup pearl barley, rinsed
    and drained
½ cup dried lima beans,
    rinsed and drained
1 large onion, chopped
3 large carrots, chopped
1 cup sliced celery
7 cups distilled water
⅛ teaspoon cayenne
¼ teaspoon fennel seeds
1 cup sliced mushrooms
2 tablespoons liquid
    aminos

European explorers found lima beans growing in Lima, Peru, hence the name. Limas are 18% protein; 1 pound contains as many nutrients as 2 pounds of meat.

1. In a large saucepan, combine barley, limas, onion, carrots, celery, water, cayenne, and fennel. Bring to a boil. Reduce heat, cover and simmer for 1 ½ hours.
2. Add mushrooms, cover and cook for an additional 15 minutes.
3. Add liquid aminos at serving time.

Makes 6 servings

148	Calories
7 g	Protein
30 g	Carbohydrates
1 g	Fat
3%	Calories from Fat
8 g	Fiber
262 mg	Sodium
0 mg	Cholesterol

The First Book of Vegetarian Cooking

Green Matrix Soup

2 English cucumbers,
    juiced (about 2 cups)
1 small onion, quartered
1 cup chopped fresh
    spinach
1/2 bell pepper, quartered
1/2 avocado, quartered
2 cloves garlic
2 tablespoons liquid
    aminos

It's necessary to have a vegetable juicer for this tasty, nutritious, uncooked soup.

Place all ingredients into a blender or food processor. Process until well blended.

Makes 4 servings

Cucumber juice is excellent for your health, flushing toxins from the body and it is also a most efficient diuretic.

63	Calories
2 g	Protein
5 g	Carbohydrates
4 g	Fat
58%	Calories from Fat
1 g	Fiber
347 mg	Sodium
0 mg	Cholesterol

Longevity Soup (Bean Soup)

½ pound mixed legumes (kidney beans, split peas, pintos, lentils, black beans, garbanzos, etc.)
1 teaspoon garlic powder
1 teaspoon cumin
2 tablespoons dehydrated onion flakes
  Distilled water to cover legumes by 4 inches
1 large onion, quartered then halved
4 stalks celery, diced
3 cloves garlic, pressed
1 bay leaf
  Pinch of cayenne
1 piece dried kombu (7-inches long)
¼ cup pearled barley, rinsed
3 whole tomatoes, diced *or* 1 cup tomato sauce
6 large carrots, peeled and cut into chunks
1 large potato, diced
2 cups chopped collard greens or kale
12 pearl onions, peeled
2 cups frozen peas
1 quart distilled water
2 tablespoons liquid aminos*

A wonderful, hearty, anti-aging soup I often have for lunch or dinner. Kombu is a mild seaweed that adds flavor and additional nutrition to recipes. Soaking beans with seasonings will improve their flavor. Make sure you have a gallon of distilled water on hand to make this recipe.

1. Soak legumes, garlic powder, cumin, and onion flakes in water to cover for 8 hours. Drain.
2. Prepare a nonstick Dutch oven or soup pot by lightly coating surface with vegetable cooking spray or by using an oiled pastry brush. Sauté the onion, celery, and garlic until soft.
3. Add drained beans and enough distilled water to cover beans by one inch. Add bay leaf, cayenne, kombu, and barley. Bring to a boil. Scoop off foam. Cover and simmer for about 1 hour or until the beans are done, but still firm. (Add more water if necessary.)
4. To the cooked beans add the remaining ingredients except liquid aminos and simmer for an additional 15 to 20 minutes or until the vegetables are tender.
5. Add liquid aminos at serving time.

Makes 10 servings

*Always add liquid aminos at the end of cooking it because should not be heated: heat destroys enzymes.

209	Calories
11 g	Protein
42 g	Carbohydrates
1 g	Fat
4%	Calories from Fat
7 g	Fiber
242 mg	Sodium
0 mg	Cholesterol

The First Book of Vegetarian Cooking

Minestrone

Minestrone comes from the Latin name "to hand out." Monks keep a kettle of this soup on the fire ready to hand out to hungry travelers.

2 cups cooked white beans *or* one 16-ounce can navy, Great Northern, or white kidney beans, undrained
1 large onion, chopped (about 2 cups)
3 stalks celery, chopped
2 cloves garlic, minced
1 small zucchini, diced
2 carrots, diced
2 potatoes, diced
1 cup frozen peas
3 cups peeled diced tomatoes *or* 1 can (28 ounces)
2 cups shredded cabbage
½ teaspoon chopped sage
1 teaspoon dried basil
1 tablespoon dried parsley
1 vegetable stock cube
1 cup uncooked elbow macaroni
Dash of cayenne pepper
Parmesan cheese alternative for garnish

1. Prepare a nonstick Dutch oven or soup pot by lightly coating surface with vegetable cooking spray or by using an oiled pastry brush. Sauté the onion, celery, and garlic until tender about 3 minutes.
2. Add remaining ingredients, cover, and cook 20 to 30 minutes or until vegetables and pasta are tender.

Makes 6 servings

I have used dried herbs in this recipe, if you have fresh available please use. A ratio of 3 (fresh) to 1 (dried) will work nicely.

262	Calories
13 g	Protein
53 g	Carbohydrates
1 g	Fat
4%	Calories from Fat
8 g	Fiber
69 mg	Sodium
0 mg	Cholesterol

Mushroom Bisque

2   large onions, sliced
1   pound mushrooms, chopped (about 4 cups)
1   clove garlic, pressed or minced
⅓   cup chopped fresh parsley
⅓   cup unbleached flour
1   teaspoon dried thyme
3   tablespoons Vogue Instant Vege Base
1 ½   quart soy or rice milk
     Liquid aminos*
     Sliced scallions for garnish

For a taste treat, try using mushrooms other than the popular button type. Oriental mushrooms can be expensive at times. Find a variety that fits your pocketbook and taste buds.

1. Prepare a nonstick Dutch oven or soup pot by lightly coating surface with vegetable cooking spray or by using an oiled pastry brush. Sauté onions, mushrooms, and garlic until soft. Stir in parsley, flour, thyme, and Vogue Instant Vege Base. Cook for another minute.
2. Place mushroom mixture into a food processor or blender. Add a little soy milk if needed to purée mixture.
3. Return mushroom mixture to pan and add remaining milk. Cook over medium heat, stirring until thickened. Add liquid aminos.
4. Serve warm and garnish with sliced scallions

Makes 8 servings

*Liquid aminos should be added after the cooking process in order to preserve their enzymes.

113	Calories
7 g	Protein
14 g	Carbohydrates
4 g	Fat
34%	Calories from Fat
4 g	Fiber
144 mg	Sodium
0 mg	Cholesterol

MUSHROOMS

Few medical benefits have been linked to the common button mushroom. In fact, button mushrooms contain hydrazides which are said to cause cancer. The hydrazides are killed by heat, so it is not recommended to eat raw button mushrooms.

Here are five oriental types that have proven results.

Enoki   *Stimulates the immune system, helping to fight viruses and tumors.*

Oyster   *In animal studies, this mushroom has shown promise in fighting cancer.*

Shiitake   *Stimulates the immune system to produce more interferon, which fights cancers and viruses.*

Tree-ear   *Can prevent heart attacks by keeping blood platelets from sticking together. In animal studies, tree-ears have been found to slow down cancer.*

Reishi   *Used for thousands of years by the Chinese for health and well being, enhancing organic functions, promoting cosmetic rejuvenation, and beautifying the skin.*

Your produce department may not have some of these mushrooms available. Ask if they can order them for you or try an oriental market, health food store, or the mail-order directory at the back of this book.

Sea Vegetable Stock

4   pieces (7 inches each) dried kombu
7   cups distilled water
2   cups carrots, cut into 1-inch pieces
2   large onions, cut into eighths
4   cups celery, cut into 1-inch pieces
3   cloves garlic
¼   teaspoon cayenne

A great stock that can be used for soups or any recipes requiring broth.

1. Rinse kombu and place into a covered Dutch oven with 5 cups of the water. Simmer covered for 45 minutes.
2. Add 2 cups water and remaining ingredients. Cover and simmer 30 minutes more.
3. Strain, reserving vegetables for future soup recipes.

Makes 1 quart

24	Calories
0 g	Protein
5 g	Carbohydrates
1 g	Fat
2%	Calories from Fat
2 g	Fiber
175 mg	Sodium
0 mg	Cholesterol

"Cream" of Mushroom Soup

2   tablespoons liquid aminos
1   medium onion
4   cloves garlic, pressed or minced
½   pound mushrooms, thinly sliced (about 2 cups)
½   teaspoon ground thyme
1   package (10.5 ounces) firm lite silken tofu, drained
1   cup distilled water
    Pinch of cayenne

A nondairy version of an all-time favorite. As a child, when I was sick, all I would eat was cream of mushroom soup with toast torn up in it.

1. In a nonstick saucepan, place 1 tablespoon water with 1 tablespoon liquid aminos. Add the onion and garlic and sauté until soft. Add mushrooms and thyme and cook an additional 5 minutes.
2. Process tofu in a food processor or blender until creamy. Add water and process.
3. Add onion mixture to the tofu in the processor and process for 1 minute. Return contents to saucepan and stir in remaining 1 tablespoon liquid aminos and cayenne.

Makes 3 cups

87	Calories
10 g	Protein
10 g	Carbohydrates
2 g	Fat
1%	Calories from Fat
2 g	Fiber
235 mg	Sodium
0 mg	Cholesterol

Vegetable Broth

1	large onion, skin left on
3	whole cloves garlic
3	stalks celery, halved with leaves
3	large carrots, quartered
2	leeks, washed well and cut into large chunks
2	medium tomatoes, quartered
2	large potatoes, quartered
10	sprigs parsley
2	bay leaves
10	peppercorns
4	whole cloves
12	cups distilled water
¼	teaspoon cayenne pepper

For a richer broth do not remove skins from the vegetables. Add a cup of this broth to your soup recipes for added flavor.

1. If not using organic vegetables, wash vegetables with Veggie Bath (page xviii).
2. Place all ingredients in stock pot or large pot. Bring to a boil, reduce heat and simmer uncovered for 1 hour.
3. Strain. Reserve vegetables for another use.
4. Cool, refrigerate, or freeze.

Makes 4 cups

You can easily double or triple this recipe and freeze in individual containers for future use, or freeze in ice cube trays when you might want just one cup of broth.

10	Calories
1 g	Protein
2 g	Carbohydrates
1 g	Fat
10%	Calories from Fat
0 g	Fiber
4 mg	Sodium
0 mg	Cholesterol

The First Book of Vegetarian Cooking

SLIM PICKIN'S

W hat are Slim Pickin's? Well, slim means the fat is cut out and pickin's are snack foods. According to the dictionary, a snack food is a light meal.

When do we eat a light meal? Children like them when they get home from school or between meals. The English call it afternoon tea and the Spanish like to relax at Tapas bars with a glass of wine. Snacking is international. And there's nothing wrong with that as long as it's healthful snacking.

People in the know recommend six light meals a day. These frequent meals facilitate weight loss and help to stabilize blood sugar. Now you can snack without guilt!

Recipes

Banana-Peanut Butter Spread

Sweet Potato "Fries"

Bean Burritos

Chick Nuggets

BLT Sandwich

Crumble Burgers

"Egg" Muffin

Broccoli Quiche

Egyptian Pitas

Falafel Sandwich

Jicama Mexicana

The Perfect Burger

Fajitas

Pita Chips

Quesadillas

Pot Stickers

Reuben Sandwich

Salad Sandwiches

Popped Corn Olé

Eggplant Sticks

Spring Rolls

Sushi Rolls

Tortilla Chips

Vietnamese Spring Rolls

Banana–Peanut Butter Spread

❧ ❧

½ cup natural peanut
    butter
1 package (10.5 ounces)
    firm lite silken tofu,
    drained
1½ bananas
1 tablespoon lemon juice
1 teaspoon honey

Want to break the butter or oleo habit? Try this spread on your morning toast or muffin.

1. Combine all ingredients in a blender or food processor and mix until smooth.
2. Chill and serve with pieces of whole grain bread, vegetable sticks, or pita.

Makes about 8 (¼ cup) servings

This recipe includes the T-word (tofu). A lot of people are turned off because they haven't tasted it when it was properly prepared. Tofu is a clone, copying the taste of the ingredient it's combined with. This recipe is sure to make believers of anyone who likes peanut butter or bananas. Tofu is so nutritious and healthful to the body that many books have been written on its beneficial properties and its ability to fight cancer and aid in the discomforts of menopause, to name two.

57	Calories
3 g	Protein
3 g	Carbohydrates
4 g	Fat
65%	Calories from Fat
1 g	Fiber
39 mg	Sodium
0 mg	Cholesterol

Sweet Potato "Fries"

❧ ❧

3   pounds sweet potatoes
    Non-aerosol vegetable
        spray

Preheat oven to 425 degrees F.

This root vegetable has been very popular for centuries in tropical countries. Because of its nutritional value, it should be eaten more frequently here, not just during the holidays. We sometimes confuse the sweet potato with the yam which is much larger. Actually, very few yams are grown here, they are mostly grown in Africa and South America. Many supermarkets interchange the names which, of course, technically is not true.

1. Scrub potatoes well with Veggie Bath (page xviii). Cut lengthwise into halves; then again into quarters. You want to have pieces about 4 to 5 inches long by 1 ½ inches wide.
2. Prepare baking sheet with non-aerosol vegetable spray. Arrange "fingers," skin-side down, over sheet keeping them separated. Spray potatoes lightly.
3. Bake for 35 to 40 minutes or until golden and tender.

Makes 4 servings

You can tell by its rich color that sweet potatoes are loaded with beta-carotene, which has the potential to reduce the risk of lung cancer. It is a good source of niacin and beneficial to the eliminative system. One cup mashed provides 43,000 IUs of vitamin A! That's 8 times the recommended daily allowance.

277	Calories
5 g	Protein
64 g	Carbohydrates
1 g	Fat
2%	Calories from Fat
8 g	Fiber
28 mg	Sodium
0 mg	Cholesterol

The First Book of Vegetarian Cooking

Bean Burritos

1 cup chopped onion
1 clove garlic, pressed or minced
½ cup chopped bell pepper
1 recipe Refried Beans (page 18) or 1 can (16 ounces) fat-free refried beans
½ cup cooked basmati or brown rice*
½ cup shredded lite Cheddar soy cheese
½ cup drained salsa
6 fat-free whole wheat tortillas

Preheat oven to 425 degrees F.

Garlic is an ancient food, one of the few mentioned in the Bible. The ancient Egyptians not only used garlic in their cooking, they felt it was magical and fed it to their soldiers before battle for courage.

1. Prepare a nonstick skillet or wok by lightly coating surface with vegetable cooking spray or by using an oiled pastry brush. Over medium-low heat, sauté onion, garlic, and pepper until vegetables are soft. Stir in remaining ingredients except tortillas.
2. Spread each tortilla with the bean mixture. Roll up jelly-roll fashion. Place on cookie sheet, seam-side down and bake for 5 minutes or until heated and cheese is melted.

Makes 6 servings

*Store uncooked brown rice in an airtight container in the refrigerator. Because of its oil-based constituents, it can become rancid.

Garlic is a member of the lily family and contains a compound called Ajoene which has proved to be toxic to malignant cells. It has long been considered medicinal and is used as a natural antibiotic.

144	Calories
8 g	Protein
29 g	Carbohydrates
1 g	Fat
7%	Calories from Fat
6 g	Fiber
556 mg	Sodium
0 mg	Cholesterol

Chick Nuggets

1   pound Meat of Wheat, chicken style, cut into bite-size pieces
2   cups soy or rice milk

Herb breading mix
1   cup finely ground cornmeal (masa harina works well)
½   cup whole wheat flour
1½ teaspoons finely cut lemon peel
1   teaspoon kelp granulars
1   teaspoon dried oregano
1   teaspoon garlic powder
½   teaspoon onion powder
½   teaspoon dried basil leaves
    Pinch cayenne pepper

Serve with barbecue, plum, or sweet and sour dipping sauces (see "Sauces, Marinades, and Dressings"). Marinate the nuggets overnight for best results.

1. In a covered container place bite-size nuggets with milk to cover. Marinate overnight.
2. Preheat the broiler. Place breading mix ingredients into pint glass jar and shake to mix. Put mixture in a plastic bag and add a few nuggets. Shake to coat well. Repeat as needed to coat remaining nuggets.
3. Place on a broiler-safe baking sheet 3 inches from coil and broil for 2 minutes on each side or just until browned. Do not overcook.
4. Place on platter surrounded by dipping sauces.

Makes approximately 16 nuggets

86	Calories
9 g	Protein
10 g	Carbohydrates
1 g	Fat
15%	Calories from Fat
1 g	Fiber
133 mg	Sodium
0 mg	Cholesterol

BLT Sandwich

4 slices whole grain
   bread
   Fat-free mayonnaise
4 strips Stripples,
   cooked per package
   directions
3 to 4 romaine lettuce
   leaves, torn into
   several pieces
1 tomato, sliced
1 cup sprouts

I found the BLT sandwich one of the things I missed when I became a vegetarian. This satisfied the yearning.

Toast the bread and apply the mayonnaise. Add Stripples and vegetables.

Makes 2 sandwiches

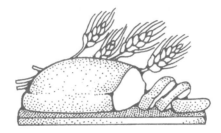

208	Calories
8 g	Protein
33 g	Carbohydrates
7 g	Fat
29%	Calories from Fat
5 g	Fiber
712 mg	Sodium
0 mg	Cholesterol

Crumble Burgers

¼ cup flax seed extract
(page 365)

1 package (10-ounces)
Tofu Crumbles*

¾ cup whole wheat bread
crumbs

1 tablespoon liquid
aminos

1. Knead all ingredients together with hands for 1 minute.
2. Form into six patties.
3. Prepare a nonstick skillet by lightly coating surface with vegetable cooking spray or by using an oiled pastry brush. Brown patties on both sides, reduce heat and cook for 5 minutes longer.

Makes 6 patties

*Available at most supermarkets.

57	Calories
5 g	Protein
4 g	Carbohydrates
3 g	Fat
40%	Calories from Fat
1 g	Fiber
145 mg	Sodium
0 mg	Cholesterol

The First Book of Vegetarian Cooking

"Egg" Muffin

1 package (10.5 ounces) extra firm, lite silken tofu, drained
¼ teaspoon powdered cumin
1 teaspoon onion powder
⅛ teaspoon curry powder
⅛ teaspoon turmeric (for color)
  Pinch of cayenne
1 teaspoon liquid aminos
4 toasted English muffins
4 slices Canadian veggie bacon (Yves)
2 slices Cheddar soy cheese, halved

Preheat the broiler.

Great snack food or good for brunch.

1. Prepare a nonstick skillet by lightly coating surface with vegetable cooking spray or by using an oiled pastry brush. In the saucepan, mash tofu into pea-size pieces with a fork. Add cumin, onion powder, curry powder, turmeric, and cayenne. Cook for 3 to 4 minutes stirring occasionally; add aminos.
2. Place four toasted muffin halves on broiler-safe pan. Top buns with bacon and cheese. Broil until cheese is melted.
3. Add scrambled tofu and top with remaining muffin half.

Makes 4 servings

241	Calories
15 g	Protein
35 g	Carbohydrates
5 g	Fat
18%	Calories from Fat
5 g	Fiber
729 mg	Sodium
0 mg	Cholesterol

Broccoli Quiche

꜊꜈ ꜉꜋

1   10-inch, unbaked, deep-
      dish, whole wheat
      pie crust
2   large onions (1 ½
      pounds), thinly sliced
⅓   cup firm tofu, drained
1   cup rice milk
1 ½ teaspoons salt
      substitute
⅛   teaspoon freshly ground
      nutmeg
2   tablespoons unbleached
      organic flour
2   tablespoons whole
      wheat flour
1   cup shredded lite Swiss-
      style soy cheese
1   package (10 ounces)
      frozen chopped
      broccoli, cooked and
      well drained

Preheat oven to 425 degrees F.

A protein-rich quiche that's dairy-free.

1. Bake pie crust for 10 minutes and cool. Lower oven temperature to 375 degrees F.
2. Prepare a nonstick skillet by lightly coating surface with vegetable cooking spray or by using an oiled pastry brush. Sauté
   the onions until soft, turning frequently.
3. In a blender, process the tofu until smooth and creamy. Add
   milk, salt substitute, nutmeg, and flours. Process to blend.
4. Spread the sautéed onion and cheese evenly over the bottom
   of the cooked pie shell. Add the cooked broccoli and the tofu
   mixture.
5. Bake for 30 to 40 minutes or until set and golden brown.
6. Cut into squares and serve at room temperature.

Makes about 20 pieces

꜊꜈ ꜉꜋

Frozen cheese is
easier to grate.

꜊꜈ ꜉꜋

*Broccoli is rich in beta-carotene. Beta-carotene and vitamin A are not
one and the same. They are related but they fulfill different functions.
Biochemists have found that beta-carotene protects the cells against free
radicals, which can cause cancer. It also appears to reduce the risk of
some heart diseases.*

130	Calories
4 g	Protein
15 g	Carbohydrates
7 g	Fat
45%	Calories from Fat
2 g	Fiber
39 mg	Sodium
0 mg	Cholesterol

Egyptian Pitas

2 tomatoes, thinly sliced
3 large pitas
1 small eggplant (about 1 pound), thinly sliced
1 tablespoon low-sodium tamari
1 cup Hummus (page 21)
1 English cucumber, thinly sliced
   Fat-free Italian dressing
   Fresh cilantro or parsley for garnish

Preheat the broiler.

Cucumbers are high in silica which helps strengthen the elasticity of the skin and muscles, even in older skin. The best way to receive silica is by juicing unpeeled European cucumbers (those long skinny ones wrapped in plastic) and drinking the fresh juice daily. Be sure to clean the cucumbers with Veggie Wash (page 000) before juicing. You will also find this juice is a wonderful natural diuretic.

---

1. Place sliced tomatoes on a paper towel to drain.
2. Split each pita in half to form 2 full circles. On a cookie sheet, place the halved pitas (inside up) and lightly brown under the broiler, about 1 minute. Set pitas aside.
3. Place eggplant slices on the cookie sheet. Brush with tamari and broil until browned and tender, about 5 minutes, turn eggplant and broil an additional 5 minutes.
4. At serving time, spread hummus on each toasted pita half. Top with eggplant, tomato slices, and cucumber slices. Drizzle lightly with Italian dressing and garnish.

Makes 6 pieces

189	Calories
8 g	Protein
28 g	Carbohydrates
6 g	Fat
29%	Calories from Fat
5 g	Fiber
180 mg	Sodium
0 mg	Cholesterol

Falafel Sandwich

৵৵ ৵৶

1 large onion, chopped
3 cloves garlic, pressed or minced
3 cups cooked chickpeas or 2 cans (16 ounces each) chickpeas or garbanzos, drained and mashed
1 medium potato, peeled, cooked and mashed
2 tablespoons chopped fresh cilantro
2 tablespoons chopped fresh parsley
2 teaspoons cumin
2 tablespoons fresh lemon juice
2 tablespoons tahini
2 teaspoons liquid aminos
  Pinch of cayenne
  Salt substitute
8 large whole wheat pitas, cut in half

Toppings

Shredded lettuce
Sliced tomatoes
Sprouts
Tahini

For years I have had fond memories of falafel and a hotel on the Nile River in Cairo. In the hotel's garden courtyard, vendors with little carts sold Egyptian soul food. This was my first taste of falafel, which I fell in love with at first bite. When I found out several years later I was returning to Egypt, my mouth started watering for those same falafel sandwiches. After my arrival in Cairo, I made a beeline (salivating all the way) to the same courtyard for this wonderful food. Alas! when I got there the vendors were unfortunately gone for good. Well, they say you can't go back.

1. In a large nonstick skillet that has been sprayed with water and lightly oiled, sauté the onions and garlic until tender. Spray additional water if necessary.
2. In a large bowl, add cooked onions and remaining ingredients except for pitas and toppings. Mix using your hands to blend well.
3. Take ¼ cup of the mixture and shape into a round, flattened patty. Repeat until all the mixture is used.
4. Prepare skillet again and brown patties well on each side.
5. Place a patty into a pita half; add vegetable toppings, and drizzle with a little tahini. At serving time, arrange on a large platter.

Makes about 16 sandwiches

146	Calories
7 g	Protein
24 g	Carbohydrates
3 g	Fat
18%	Calories from Fat
3 g	Fiber
166 mg	Sodium
0 mg	Cholesterol

The First Book of Vegetarian Cooking

Jicama Mexicana

1 lime, halved
1 jicama* (2 pounds),
   peeled and cut into
   ½-inch slices
   Chili powder

Jicama (pronounced HEE-ka-mah) brings back pleasant memories of strolling down the streets of Merida (in the Yucatan) and seeing vendors of every description selling these snacks.

1. Rub lime over jicama slices and sprinkle with chili powder.
2. Chill until ready to serve.

Makes 6 servings

*Jicama (sometimes called the Mexican potato) is a crisp root vegetable with a slightly sweet, nutty flavor resembling a turnip. A source of vitamin C and potassium.

59	Calories
1 g	Protein
14 g	Carbohydrates
1 g	Fat
2%	Calories from Fat
1 g	Fiber
6 mg	Sodium
0 mg	Cholesterol

The Perfect Burger
❧ ❧

1   package (5.3 ounces)
        Burger 'n' Loaf,
        original
4   ounces mushrooms,
        minced
1   cup minced onion
1   tablespoon liquid
        aminos
        Pinch of cayenne
        Freshly ground pepper
6   whole wheat burger
        buns, split
        Vegetable cooking spray
        Mayonnaise, lettuce,
        ketchup, tomatoes,
        onions, or sprouts for

❧ ❧

I individually wrap and
freeze these patties for
a quick sandwich.

❧ ❧

Perfect in nutrition and taste. One of the first lessons I learned in the restaurant business was "always toast the buns." And please use a whole grain bun for the extra nutrition. White bread is like paste in your stomach and not much else.

1. Prepare burger according to package directions, omitting the oil. Add mushrooms, onion, aminos, and seasonings. Mix thoroughly with your hands.
2. Divide into 6 patties. Prepare a nonstick skillet by lightly coating surface with vegetable cooking spray or by using an oiled pastry brush. Cook burgers over medium heat for 3 to 4 minutes on each side. Spray burgers and pan with vegetable cooking spray as needed.
3. Spray the inside of buns and brown in skillet. This will add a new dimension to the humble bun.
4. Garnish as desired.

Makes 6 burgers

207	Calories
20 g	Protein
28 g	Carbohydrates
4 g	Fat
15%	Calories from Fat
8 g	Fiber
616 mg	Sodium
0 mg	Cholesterol

The First Book of Vegetarian Cooking

Fajitas

1	bell pepper, seeded and cut into quarters and then sliced
1	large onion, sliced
1	clove garlic, pressed or minced
1/4	cup cleaned and sliced mushrooms
1	package Yves Burger Burgers, cut into 1/2-inch strips
4	large whole wheat, fat-free tortillas
1/4	cup drained salsa

1. Prepare a nonstick skillet by lightly coating surface with vegetable cooking spray or by using an oiled pastry brush. Sauté bell peppers, onion, and garlic until tender, but still crisp. Just before done, add mushrooms and cook a little longer.
2. Re-oil skillet if necessary and brown burger strips on both sides. Slightly brown tortillas in pan. They should remain flexible.
3. Fill tortillas with vegetable mixture and burger strips and top with salsa.

Makes 4 servings

You are only limited by your imagination as to the vegetables you can substitute in this recipe. Large whole wheat pitas may be substituted for the tortillas.

150	Calories
9 g	Protein
23 g	Carbohydrates
2 g	Fat
15%	Calories from Fat
10 g	Fiber
432 mg	Sodium
0 mg	Cholesterol

Pita Chips

3   large pitas
     Vegetable cooking spray
     Tex-Mex seasoning,
       Parmesan cheese
       substitute or season-
       ing of choice

Preheat oven to 400 degrees F.

Tortillas or wonton wrappers
can be substituted for the
pitas. CedarLane makes
fat-free, organic, whole
wheat flour tortillas.

For healthier chips use whole wheat, fat-free pitas.

1. Split pitas in two, making 6 rounds. Cut into desired shape: pieces, strips, triangles etc.
2. Place on cookie sheet, spray pitas lightly with vegetable spray and sprinkle with seasoning. Bake 10 minutes or until crisp.

Makes approximately 40 chips

Illness tells us what we are.

—ITALIAN PROVERB

89	Calories
4 g	Protein
15 g	Carbohydrates
1 g	Fat
14%	Calories from Fat
2 g	Fiber
183 mg	Sodium
0 mg	Cholesterol

The First Book of Vegetarian Cooking

Quesadillas

1	bell pepper, seeded, cut into quarters, and sliced into ¼-inch slices
1	zucchini, chopped
1	large onion, sliced
1	clove garlic, pressed or minced
¼	cup sliced mushrooms
6	large tortillas
6	ounces shredded lite Cheddar-style soy cheese*
	Guacamole for garnish

To turn over large items like tortillas and cooked omelets, place a plate (the size of the tortilla or a little larger) over the food. With a hand on the plate, turn pan over leaving food on the plate. Slip food from plate back into pan and continue cooking.

I adapted this Mexican-restaurant favorite to compliment a healthier lifestyle.

1. Prepare a nonstick skillet by lightly coating surface with vegetable cooking spray or by using an oiled pastry brush. Sauté bell peppers, zucchini, onion, and garlic until tender but still crisp. Add mushrooms and cook an additional minute. Remove from skillet.
2. Place a tortilla in the heated skillet and top with ⅓ of the vegetable mixture and ⅓ cheese. Top with a tortilla. When bottom is golden and cheese, melted turn over and brown the other side. Repeat, making three quesadillas.
3. Using scissors, cut into eighths. You can refrigerate at this point and reheat at serving time. Just before serving, garnish with a dollop of guacamole on each wedge.

Makes 24 wedges

*Frozen cheese will shred easier.

29	Calories
2 g	Protein
4 g	Carbohydrates
1 g	Fat
3%	Calories from Fat
3 g	Fiber
108 mg	Sodium
0 mg	Cholesterol

Pot Stickers

୧୨ ୧୨

6	dried shiitake mushrooms, soaked in warm distilled water for 20 minutes
6	finely minced scallions, include 2 inches of green (1 cup)
2	cloves garlic, pressed
3	cups finely chopped napa cabbage
1	cup shredded carrots
1	teaspoon fresh grated gingerroot
1	tablespoon low-sodium tamari sauce
1	tablespoon dry sherry
1	package (14 ounce) round pot sticker wrappers*

Dipping sauce

2	tablespoons sugar-free, all-fruit strawberry jam
1/4	cup low-sodium tamari
1/4	cup balsamic vinegar
2	teaspoons mirin
2	scallions, thinly sliced

Some Chinese recipes require lots of chopping. It's easier if you do all the prep work before starting to cook. This way everything is ready to pop into the skillet.

1. Drain mushrooms, reserving liquid for later use in soups, etc. Discard stems and tough root from mushrooms and finely chop the caps.
2. Prepare a nonstick skillet by lightly coating surface with vegetable cooking spray or by using an oiled pastry brush. Sauté scallions and garlic until tender. Add mushrooms and remaining pot sticker ingredients (excluding wrappers) and cook for an additional 5 minutes. Place filling in a bowl and wipe out skillet in preparation for the wrappers.
3. Place 1 heaping teaspoonful of filling into the center of each pot sticker circle. Moisten edges of circle with water and fold in half pressing edges together to form a half-circle. Keep completed pot stickers covered with a damp cloth to prevent drying out.

The First Book of Vegetarian Cooking

4. Respray skillet and lightly brown pot stickers on each side. When brown, add ¼ cup of water, cover pan, and steam over low heat until all the water is evaporated, about 3 minutes. It might be necessary to do a couple of batches. If the pan gets too hot you'll see how they got their name.
5. Combine dipping sauce ingredients and serve with pot stickers.

Makes about 30 pot stickers and about ⅔ cup sauce

*Available at oriental markets.

46	Calories
2 g	Protein
9 g	Carbohydrates
0 g	Fat
5%	Calories from Fat
1 g	Fiber
129 mg	Sodium
0 mg	Cholesterol

Reuben Sandwich

2 slices rye or whole grain bread
  Vegetable cooking spray
2 tablespoons fat-free Thousand Island Dressing (page 273)
½ cup sauerkraut, rinsed and squeezed dry
2 tablespoons dark and grainy mustard
1 slice fat-free meatless corned beef deli slices
1 slice fat-free Swiss soy cheese

The pre-Christian-era Romans are credited with the first sandwiches which they called offula: *a between-meal snack. Being master bread bakers, eating food between slices of bread came naturally.*

1. Spray both sides of bread slices with vegetable oil and brown one side in a nonstick skillet.
2. Spread the browned side with dressing. Add sauerkraut, mustard, corned beef, and cheese. Top with bread, browned-side down.
3. Place sandwich back in skillet and brown both sides until golden.
4. Serve warm. Keep warm in a 200 degree F oven if making more than one batch.

Makes 1 sandwich

Nearly all men die of their medicines,
and not of their illnesses.

—MOLIÈRE

Drugs prescribed by doctors and approved by the FDA kill 146,000 people each year.

242	Calories
14 g	Protein
36 g	Carbohydrates
5 g	Fat
18%	Calories from Fat
3 g	Fiber
1761 mg	Sodium
0 mg	Cholesterol

The First Book of Vegetarian Cooking

Salad Sandwiches

2   large fat-free whole
        wheat pitas
      Fat-free mayonnaise
¼   avocado, sliced
1   tomato, sliced
8   cucumber slices
1   cup sprouts
2   teaspoons soy "bacon"
        bits
2   onion slices

I have this sandwich quite often for lunch, warming the pita in the toaster before stuffing.

1. Cut the top from each pita, making room to put in the vegetables.
2. Spread inside of pitas with mayonnaise and add vegetables.

Makes 2 pitas

224	Calories
9 g	Protein
33 g	Carbohydrates
7 g	Fat
27%	Calories from Fat
5 g	Fiber
470 mg	Sodium
0 mg	Cholesterol

Popped Corn Olé

❧ ❧

10 cups popped corn
Non-aerosol flavored
oil spray
¼ cup Parmesan cheese
substitute
½ teaspoon onion powder
½ teaspoon ground cumin
Pinch of cayenne
1 teaspoon paprika

The art of popping corn is at least five thousand years old and was perfected by the American Indians. Columbus bought popcorn necklaces from the natives in the West Indies. It is said the Plymouth pilgrims popped corn as part of the first Thanksgiving dinner in 1621. In 1897 you could order popping corn from the Sears Roebuck catalog, 25 pounds for $1.00.

Spray popped corn with oil. Mix seasonings together and toss with sprayed popped corn.

Makes 10 cups

36	Calories
1 g	Protein
6 g	Carbohydrates
1 g	Fat
21%	Calories from Fat
1 g	Fiber
17 mg	Sodium
0 mg	Cholesterol

Eggplant Sticks

1   eggplant (1 pound)
1   cup lite soy or rice milk
1   cup whole grain bread
        crumbs
        Freshly cracked pepper
$1/2$ teaspoon dried oregano
$1/4$ cup grated Parmesan
        cheese substitute

Preheat oven to 400 degrees F.

1. Peel and slice eggplant into $1/2$-inch slices. Cut slices into $1/2 \times 4$-inch sticks.
2. Dip sticks into milk then roll in bread crumbs.
3. Place sticks onto a sprayed or oiled cookie sheet and bake for 10 minutes. Turn sticks over and bake an additional 5 minutes.
4. Sprinkle with pepper, oregano, and Parmesan substitute.

Makes 4 servings

Oregano is actually a wild species of marjoram that has been used sucessfully for digestion and as an expectorant for coughs, colds, and chest congestion.

94	Calories
3 g	Protein
19 g	Carbohydrates
1 g	Fat
13%	Calories from Fat
2 g	Fiber
122 mg	Sodium
0 mg	Cholesterol

Spring Rolls

❧ ❧

3   dried shiitake mushrooms, soaked for 20 minutes in warm distilled water
3   tablespoons low-sodium tamari
½   cup chopped onion
½   tablespoon minced fresh gingerroot
2   cloves garlic, pressed or minced
1½   cups chopped green cabbage
4   fresh mushrooms, chopped
½   cup bamboo shoots, drained and chopped
½   can (8 ounces) water chestnuts, drained and chopped
1   cup fresh bean sprouts, slightly chopped
½   tablespoon mirin rice wine
½   tablespoon honey
12   spring roll wrappers*
      Pronto Plum Sauce for dipping (page 261)

As with most oriental recipes, it is easier to have all the ingredients prepared before starting to cook. If any older children are around the house, why not bring them into the kitchen to help with the chopping. Makes for great quality time.

1. Drain the shiitake mushrooms and remove and discard the stems. Slice the caps thinly.
2. In a nonstick wok or large skillet, heat 2 tablespoons water with 2 tablespoons tamari and bring to a simmer. Add onion, gingerroot, and garlic and sauté until onion is soft. Add cabbage and cook until crisp-tender. Add remaining vegetables and cook an additional 5 minutes, tossing occasionally. Vegetables should be crisp.
3. Stir in remaining 1 tablespoon tamari, mirin, and honey. The filling should be moist but not soupy. Remove from heat.
4. Stack wrappers with the point facing you. Moisten the edges of each wrapper with water before spooning about ¼ cup of filling into the center of the wrapper. Bring bottom up to center and tuck point under the filling. Bring in the sides toward the center (envelope-fashion). Tightly roll up into cylinders, pressing top corner to seal.

*Sold in most oriental food stores. If not available, egg roll wrappers may be substituted.

The First Book of Vegetarian Cooking

5. Place rolls in a nonstick skillet, seam-side down. Do not crowd. Lightly coat with vegetable spray and completely brown rolls over medium heat. To speed up the process, pop under a hot broiler for 1 to 2 minutes.
6. Serve warm with plum sauce or Sweet and Sour sauce (see "Sauces, Marinades, and Dressings").

Makes 12 rolls

Our forests are the lungs of our planet, removing carbon dioxide from the air we breathe and replacing it with oxygen. Ten thousand acres a day are being cut down to make pasture land for cattle. By not eating meat we can help save our planet, ourselves, and our loved ones. Nothing can exist without oxygen.

79	Calories
3 g	Protein
17 g	Carbohydrates
1 g	Fat
2%	Calories from Fat
1 g	Fiber
87 mg	Sodium
0 mg	Cholesterol

Sushi Rolls

❧ ❧

1 tablespoon mirin vinegar
2 cups cooked medium-grain brown rice (rice should be cooked to a soft, sticky consistency)
2 scallions, finely minced (1 tablespoon)
¼ cup finely chopped almonds
5 sheets sushi nori
1½ teaspoons prepared wasabi (Japanese horseradish)

Prepare and divide the following vegetables into fifths

½ large avocado, cut into ¼-inch strips
2 stalks celery, quartered crosswise and cut into ¼-inch strips
1 cup shredded carrots
1 cup alfalfa sprouts
½ cup sweet pickled ginger, drained

❧ ❧

A dipping sauce can be made with tamari sauce mixed with a little wasabi to taste. Watch out—wasabi is hot.

❧ ❧

Sushi rolls have become a very popular food which is most fortunate as they are very healthful. This recipe might require a trip to the oriental market.

1. In a large glass or ceramic bowl, gently combine the vinegar and rice. Fold in the scallions and almonds.
2. Place one nori sheet (shiny side out) on wax paper or bamboo nori mat. The nori sheet and wax paper should be even at the bottom edge.
3. Spread ¼ teaspoon of wasabi along the bottom of nori sheet. Spread ⅕ rice mixture over the nori sheet leaving a 1-inch border at the top edge.
4. In the center of the roll make horizontal rows with ⅕ of the vegetables.
5. Roll nori from the bottom, gripping both nori and wax paper using the paper to help make a firm, tight roll. Don't roll the wax paper in! When completed, set aside seam-side down.
6. Repeat making four additional rolls using remaining ingredients. Cut each roll into 8 pieces using a very sharp, wet knife. Serve with small dishes of extra wasabi, pickled ginger, and tamari (optional).

Makes 5 sushi rolls or 40 pieces

Many Japanese take a spoonful of wasabi each day to prevent allergies, especially hay fever. They only use it when the symptoms are apparent.

23	Calories
1 g	Protein
3 g	Carbohydrates
1 g	Fat
33%	Calories from Fat
1 g	Fiber
4 mg	Sodium
0 mg	Cholesterol

The First Book of Vegetarian Cooking

Tortilla Chips

6   large corn tortillas

Preheat oven to 300 degrees F.

Sprinkle with your favorite seasonings for a different taste treat.

These chips are baked to cut down on those unnecessary fat calories and free radicals that are harmful to our bodies.

1. Cut each tortilla into eight pie-shaped pieces.
2. Place pieces on baking sheet and bake for 10 to 15 minutes or until chips are crisp.

Makes 48 chips

50	Calories
1 g	Protein
10 g	Carbohydrates
1 g	Fat
8%	Calories from Fat
1 g	Fiber
40 mg	Sodium
0 mg	Cholesterol

Vietnamese Spring Rolls

~~

3 ounces rice sticks
1 medium carrot, shredded or julienned
1 English cucumber, julienned
3 scallions, thinly sliced
¼ pound bean sprouts
12 sheets rice paper (dried pastry flake)

Peanut Sauce Dip

¼ cup natural chunky peanut butter
⅛ cup lite rice milk
1 teaspoon reduced-sodium tamari sauce
2 tablespoons frozen orange juice concentrate
1 teaspoon fresh lime juice
1 teaspoon honey
½ teaspoon freshly grated ginger
⅛ teaspoon cayenne
Dash of coconut extract (scant ⅛ teaspoon)

A trip to an Asian market is required to make this live-food snack. Rice sticks are a pasta, and rice paper is the wrapper that holds everything together. Traditionally they are served with hoisin sauce for dipping. I have substituted a more health-ful peanut sauce.

1. Prepare rice sticks by cooking in boiling water for no more than 3 minutes (they become mushy if overcooked). Drain and rinse with cold water; drain again. Save boiling water for rice paper.
2. Put prepared carrots, cucumber, scallions, bean sprouts, and rice sticks in bowls on your work surface.
3. Plunge one sheet of rice paper into boiling water until edges just begin to curl; this takes only a few seconds. Remove with slotted spoon and pat both sides dry with paper towel.
4. Prepare only one roll at a time. Place rice sticks and vege-tables into wrapper and roll up cigar fashion.
5. Mix all sauce ingredients together and serve with spring rolls.

Makes 12 rolls and ¾ cup sauce

98	Calories
3 g	Protein
16 g	Carbohydrates
3 g	Fat
26%	Calories from Fat
1 g	Fiber
53 mg	Sodium
0 mg	Cholesterol

The First Book of Vegetarian Cooking

GREEN BEANS AND VEGGIE DREAMS

"Eat your vegetables." How many times have we heard that? It brings to mind a picture of a little boy sitting at the table with a portion of peas remaining on his plate. As he stirs the peas around, the look on his face would make you think he was being forced to eat poison. You won't have to bribe anyone to eat the vegetable recipes in this chapter because they are delicious as well as nutritionally sound. They can be eaten as side dishes or enjoyed as a main course.

Eating vegetables is good for you. Did you know vegetarians have lower rates of heart disease, high blood pressure, some forms of cancer, adult onset diabetes, immune dysfunction, and obesity? A recent British study concluded that 400 to 800 IUs of vitamin E can reduce heart attacks by 75 percent when taken by people with bad hearts. A vegetable source of vitamin E is dark green leafy vegetables.

Bioflavonoids are big news in nutrition (along with other phytomins) as cancer fighters. Immune-enhancing foods rich in bioflavonoids have a powerful antioxidant effect. They also have an antibacterial effect and enhance vitamin C action. Your body can not produce this, it has to be introduced through eating food rich in bioflavonoids. Vegetable sources include cabbage (with hearts), whole green peppers, citrus (including inner white membranes), parsley, carrots, broccoli, brussels sprouts, turnips, parsnips, horseradish, scallions, onions, garlic, potatoes, yams, squash, pumpkins, and eggplant.

Vegetables are also a source of protein. And don't worry about complete proteins anymore. The body makes it own complete protein in the variety of foods we eat. Broccoli, spinach, peas, and kale are a few sources of protein.

So eat your vegetables and enjoy!

Recipes

Caramelized Onions

"Fried" Green Tomatoes

"Creamed" Spinach

Eggplant Casserole

Carrot Cakes

French "Fries"

Kale and Tomatoes

Marinated Carrots

Rolled Sweet Potatoes

Marinated Green Beans

Vegetable al Forno

Moroccan Couscous

Oriental Broccoli

Pickled Cucumbers

Ratatouille

Snow Peas in Orange Sauce

Spaghetti Squash Parmesan

Stuffed Squash

Tangy Green Beans

Vegetable Curry

"Fried" Eggplant

Zucchini Boats

Caramelized Onions

2   large red onions, thinly
       sliced
2   teaspoons maple syrup
2   teaspoons balsamic
       vinegar
1 1/2 teaspoons dried basil

This can be enjoyed as a side dish or be part of a nutritious salad sandwich.

1. Prepare a nonstick skillet by lightly coating surface with vegetable cooking spray or by using an oiled pastry brush. Over medium-high heat, sauté onions until soft and deep golden-brown.
2. Stir in maple syrup, vinegar, and basil. Cook another minute.

Makes 2 cups

36	Calories
1 g	Protein
8 g	Carbohydrates
1 g	Fat
4%	Calories from Fat
1 g	Fiber
1 mg	Sodium
0 mg	Cholesterol

"Fried" Green Tomatoes

½ cup unbleached flour
½ cup cornmeal
½ teaspoon Spike
   seasoning or salt
   substitute
½ teaspoon freshly ground
   pepper
4 large green tomatoes,
   sliced into ½-inch
   slices
2 cups cold distilled water
1 tablespoon grated
   Parmesan cheese
   alternative

Preheat oven to 400 degrees F.

Forget the lard and bacon grease, these tomatoes are baked and you can't tell the difference.

1. In a shallow dish combine the flour, cornmeal, Spike seasoning, and pepper.
2. Dip each tomato slice into cold water then dredge in flour mixture.
3. Place tomatoes on sprayed or oiled cookie sheet. Bake 15 minutes. Turn and bake another 5 minutes.
4. Sprinkle with Parmesan cheese substitute and serve immediately.

Makes 6 servings

99	Calories
3 g	Protein
21 g	Carbohydrates
1 g	Fat
5%	Calories from Fat
1 g	Fiber
69 mg	Sodium
0 mg	Cholesterol

The First Book of Vegetarian Cooking

"Creamed" Spinach

1 medium onion, chopped
2 cloves garlic, minced or
   pressed
2 packages (10 ounces
   each) frozen spinach
1 package (10.5 ounces)
   extra-firm lite silken
   tofu, drained
   Pinch of cayenne
1/4 teaspoon nutmeg
2 tablespoons grated
   Parmesan cheese
   substitute
1 tablespoon liquid
   aminos
1/4 teaspoon freshly ground
   pepper
2 tablespoons Vogue
   Instant Vege Base

Garnish
1/2 teaspoon grated
   Parmesan cheese
   substitute
1/4 cup whole grain Italian
   bread crumbs
   Non-aerosol vegetable
   spray

Preheat oven to 350 degrees F.

A healthful substitute for the fat-, calorie-, and cholesterol-laden standard recipe. Kale, mustard greens, or collards can be substituted for the spinach.

1. Prepare a nonstick skillet by lightly coating surface with vegetable cooking spray or by using an oiled pastry brush. Sauté onion and garlic until soft. Add spinach and cook until defrosted.
2. In a food processor or blender, process tofu until smooth and creamy. Add to spinach mixture.
3. Mix in remaining ingredients (excluding garnish). Cook over low heat until excess moisture is absorbed.
4. Transfer to an oiled soufflé dish (or high-sided baking dish). Top with Parmesan substitute and bread crumbs. Spray lightly with non-aerosol vegetable spray.
5. Bake for 30 minutes.

Makes 6 servings

70	Calories
6 g	Protein
12 g	Carbohydrates
1 g	Fat
12%	Calories from Fat
3 g	Fiber
440 mg	Sodium
0 mg	Cholesterol

Eggplant Casserole

1 large eggplant
2 large onions, peeled and sliced
3 cloves garlic, pressed or minced
1 pound fresh mushrooms, sliced (about 4 cups)
4 tomatoes, peeled and chopped
2 bell peppers, cut into chunks
¼ teaspoon freshly ground black pepper
1 bay leaf
¼ teaspoon dried basil
¼ teaspoon dried oregano
Pinch of ground cloves
2 teaspoons liquid aminos
2 teaspoons grated Parmesan cheese substitute

Preheat oven to 275 degrees F.

1. Peel eggplant and cut into 1-inch slices. Steam 10 minutes. Drain and set aside.
2. Prepare a nonstick skillet by lightly coating surface with vegetable cooking spray or by using an oiled pastry brush. Sauté the onions and garlic until tender. Add mushrooms and cook 5 minutes longer. Add tomatoes, bell peppers, and seasonings. Simmer 10 additional minutes. Add aminos.
3. In an oiled/sprayed 2-quart casserole dish arrange alternate layers of eggplant and tomato mixture.
4. Top with Parmesan cheese substitute and bake for 1½ hours.

Makes 8 servings

62	Calories
3 g	Protein
13 g	Carbohydrates
1 g	Fat
10%	Calories from Fat
3 g	Fiber
67 mg	Sodium
0 mg	Cholesterol

Carrot Cakes

1 pound carrots, peeled
  and sliced into
  1/4-inch slices
1 cup whole grain bread
  crumbs
4 ounces lite shredded
  Cheddar cheese
  substitute
2 teaspoons liquid aminos
1 tablespoon egg replacer
  (Ener-G), whisked
  with 1/4 cup distilled
  water
1/4 teaspoon allspice
1/8 teaspoon fresh cracked
  pepper
  Pinch of cayenne
1 cup whole wheat corn
  flake cereal, coarsely
  crushed

Preheat oven to 375 degrees F.

1. Steam carrots until tender, about 20 minutes; remove to large bowl and mash.
2. Add bread crumbs, cheese substitute, liquid aminos, egg replacer, allspice, pepper, and cayenne. Mix well.
3. Scoop 1/3 cup of mixture and form into patty. Press patty into corn flakes, coating each side. Continue making 6 patties.
4. Place on sprayed baking sheet and bake for 30 minutes.

Makes 6 servings

82	Calories
6 g	Protein
13 g	Carbohydrates
0 g	Fat
3%	Calories from Fat
1 g	Fiber
338 mg	Sodium
0 mg	Cholesterol

French "Fries"

꿈꿈 꿈꿈

2 large baking potatoes
1 large bowl of ice water
1 cup distilled water
¼ cup flax seeds
1 teaspoon Cajun Spice
 (page 379)

Preheat oven to 425 degrees F.

꿈꿈 꿈꿈

The leftover extract can be stored for two weeks in the refrigerator. The liquid can be used in recipes calling for eggs, and the flax seeds are a wonderful nutritious addition to muffins, breads or soups.

꿈꿈 꿈꿈

Regular French fries are not only fattening, they can cause cancer. Once fat is heated it becomes rancid and when entering the body becomes a source of free radicals (a cause of cancer). This recipe uses no fat so you can enjoy the healthful benefits of the potatoes which are an excellent source of vitamins A, B, C, and potassium.

1. Peel potatoes and cut into French fry-size pieces. Place pieces into the ice water. Set aside.
2. Mix distilled water and flax seeds and set aside for 20 minutes. Stir once or twice.
3. Place flax seed mixture in a small strainer and strain, stirring the seeds well to remove all the liquid. Reserve the seeds for future use.
4. In a large bowl, mix ¼ cup flax seed extract with Cajun spice.
5. Drain potatoes and add to flax extract mixture. Toss to coat.
6. Spray two cookie sheets with non-aerosol vegetable spray. Add single layers of potatoes and bake for 20 minutes. Turn potatoes over and cook for 15 minutes more or until golden.

Makes 4 to 6 servings of potatoes and ¾ cup extra flax seed extract

76	Calories
2 g	Protein
17 g	Carbohydrates
1 g	Fat
5%	Calories from Fat
2 g	Fiber
6 mg	Sodium
0 mg	Cholesterol

Kale and Tomatoes

1½ pounds fresh kale,
    washed with stems
    removed
1 large onion, chopped
1 clove garlic, pressed or
    minced
1 cup chopped fresh
    tomatoes
2 teaspoons lemon juice
    Pinch of black pepper

1. Roll wet kale into cigar-shape tubes. Cut into ½-inch slices; place into Dutch oven and cook over medium heat, uncovered, until tender, about 20 to 30 minutes.
2. Prepare a nonstick skillet by lightly coating surface with vegetable cooking spray or by using an oiled pastry brush. Sauté onion and garlic until tender. Add remaining ingredients, including the cooked kale. Cook for 5 minutes, stirring constantly.

Makes 8 servings

40	Calories
2 g	Protein
8 g	Carbohydrates
1 g	Fat
12%	Calories from Fat
2 g	Fiber
28 mg	Sodium
0 mg	Cholesterol

Marinated Carrots

❧ ❧

2 pounds carrots, peeled and cut into sticks
1 cup orange juice
1 teaspoon fresh grated ginger
1 teaspoon honey
1 teaspoon fresh lemon juice
1 tablespoon chopped fresh mint for garnish

Just about any vegetable may be substituted for the carrots.

1. In a large saucepan, combine carrots with orange juice, ginger, honey, and lemon juice and simmer until carrots are tender but crisp.
2. Place carrots and juice in covered dish and refrigerate overnight.
3. To serve, pour off liquid and arrange carrots on a plate garnished with fresh mint.

Makes 6 cups

Carrots are a wonderful source of beta-carotene, 1 cup (raw, shredded) provides 31,000 international units with only 48 calories. Fat-free and high in soluble fiber they make a good, nutritious diet food. I find more and more markets are stocking organic carrots. We've come a long way, baby!

41	Calories
1 g	Protein
10 g	Carbohydrates
1 g	Fat
3%	Calories from Fat
1 g	Fiber
42 mg	Sodium
0 mg	Cholesterol

Rolled Sweet Potatoes

2   pounds sweet potatoes
          (about 4)
½   cup orange juice
1   tablespoon sugarless
          orange fruit spread
2   tablespoons honey
1   teaspoon minced fresh
          gingerroot
        Pinch of cayenne
2   tablespoons liquid
          aminos
¼   cup pecan meal or finely
          processed pecans

Preheat oven to 425 degrees F.

1. Bake sweet potatoes until tender, about 40 minutes.
2. When potatoes are cool enough to handle, remove skins with a paring knife. The potatoes should retain their shape. Set aside.
3. Combine remaining ingredients (except pecan meal) in a shallow dish. Place pecan meal into another shallow dish. Dip potatoes into liquid, coating well, then roll in the pecan meal.
4. Place on oiled/sprayed cookie sheet and bake for 15 minutes or until lightly brown and crisp.

Makes 4 servings

302   Calories
5 g   Protein
61 g   Carbohydrates
5 g   Fat
15%   Calories from Fat
6 g   Fiber
350 mg   Sodium
0 mg   Cholesterol

Marinated Green Beans

֍ ֎

1 cup green beans, cooked but firm

2 cups pearl onions, peeled and cooked but firm

$1/2$ cup fat-free Italian dressing

Green beans are alkaline in nature, high in protein and iron, and low in calories. Try this recipe with a variety of vegetables.

1. Combine all ingredients and marinate for at least 4 hours or overnight.
2. Store in a glass jar in the refrigerator.

Makes 3 $1/2$ cups

֍ ֎

To peel pearl onions; place in a heat-proof bowl and cover with boiling water. Let rest 5 to 10 minutes. The skin will peel right off.

֍ ֎

One cup of fresh cooked green beans gives you 2 milligrams of iron and has only 20 calories. A 3$1/2$-ounce T-bone steak has 2$1/2$ milligrams of iron and 324 calories.

30	Calories
1 g	Protein
5 g	Carbohydrates
1 g	Fat
37%	Calories from Fat
1 g	Fiber
245 mg	Sodium
0 mg	Cholesterol

Vegetable al Forno

1   large eggplant
2   green bell peppers
2   red bell peppers
1   large onion
1   pound potatoes
    Salt substitute
    Fresh ground pepper
3   cloves garlic, pressed or
      minced
1   teaspoon dried basil
4   large tomatoes, diced or
      1 can (28 ounces)
      crushed plum
      tomatoes

Preheat oven to 375 degrees F.

1. Slice eggplant, peppers, onions, and potatoes into a little thicker than $1/4$-inch slices.
2. Prepare a nonstick skillet by lightly coating surface with vegetable cooking spray or by using an oiled pastry brush. Sauté vegetables individually. This will take 3 pans: one for the potatoes, one for the eggplant, and one for the peppers and onions. You can use one pan, wiping it clean and re-oiling it after cooking each vegetable. Sauté vegetables until tender and beginning to brown. The potatoes and eggplant should be golden.
3. Place potatoes, peppers, onions, eggplant, and salt and pepper into a 2-quart casserole dish. Top with garlic, basil, and tomatoes. Toss lightly.
4. Bake for 35 minutes.

Makes 4 servings

188	Calories
6 g	Protein
42 g	Carbohydrates
2 g	Fat
7%	Calories from Fat
6 g	Fiber
23 mg	Sodium
0 mg	Cholesterol

Moroccan Couscous

1   large onion, chopped
1   small chili pepper,
      minced (or jalapeño)
2   cups vegetable broth*
1   can (14½ ounces)
      chopped tomatoes
1¼ teaspoons ground
      coriander
1   teaspoon ground cumin
1   cup couscous
1   tablespoon liquid
      aminos

Couscous, a granular semolina, is a staple of North African cuisine. Piles of meat are usually heaped on top of a mound of this delicious food. You can add seitan to this recipe for a main course dish or serve as below for a main course accompaniment.

1. Combine onion and pepper with ½ cup of the broth; cook over medium heat until onions are soft.
2. Add remaining 1¾ cup broth, tomatoes, and spices. Cover and simmer for 10 minutes.
3. Stir in couscous and liquid aminos, cover and remove from heat. Rest for 5 minutes or until all the liquid is absorbed. Fluff with a fork.

Makes 4 servings

*Prepared broth or 2 rounded tablespoons Vogue Instant Vege Base dissolved in 2 cups water.

236	Calories
9 g	Protein
49 g	Carbohydrates
1 g	Fat
3%	Calories from Fat
3 g	Fiber
843 mg	Sodium
0 mg	Cholesterol

The First Book of Vegetarian Cooking

Oriental Broccoli

1 head broccoli, cut into florets or 1 package (10 ounces) frozen broccoli spears, partially thawed
1 large onion, sliced
1/2 pound mushrooms, sliced (2 cups)
2 cloves garlic, pressed or minced
1/4 cup teriyaki sauce

1. Prepare a nonstick skillet by lightly coating surface with vegetable cooking spray or by using an oiled pastry brush. Sauté broccoli, onion, mushrooms, and garlic with teriyaki sauce, stirring constantly.
2. Cook until broccoli is just tender but still crisp, about 5 minutes.

Makes 4 servings

61	Calories
5 g	Protein
11 g	Carbohydrates
1 g	Fat
8%	Calories from Fat
4 g	Fiber
710 mg	Sodium
0 mg	Cholesterol

Pickled Cucumbers

❧ ❧

½ cup apple cider vinegar*
3 cups distilled water
1½ teaspoons powdered barley malt sweetener (Dr. Bronner's)
2 European cucumbers, cut into ¼-inch slices
1 small onion, cut into ¼-inch slices

I remember when I was growing up that pickled cucumbers were served quite often with our evening meals. I never get tired of them and the European variety is very high in silica.

1. In a 1½-quart glass jar, mix the vinegar, water, and sweetener. Stir until sweetener is dissolved.
2. Add the cucumber and onion slices, submerging in the marinade. Cover (use the jar's lid if not metal).
3. Refrigerate overnight. Keeps well for a week or so.

Makes 4 to 6 servings

*Use raw and unfiltered organic vinegar (available at health food stores). When vinegar is processed the beneficial ingredients are removed. Raw apple cider vinegar is a wondrous food. Two teaspoons mixed with 1 teaspoon honey in a cup of distilled water, taken daily, is most beneficial to the body. There are books on the market describing the benefits that range from arthritis-reversal to weight-loss.

CRUCIFEROUS VEGETABLES

The vegetables of this family (pronounced crew-SIF-er-us) bear flowers that resemble the cross or crucifix, hence their name. They are:

Broccoli	*Turnips*	*Cauliflower*
Radishes	*Bok choy*	*Rutabaga*
Kale	*Cabbage*	*Watercress*
Mustard greens	*Brussels sprouts*	
Horseradish	*Kohlrabi*	

Cruciferous vegetables are important cancer and heart disease fighters that should be included in your diet.

All vegetables contain protein as well as other nutrients. Contrary to popular belief, you don't have to have a rare steak to get your protein.

19	Calories
1 g	Protein
4 g	Carbohydrates
1 g	Fat
8%	Calories from Fat
1 g	Fiber
2 mg	Sodium
0 mg	Cholesterol

Ratatouille

2 cups eggplant, peeled and cubed
2 cups zucchini, cubed
5 large tomatoes, peeled and sliced
2 large onions, diced
2 medium red or yellow bell peppers, sliced
4 cloves garlic, minced
1 teaspoon dried oregano
$1/2$ teaspoon dried marjoram
1 tablespoon chopped fresh basil
$1 1/2$ teaspoons salt substitute
Pinch of cayenne pepper

Preheat oven to 350 degrees F.

Combine all the ingredients and place in an oiled 2-quart baking dish. Cover and bake for 45 minutes. Uncover and bake an additional 10 minutes.

Makes 4 servings

Remedy for coughs and sore throats:

An old wives tale? I think not! To 1 cup of near boiling water add the juice of 1 lemon, 1 to 2 teaspoons of honey, and a good pinch of cayenne pepper.

90	Calories
3 g	Protein
20 g	Carbohydrates
1 g	Fat
11%	Calories from Fat
5 g	Fiber
19 mg	Sodium
0 mg	Cholesterol

Snow Peas in Orange Sauce

❧ ❧

½ cup freshly squeezed
   orange juice
2 tablespoons slivered
   orange zest
2 tablespoons honey
⅛ teaspoon ground
   cardamom
   Pinch of ground cloves
1¼ pounds snow peas

1. Combine all ingredients except peas in a small pan and simmer until reduced by half.
2. Plunge snow peas into boiling water for 30 seconds. Drain and transfer to warm serving dish.
3. Pour sauce over snow peas and toss lightly to coat.

Makes 6 servings

72	Calories
3 g	Protein
15 g	Carbohydrates
1 g	Fat
3%	Calories from Fat
3 g	Fiber
5 mg	Sodium
0 mg	Cholesterol

The First Book of Vegetarian Cooking

Spaghetti Squash Parmesan

1   spaghetti squash (about 3 pounds), halved
1   tablespoon Vogue Instant Vege Base
½   cup warm distilled water
1   red bell pepper, cut into thin strips
1   green bell pepper, cut into thin strips
1   large onion, sliced
2   cloves garlic, pressed or minced
¼   cup fresh basil leaves, rolled and thinly sliced
¼   cup plus 2 tablespoons grated Parmesan cheese alternative
1   tablespoon arrowroot
    Fresh cracked pepper for garnish
2   tablespoons ground hazelnuts for garnish

Spaghetti squash is not a true squash—it is really a gourd. Outside it resembles an oval, yellow pumpkin with smooth skin; inside the flesh looks like spaghetti strands. A good source of vitamin A and potassium that is low in calories and lends itself well to pasta sauces.

1. Scrape seeds from halved squash. Place cut sides down on a steamer rack. Steam until tender about 20 minutes. When cool enough to handle, scrape out the flesh with the tines of a fork. It will look like spaghetti strands. Set aside.
2. Mix Vogue Instant Vege Base with water to make broth. Set aside.
3. Prepare a nonstick skillet by lightly coating surface with vegetable cooking spray or by using an oiled pastry brush. Sauté peppers, onion, and garlic until tender. Add ¼ cup broth, squash strands, and basil and toss to coat. Add 2 tablespoons grated cheese and toss again. Mix arrowroot with the remaining ¼ cup broth, add to squash mixture, and toss.
4. Transfer to a squash shell or warm platter and garnish with ¼ cup cheese, pepper to taste, and nuts.

Makes 4 to 6 servings

96	Calories
4 g	Protein
16 g	Carbohydrates
3 g	Fat
25%	Calories from Fat
3 g	Fiber
154 mg	Sodium
0 mg	Cholesterol

Stuffed Squash

❧ ❧

6	pounds butternut squash (about 2 large squash), cut in half lengthwise
3	ounces dried shiitake mushrooms
4	cups hot distilled water
1	cup uncooked basmati brown rice
1	tablespoon Vogue Instant Vege Base
1	bay leaf
	Dash of cayenne
1/2	cup uncooked wild rice
2	teaspoons poultry seasoning
4	large stalks celery, chopped
1	large onion (about 1 pound), chopped
2	cloves garlic, minced
1/2	pound Meat of Wheat, sausage style
1/4	cup liquid aminos
1	bag (8 ounces) herb stuffing mix (not cubed)
1/4	cup minced fresh parsley
2	ounces pine nuts

Preheat oven to 350 degrees F.

A festive dish for the holidays and special occasions.

1. Place squash, cut side down, in a baking dish that has been sprayed or oiled. Bake for 45 minutes or until squash is tender.
2. Reconstitute mushrooms in the distilled water for 20 minutes. Drain and reserve the mushroom broth. Discard stems from mushrooms. Thinly slice mushrooms.
3. Bring basmati rice, Vogue Instant Vege Base, bay leaf, cayenne, and 2 cups of mushroom broth to a boil. Cover and simmer for 45 minutes or until all the water is absorbed.
4. At the same time, in another pot, bring wild rice, poultry seasoning, and the 1 cup of mushroom broth to a boil. Cover and simmer for 45 minutes or until all the water is absorbed.
5. Prepare a nonstick skillet by lightly coating surface with vegetable cooking spray or by using an oiled pastry brush. Sauté the celery, onion, and garlic until tender. Stir in the mushrooms and cook an additional 2 minutes.

The First Book of Vegetarian Cooking

6. Combine all ingredients except squash in a large bowl.
7. Peel the skin from the squash and mash the pulp. Line the bottom of a large oiled baking dish with the squash and top with the stuffing. Bake for 30 to 45 minutes.

Makes 12 servings

Wild rice is actually a grass that grows in water. It is rich in protein, minerals, and B vitamins. Squash is an excellent source of the antioxidant beta-carotene.

227	Calories
11 g	Protein
40 g	Carbohydrates
4 g	Fat
15%	Calories from Fat
7 g	Fiber
725 mg	Sodium
0 mg	Cholesterol

Tangy Green Beans

꿍ꍷ ꍷꍆ

1 pound fresh green beans
2 large onions, sliced
3 cloves garlic, pressed or minced
¼ cup balsamic vinegar
¼ teaspoon powdered barley malt sweetener (Dr. Bronner's)

One of my favorite vegetable dishes.

1. Steam beans for 10 minutes.
2. Prepare a nonstick skillet by lightly coating surface with vegetable cooking spray or by using an oiled pastry brush. Sauté onions and garlic until tender.
3. Add green beans and cook with the onions for 5 minutes, tossing frequently. Add vinegar and cook an additional 10 minutes, tossing frequently. The liquid should be almost absorbed.
4. Add sweetener and toss to blend.

Makes 5 servings

64	Calories
2 g	Protein
15 g	Carbohydrates
1 g	Fat
5%	Calories from Fat
2 g	Fiber
5 mg	Sodium
0 mg	Cholesterol

The First Book of Vegetarian Cooking

Vegetable Curry

1 teaspoon turmeric
1 teaspoon ground cumin
1 teaspoon ground
     coriander
½ teaspoon cayenne
2 teaspoons paprika
1 large onion, chopped
     (2 cups at least)
1 bell pepper, chopped
2 cloves garlic, minced
1 pound cooked potatoes,
     cut into 1-inch pieces
½ pound cooked carrots,
     cut into ½-inch
     pieces
1 can (16 ounces) peeled
     tomatoes, undrained
1 cup frozen peas
1 tablespoon liquid
     aminos

I discovered this dish during a brief stay in London and still have fond memories of that Indian Tandoori. This tastes just as good.

1. Mix the turmeric, cumin, coriander, cayenne, and paprika with a little water to form a paste.
2. Prepare a nonstick skillet by lightly coating surface with vegetable cooking spray or by using an oiled pastry brush. Sauté onion, bell pepper, and garlic until tender. Continue cooking and add seasoning paste and stir until spices become aromatic; about 5 minutes.
3. Combine potatoes and carrots with onion mixture. Cook for a minute or so.
4. Add tomatoes and peas and simmer covered for 15 to 20 minutes longer. Uncover after 10 minutes. Add liquid aminos before serving.

Makes 4 to 6 servings

157 Calories
5 g Protein
34 g Carbohydrates
1 g Fat
5% Calories from Fat
4 g Fiber
294 mg Sodium
0 mg Cholesterol

"Fried" Eggplant

1 cup organic whole grain pastry flour

$1/2$ teaspoon garlic powder

1 tablespoon Old Bay Seasoning or Cajun spice (page 379)

1 cup lite rice or soy milk

$1/4$ cup flax seed extract (see page 365)

1 tablespoon liquid aminos

1 eggplant (1 pound)

1. In a medium bowl combine flour, garlic powder, and spice. Whisk in milk, flax seed extract, and liquid aminos.
2. Peel and slice eggplant into $1/2$-inch slices; dip into batter. Shake off excess batter.
3. Prepare a nonstick skillet by lightly coating surface with vegetable cooking spray or by using an oiled pastry brush. Cook the eggplant 5 minutes on each side over low heat.

Makes 4 servings

Vitamins should not be taken on an empty stomach, they can pass through the system too quickly.

168	Calories
5 g	Protein
35 g	Carbohydrates
2 g	Fat
11%	Calories from Fat
2 g	Fiber
329 mg	Sodium
0 mg	Cholesterol

The First Book of Vegetarian Cooking

Zucchini Boats

2   medium zucchini
1   large onion, chopped
1/2   pound mushrooms,
          sliced (2 cups)
1   red bell pepper, chopped
1   cup corn kernels
1/2   cup salsa
2   tablespoons whole
          wheat bread crumbs
2   tablespoons grated soy
          Parmesan cheese

Preheat oven to 350 degrees F.

1. Cut zucchini in half lengthwise. Remove pulp and cut pulp into 1/2- inch pieces. Reserve the shells.
2. Prepare a nonstick skillet by lightly coating surface with vegetable cooking spray or by using an oiled pastry brush. Sauté onion, mushrooms, zucchini pulp, and pepper until tender-crisp. Add corn, salsa, crumbs, corn, and cheese. Toss to coat.
3. Stuff zucchini shells with sautéed mixture and place on a cookie sheet. Bake for 20 minutes.

Makes 4 boats

101	Calories
5 g	Protein
22 g	Carbohydrates
1 g	Fat
10%	Calories from Fat
3 g	Fiber
305 mg	Sodium
0 mg	Cholesterol

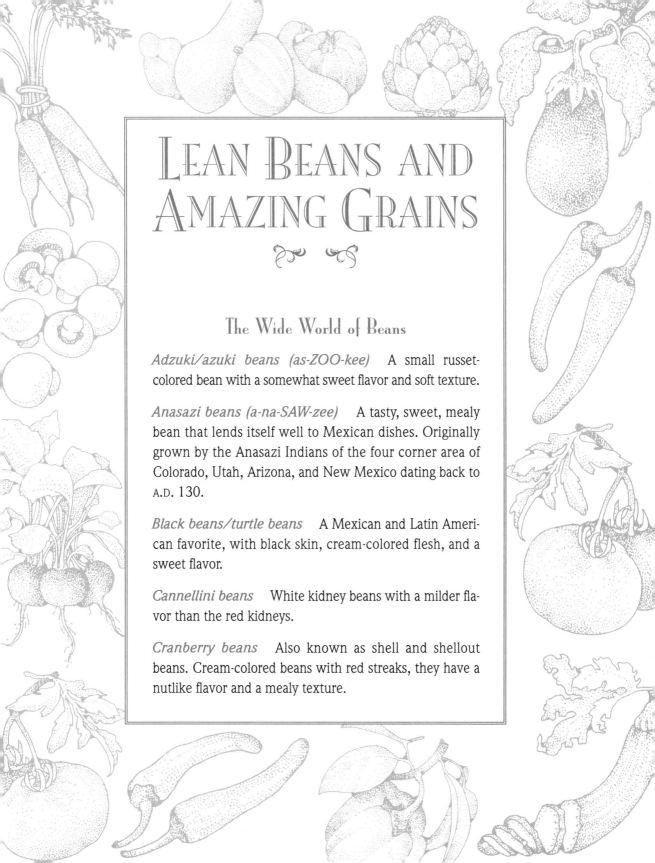

LEAN BEANS AND AMAZING GRAINS

The Wide World of Beans

Adzuki/azuki beans (as-ZOO-kee)   A small russet-colored bean with a somewhat sweet flavor and soft texture.

Anasazi beans (a-na-SAW-zee)   A tasty, sweet, mealy bean that lends itself well to Mexican dishes. Originally grown by the Anasazi Indians of the four corner area of Colorado, Utah, Arizona, and New Mexico dating back to A.D. 130.

Black beans/turtle beans   A Mexican and Latin American favorite, with black skin, cream-colored flesh, and a sweet flavor.

Cannellini beans   White kidney beans with a milder flavor than the red kidneys.

Cranberry beans   Also known as shell and shellout beans. Cream-colored beans with red streaks, they have a nutlike flavor and a mealy texture.

Fava beans   (FAH-vuh) These broad beans look like large lima beans with tan skin and are a Mediterranean and Middle Eastern favorite. They have a very tough outer skin, which should be removed by blanching.

Great Northern beans   Large white beans resembling lima beans but with a delicate mild flavor and mealy texture.

Kidney beans   A dark red skin with cream-colored flesh. Its full-bodied flavor makes it a favorite in chili. White kidney beans are cannellini beans.

Lima beans/butter beans   Available in large or small. Rather bland flavor with soft texture.

Mung beans   A small dried bean with yellow flesh and skin of green, brown, or black. Used to grow bean sprouts mostly, but when cooked has a tender texture with a sweet flavor.

Navy bean/pea bean/Yankee bean   Commonly used white legume with a mild flavor and mealy texture. Used mostly in baked beans and soups. Gets its name from the fact the U.S. Navy has used this bean as a staple since the 1800s.

Pink beans   This smooth, reddish-brown bean is very popular in the west. These beans have a meaty flavor and mealy texture. A favorite in refried beans and chili.

Pinto beans   Pinto is the Spanish word for "painted." A pale pink bean mottled with reddish-brown, these beans are interchangeable with pink beans. Full-bodied flavor and mealy texture.

Red beans   Popular in Mexico and the U.S. Southwest. A bean with a mealy texture and sweet flavor. Also used in refried beans and chili dishes.

Soybeans   This legume dates back to about 3,000 B.C. There are over a thousand varieties. Their taste is quite bland with a firm texture. Low in carbohydrates, high in protein and oil, these beans are used to make tofu, soybean oil, soy flour, soy milk, soy sauce, miso, and tamari as well and are cooked in bean dishes like other dried beans. They are also sprouted and their byproducts are used in food and nonfood products. Truly a wonder food.

Flageolets (fla-zhoh-LAY)   Tiny French kidney beans that range in color from green to pale cream. A delicate sweet flavor with a soft texture.

Lentils   A staple throughout the Middle East and India and popular in Europe and in vegetarian cooking. There are two varieties of lentils; the French/European and the Egyptian/red. Both are small; oval to round in shape. Green lentils are pungent in flavor with a soft texture whereas the pink are more bland.

Legume Cooking Chart

Dry Legumes (1 cup)	Water (cups)	Cooking Time (approximate hours)	Yield (cups)
Adzuki beans*	3 ¼	1	3
Anasazi beans	2	1	2 ¼
Black beans	3	1–2	2 ¼
Black-eyed peas	3	1	2
Chickpeas	4	2–3	2
Great Northern beans	3 ½	1 ½–2	2 ⅔
Kidney beans	2 ¼	1 ½–2	2 ¼
Lentils, brown*	3	½	2 ¼
Lentils, red*	3	½	1 ⅔
Navy beans	3	1–1 ½	2 ⅔
Pinto beans	3	1 ½–2	2 ⅔
Split peas	3	1	2

Soak legumes with seasonings at least 8 hours before cooking.
*do not require soaking

Peas

Black-eyed peas/cowpea   Beige in color with a black circular eye at its inner edge. Succulent, earthy flavor with a mealy texture. Very popular in the southern United States.

Chickpeas/garbanzo   Round, irregular-shaped with a beige color. Nutlike in flavor with a crunchy texture. Used extensively in the Mediterranean, India, and Middle East.

Field/garden peas   Available dried in green or yellow and usually sold split. Sweet taste with a soft texture.

Pigeon peas   A gray-yellow pea about the size of a garden pea. A pungent flavor and mealy texture.

Split peas   The split form of garden or field peas.

The Wide World of Grains

Whenever available always purchase stone-ground grains, which retain more nutrients. Store grains in the refrigerator to avoid infestations and rancidity.

Amaranth   The food of the gods for over five thousand years to the Aztecs and Incas. A nutty and somewhat sweet grain available in whole grain, flour, and cereal forms. Used in porridge, puddings, casseroles, and loaves. If rising is desired in a recipe, this flour should be mixed with other flours (1/4 to 1/2 cup per recipe).

Barley groats   Unpolished whole kernels of barley. Mild in flavor with a chewy texture.

Barley, pearl   Whole kernels that have been polished four to six times. Mild in flavor with a tender texture. A favorite in soups.

The First Book of Vegetarian Cooking

Whole Grains Cooking Chart

Grain (1 cup dry)	Water (cups)	Cooking Time (minutes)	Yield (cups)
Amaranth	1 1/2	20–25	2
Barley	3	45–70	2 1/2
Basmati rice (white)	2 1/2	20–25	3
Basmati rice (brown)	2 1/4	35 to 40	3
Brown rice	2	45–60	3
Buckwheat (kasha)	2	15–20	2 1/2
Cornmeal (Polenta)	4	25–40	3
Cracked rye wheat	2	25–40	2 1/2
Millet*	2 1/2–3	35–45	3 1/2
Quinoa*	2	15–20	3
Rye berries	2 1/2–3	1 hr.	2
Wild rice	3	50–65	3 1/2
Whole wheat berries	2 1/2–3	2 hours	2 3/4

*Millet and Quinoa are even more flavorful if dry-roasted prior to cooking in water. Spread grain over a heavy skillet, and cook, over medium heat, until you begin to smell the grain's aroma. Transfer to water and simmer as per chart above.

Barley grits Ground pearl barley. Comes in coarse, medium, and fine.

Buckwheat groats Whole unpolished kernels. Mild in flavor with a nutty taste and soft texture. Cooked in a manner similar to rice.

Buckwheat groats, toasted (whole kasha) Oven toasted to bring out the flavor. Can be used as a substitute for rice in recipes.

Buckwheat grits (kasha) Ground groats. Available in coarse, medium, or fine. Buckwheat is native to Russia and is used (flour-form) in their famous blinis. Can be used in rice recipes.

Bulgur   Wheat berries that are steamed, dried, and cracked. Has a mild nutty flavor and a soft chewy texture. Excellent in pilaf and salads. The base grain for tabbouleh.

Cornmeal   Dried corn kernels that have been ground into fine, medium, or coarse textures. The stone-ground variety is the most nutritious, retaining more nutrients. Available in white yellow, or blue. A sweet flavor.

Kamut (ka-MOOT)   Available in whole grain, rolled whole grains, whole-grain flours, pancake mix, and cereal. Another ancient grain, a staple in the Nile region over six thousand years ago. Makes light textured pastas and baked goods. It has a light buttery flavor. Used in breads, soups, salads, and stews for texture; rolled grain as a hot cereal, in loaves and casseroles, and to thicken soups.

Quinoa (KEEN-wa)   This Peruvian staple is good in pilafs, cold salads, casseroles, and even as a pudding. Always rinse well to avoid a bitter taste. One of the finest sources of protein in the vegetable kingdom. Available in whole-grain or pasta form. Has a mild, pleasant flavor; can be substituted for rice in any recipe.

Masa harina   Finely ground kernels of yellow or white hominy.

Millet   A cereal grass, rich in protein; available whole or in flour form. Use whole, cooked in hot cereals or in pilaf. The powdered form is used in puddings, breads, and cakes.

Oat groats   Unpolished whole kernels of oats still retaining most of the original nutrients. Mostly eaten as cereal, salad, or stuffing, they are nutlike in flavor and have a chewy texture. When steamed and flattened (rolled) they become the old-fashioned rolled oats.

Rolled oats (oat flakes)   Steamed and flattened oat groats.

Oatmeal Ground oat groats; available in coarse, medium, or fine.

Rice, arborio Polished whole kernels of a round short-grain rice with a rather bland taste and soft texture.

Rice, basmati Meaning "queen of fragrance." A fragrant long-grain rice with a fine texture and nutlike flavor, aged to decrease its moisture content.

Rice, brown The entire grain with only the inedible outer husk removed. Nutlike in flavor with a chewy texture. Available in long, medium, or short kernels.

Rice, glutinous Polished whole kernels of short-grain rice with a slightly sweet flavor and very sticky texture.

Rice, white The husk, bran, and germ is removed. Available long, medium, and short grain. Rather bland in flavor.

Rice, wild (actually a grass) Unpolished whole kernels with a strong nutty flavor and chewy texture.

Rye, cracked Unpolished rye that has been cracked with a soft texture and slightly sour in flavor.

Spelt One of the most ancient grains dating back to Europe about nine thousand years ago. Especially favored by people that are gluten intolerant. Favored in pastas for its rich wheat flavor. Available in whole-grain flour, rolled grain, bran, breads (including bagels and pita), cereal, and pastas.

Teff Used in Ethiopia for thousands of years; the world's tiniest grain. Having a strong, distinct flavor and aroma, it is used mostly in porridges, puddings, pancakes, and baked goods or added to soups and stews. The delicious Ethiopian bread, Injera is made with teff flour.

Wheat berries   Unpolished whole kernels with a very chewy texture and robust flavor. Not only used cooked but sprouted to make the most beneficial wheat grass, which is juiced and drunk.

Wheat, cracked   Cracked wheat berries. Available in coarse, medium, and fine.

Whole grains are a good source of zinc. Zinc is needed by 100 enzymes in human cells to function properly. While a mild deficiency of this mineral may not produce obvious symptoms, it is thought to accelerate the aging process.

Recipes

Cooking Legumes	Chili Pie
Beans and Franks	Hopping John
Bhat Aur Savia	Lentil Patties
Black Lentil Curry	Macaroni and Lentils
Bulgur Pilaf	Spanish Rice
Cabbage Rolls	Tamale Pie
Chile (no con) Carne	Stuffed Peppers

The First Book of Vegetarian Cooking

Cooking Legumes

1	cup dry beans
3	cups distilled water (for soaking beans)
½	teaspoon garlic powder
½	teaspoon cumin
	Distilled water for cooking (see chart)
1	small onion, chopped
2	stalks celery
1	clove garlic, pressed or minced
1	bay leaf
	Pinch of cayenne
	Salt/salt substitute*

1. Rinse beans and pick out any impurities. Place in a bowl and cover with distilled water, garlic powder, cumin, and desired seasoning. Soak for at least 8 hours or overnight (soaking beans with seasoning will improve their flavor).

2. Drain beans and place in a saucepan with indicated amount of water (see chart, page 155). Bring to a boil. Skim off foam and add onion, celery, garlic, bay leaf, and cayenne. Cover, reduce heat to a simmer, and cook for amount of time indicated on the chart. Add salt or salt substitute to taste when legumes are soft.

Makes 2 to 3 cups (see chart)

*Do not add salt or tomato products to uncooked beans. Doing this will prolong the cooking time. Add only when beans are done.

Discarding the soaking water and replacing with fresh water for cooking reduces the amount of gas you will experience from eating legumes. Cooking beans with celery makes for a more digestible bean.

118	Calories
7 g	Protein
23 g	Carbohydrates
1 g	Fat
3%	Calories from Fat
4 g	Fiber
20 mg	Sodium
0 mg	Cholesterol

Beans and Franks

1 pound navy beans, cooked
1 large onion, roughly chopped
¼ cup honey
1 teaspoon dry mustard
½ teaspoon cinnamon
1 can (14 ounces) crushed tomatoes, undrained
2 teaspoons liquid aminos
5 Yves Veggie Tofu wieners

Preheat oven to 350 degrees F.

For another great barbecue dish take a look at the Jerk Kebobs (page 239)

I saw a commercial on TV mentioning not taking a certain girl to a barbecue because she was a vegetarian. One vegetarian complained and guess what? They cut that part from the commercial. Who says we can't make a difference. Here's a recipe that certainly would be good barbecue food. Serve with garlic bread.

1. Place cooked beans into a baking pan (a lasagna baking dish works well). Add remaining ingredients (excluding the wieners and aminos) and mix.
2. Bake uncovered for 1 hour, then cover and bake an additional 30 minutes. Add aminos.
3. Just before serving time, cook the wieners on the barbecue grill or inside on a griddle. Arrange wieners on top of beans and serve.

Makes 5 servings

453	Calories
33 g	Protein
80 g	Carbohydrates
2 g	Fat
3%	Calories from Fat
38 g	Fiber
454 mg	Sodium
0 mg	Cholesterol

The First Book of Vegetarian Cooking

Bhat Aur Savia (Rice and Pasta)

1 large onion, chopped
2 cloves garlic, pressed or minced
3 whole cloves
1 inch cinnamon stick
¼ teaspoon cumin seed
¼ teaspoon whole allspice
1 teaspoon salt substitute
½ teaspoon turmeric
   Pinch of cayenne
1 cup uncooked basmati rice
3 ounces spinach elbow pasta

A slimmed-down Indian dish.

1. Prepare a nonstick skillet by lightly coating surface with vegetable cooking spray or by using an oiled pastry brush. Sauté onion and garlic until tender.
2. Add spices, rice, and pasta. Sauté for 3 minutes.
3. Add just enough boiling water to cover rice and pasta. Simmer, covered, until rice is tender and all the liquid is absorbed, about 30 minutes. Add more water if necessary.

Serves 4

223	Calories
6 g	Protein
47 g	Carbohydrates
1 g	Fat
3%	Calories from Fat
2 g	Fiber
540 mg	Sodium
0 mg	Cholesterol

Black Lentil Curry (Maahn)

୬ ୬

2	cups Urads* (black lentils), rinsed well
1/2	cup kidney beans, rinsed and soaked 8 hours
5	cups distilled water
3	carrots, diced
1	piece (1 inch) gingerroot
1	large onion, chopped
2 1/2	tablespoons curry powder
2	teaspoons ground cumin
1/4	teaspoon cayenne pepper
2	cinnamon sticks
7	whole cardamom pods or 1/8 teaspoon ground cardamom seeds
2	large tomatoes, chopped
1	tablespoon salt-free tomato paste
3	tablespoons liquid aminos

The Urad (black lentils) are different from regular varieties of lentils and must be cooked very slowly or they become mushy. A Crock-Pot is ideal for this recipe. Freeze unused curry for future meals.

1. Place Urads, kidney beans, water, carrots, gingerroot, onion, curry powder, cumin, cayenne, cinnamon, and cardamom in a Crock-Pot, stir, cover and cook on low heat until beans and carrots are tender, 6 to 8 hours, depending upon pot. Add tomatoes and tomato paste and cook another 1 hour.
2. Remove 1 cup of the cooked bean mixture and mash or process in a food processor. Return to the pot, add liquid aminos and stir to blend.

Makes 16 servings

*Available at East Indian food stores.

124	Calories
9 g	Protein
22 g	Carbohydrates
1 g	Fat
4%	Calories from Fat
5 g	Fiber
146 mg	Sodium
0 mg	Cholesterol

Bulgur Pilaf

1 cup raisins
  Hot distilled water
1 cup chopped celery
2 cups chopped onion
3 cups uncooked course
  bulgur
1 tablespoon poultry
  seasoning
¼ cup Vogue Instant
  Vege Base
5 cups warm distilled
  water
2 tablespoon liquid
  aminos
½ cup chopped walnuts

Bulgur is a staple grain of eastern Mediterranean countries. It is a wheat that has been parboiled, dried, and cracked; a good source of protein, niacin, and iron. I quite often bring this dish to Thanksgiving or Christmas dinners.

1. In a small bowl, add enough hot water to cover the raisins.
2. Prepare a nonstick skillet by lightly coating surface with vegetable cooking spray or by using an oiled pastry brush. Sauté the celery and onion until soft.
3. Add bulgur and sauté while stirring for about 5 minutes. Add poultry seasoning.
4. Mix Vogue Instant Vege Base with the warm water to make a broth. Stir in broth, bring to a boil, cover and reduce heat to a simmer and cook for 20 minutes or until the liquid is absorbed.
5. Drain raisins. Stir raisins, liquid aminos, and nuts into the bulgur mixture.
6. Transfer to large warmed casserole dish and serve.

Makes 10 servings

253	Calories
7 g	Protein
49 g	Carbohydrates
5 g	Fat
18%	Calories from Fat
7 g	Fiber
279 mg	Sodium
0 mg	Cholesterol

Cabbage Rolls

1   cup uncooked brown basmati rice, rinsed
1¼ cups distilled water
1   large onion, chopped (1 pound)
1   bell pepper, chopped
2   cloves garlic, minced or pressed
6   ounces portabello mushrooms, chopped
2   carrots, shredded (1 cup)
2   tablespoons salt-free tomato paste
    Pinch of cayenne
1   tablespoon liquid aminos
2½ pounds savoy cabbage, rinsed and cored, remove outside leaves
3   cups fat-free, drained, stewed tomatoes, spaghetti sauce, tomato sauce, or salsa

Preheat oven to 375 degrees F.

If time is short, steps 1 to 3 can be prepared a day or two in advance. I ran into a gentleman in the flea market the other day, and he swears juicing raw cabbage cured his ulcer after all else failed. Speaking of flea markets, the first things I do when arriving in a foreign country is check out the book stores that sell English translations of local recipes and find out when the flea markets are open. I haven't found a country that doesn't have some sort of flea market.

1. Bring rice and water to a boil, reduce heat, cover and cook rice for 25 minutes. If too moist uncover and cook for an additional minute or two. All the liquid should be absorbed.
2. Prepare a nonstick skillet by lightly coating surface with vegetable cooking spray or by using an oiled pastry brush. Sauté onion, bell pepper, and garlic until soft. Add mushrooms, carrots, tomato paste, and cayenne. Cook an additional 2 minutes; liquid should be absorbed.
3. Add rice and liquid aminos; mix well. Set aside.
4. Carefully remove 10 leaves from the cabbage and place on a steamer rack in an 8-quart Dutch oven with 1 inch of boiling water. Cover and steam for 10 minutes. Drain in colander.
5. When cool enough to handle, pat leaves dry with towel. Make an upside-down V cut in each leaf and remove 1½ to 2 inches of the remaining core.

6. Save leftover cabbage for the soup pot. Place ⅓ cup of filling onto each leaf. Fold cabbage (stem-end side) over filling, tucking up under filling, bring in sides and fold over, envelope fashion.

7. Place rolls, seam-side down, into a sprayed 2-quart lasagna pan. Top with stewed tomatoes, completely covering the rolls, cover and bake for 30 minutes. Uncover and bake an additional 30 minutes.

Makes 10 rolls (5 generous servings)

277	Calories
10 g	Protein
60 g	Carbohydrates
2 g	Fat
7%	Calories from Fat
9 g	Fiber
420 mg	Sodium
0 mg	Cholesterol

Chili (no con) Carne

<table>
<tr><td>1</td><td>extra large onion, chopped</td></tr>
<tr><td>1</td><td>green bell pepper, chopped</td></tr>
<tr><td>3</td><td>cloves garlic, pressed</td></tr>
<tr><td>3</td><td>tablespoons chili powder</td></tr>
<tr><td>1</td><td>teaspoon cumin</td></tr>
<tr><td></td><td>Salt substitute</td></tr>
<tr><td>½</td><td>teaspoon Tabasco sauce</td></tr>
<tr><td>1</td><td>carrot, shredded</td></tr>
<tr><td>1½</td><td>cups distilled water</td></tr>
<tr><td>1</td><td>can (28 ounces) crushed tomatoes</td></tr>
<tr><td>¼</td><td>cup TVP granules (textured vegetable protein—optional)</td></tr>
<tr><td>2</td><td>cups cooked kidney beans</td></tr>
</table>

Prepare a nonstick skillet by lightly coating surface with vegetable cooking spray or by using an oiled pastry brush. Sauté onion, pepper, and garlic until soft. Add seasonings and cook an additional 3 minutes. Add remaining ingredients and cook covered for 30 minutes.

Makes 4 servings

206	Calories
11 g	Protein
40 g	Carbohydrates
2 g	Fat
10%	Calories from Fat
7 g	Fiber
419 mg	Sodium
0 mg	Cholesterol

The First Book of Vegetarian Cooking

Chili Pie

ॐ ॐ

10 ounces prepared polenta (San Gennaro)*

1 medium onion, halved, sliced thinly

1 can (15 ounces) fat-free vegetarian chili with black beans (Health Valley)

1 can (4 ounces) chopped green chiles

1 tomato, diced

1 tablespoon Parmesan cheese alternative

Preheat oven to 350 degrees F.

I was very pleased when I found a two pound tube of prepared organic polenta at the health food store and it's fat-free to boot. What a time saver!

1. Slice polenta into ¼-inch slices. Spray or oil a 9-inch or 10-inch deep-dish pie pan with vegetable oil and arrange sliced polenta over bottom of pan, cutting pieces to fit where necessary.
2. Add remaining ingredients in layers, spreading out to cover preceding layer.
3. Place in oven and bake for 30 minutes.

Makes 4 servings

*Or make your own (page 374).

152	Calories
9 g	Protein
30 g	Carbohydrates
0 g	Fat
1%	Calories from Fat
9 g	Fiber
408 mg	Sodium
0 mg	Cholesterol

Hopping John

❧ ❧

2 cups dried black-eyed peas, rinsed and soaked for 8 hours
1 large onion, chopped (2 cups)
1 bell pepper, chopped (1 cup)
⅛ teaspoon cayenne
1½ tablespoon Vogue Instant Vege Base
4½ cups distilled water
1 cup uncooked brown rice
¼ teaspoon fresh cracked pepper
1 tablespoon liquid aminos

Soak the black-eyed peas on New Year's Eve so you can enjoy this traditional dish of the South the next day.

1. Place peas, onion, bell pepper, cayenne, Vogue Instant Vege Base, and 2½ cups distilled water in Dutch oven. Cover and cook for 1¼ hours. Almost all the liquid should be absorbed.
2. Add rice, additional 2 cups distilled water, and pepper. Cover and cook for 45 minutes or until rice is done. Add liquid aminos before serving.

Makes 8 servings

❧ ❧

Serve with cornbread and greens for a typical southern New Year's feast that will ensure good luck for the coming year.

❧ ❧

255	Calories
13 g	Protein
49 g	Carbohydrates
2 g	Fat
5%	Calories from Fat
13 g	Fiber
154 mg	Sodium
0 mg	Cholesterol

The First Book of Vegetarian Cooking

Lentil Patties

3	cups lentils, cooked and mashed
1	medium onion, minced
½	medium carrot, grated
2	tablespoons sunflower seeds
2	tablespoons tahini
1	teaspoon garlic powder
1	teaspoon cumin powder
⅛	teaspoon cayenne
1	teaspoon chili powder
1	teaspoon low-sodium tamari
¾	ounce oat bran
¾	ounce cornmeal

Preheat oven to 400 degrees F.

1. Mix all ingredients together (excluding the cornmeal).
2. Form into five patties and lightly dust each patty with cornmeal.
3. Bake on a sprayed or oiled cookie sheet for 15 minutes. Turn patties over and cook an additional 15 minutes.

Makes 5 patties

Patties can also be prepared in a nonstick skillet that has been sprayed with non-aerosol vegetable spray. Brown patties on both sides.

242	Calories
15 g	Protein
36 g	Carbohydrates
6 g	Fat
24%	Calories from Fat
7 g	Fiber
61 mg	Sodium
0 mg	Cholesterol

Macaroni and Lentils

1   large onion, chopped
2   cloves garlic, minced or
      pressed
1¾ cups cooked lentils or
      1 can (15 ounces)
      lentils, drained
1   can (8 ounces) salt-free
      tomato sauce
2   tablespoons chopped
      fresh Italian flat-leaf
      parsley
½   teaspoon dried oregano
      Pinch of cayenne
8   ounces dry whole wheat
      elbow macaroni,
      cooked

1. Prepare a nonstick skillet by lightly coating surface with vegetable cooking spray or by using an oiled pastry brush. Sauté onions and garlic until soft.
2. Mix in remaining ingredients. Cook until thoroughly heated.

Makes 4 servings

183	Calories
11 g	Protein
36 g	Carbohydrates
1 g	Fat
4%	Calories from Fat
7 g	Fiber
17 mg	Sodium
0 mg	Cholesterol

The First Book of Vegetarian Cooking

Spanish Rice

1 cup 1-inch chunks TVP (textured vegetable protein)*

1 large bell pepper, chopped

1 extra large onion, chopped

4 cloves garlic, minced

2 cups uncooked brown rice, rinsed

1 can (6 ounces) tomato paste

2¼ cups distilled water (incl. the reserved TVP liquid)

⅛ cup liquid aminos

1 tablespoon Vogue Instant Vege Base

⅛ teaspoon cayenne

2 tablespoons pimiento, diced

1 bay leaf

⅛ teaspoon saffron threads (optional)

¼ teaspoon ground annatto seeds

This recipe is one of my favorites. I enjoy it both with or without the TVP.

1. Reconstituted the TVP*. Set aside and reserve the liquid.
2. Prepare a nonstick skillet by lightly coating surface with vegetable cooking spray or by using an oiled pastry brush. Sauté the bell pepper, onion, and garlic until soft.
3. Add the rice and cook for about 2 minutes, stirring frequently. Add the prepared TVP and the remaining ingredients. Simmer, covered, for about 40 minutes or until the rice is done and liquid is absorbed. Add more water as needed.

Makes 8 servings

*See TVP Reconstituting, page 383.

Ground annatto seeds can be found in the Spanish section of supermarkets or ethnic shops and is used for the coloring in this dish.

248	Calories
11 g	Protein
48 g	Carbohydrates
2 g	Fat
7%	Calories from Fat
5 g	Fiber
415 mg	Sodium
0 mg	Cholesterol

Tamale Pie

ào⁓ ⇜ɕ

Filling

1 extra large onion, chopped
1 green bell pepper, chopped
3 cloves garlic, pressed
3 tablespoons chili powder
1 teaspoon cumin
   Salt substitute
1/2 teaspoon Tabasco sauce
1 carrot, shredded
1 1/2 cups distilled water
1 can (28 ounces) crushed tomatoes
1/4 cup TVP granules (textured vegetable protein), optional
2 cups cooked kidney beans

If you like chili and cornbread, you'll love this dish.

1. Prepare a nonstick skillet by lightly coating surface with vegetable cooking spray or by using an oiled pastry brush. Sauté onion, pepper, and garlic until soft. Add chili powder, cumin, salt substitute, and Tabasco and cook an additional 3 minutes. Add remaining filling ingredients and cook, covered, for 30 minutes.
2. While chili is cooking, prepare the cornbread topping. Sift dry topping ingredients into a large bowl. In a separate bowl mix the remaining topping ingredients together. Combine wet and dry ingredients.

ào⁓ ⇜ɕ

In a rush? Use 2 cans (15 ounces each) fat-free vegetarian chili and cornbread from a mix.

ào⁓ ⇜ɕ

Cornbread topping

1   cup organic cornmeal
1   cup organic enriched
        unbleached flour
¼   teaspoon powdered
        barley malt sweet-
        ener (Dr. Bronner's)
1½ tablespoons baking
        powder
½   teaspoon salt substitute
½   teaspoon cumin powder
1   cup lite soy or rice milk
1½ teaspoons egg replacer
        (see "Ingredient
        Exchanges"), whisked
        with ¼ cup distilled
        water
2   tablespoons applesauce
1   teaspoon minced
        jalapeño pepper
        (optional)

Preheat oven to 400 degrees F.

3. Spoon chili into a sprayed 10-inch deep-dish pie plate or 2-quart casserole. Top with cornbread mixture, smoothing out to edges of dish. Bake for 30 to 45 minutes until chili is hot and bubbly and cornbread is golden brown.

Makes 6 servings

328	Calories
12 g	Protein
68 g	Carbohydrates
2 g	Fat
7%	Calories from Fat
7 g	Fiber
549 mg	Sodium
0 mg	Cholesterol

Stuffed Peppers

~ ~

6   bell peppers
1   extra-large onion,
      chopped (3 cups)
3   cloves garlic, minced
1   tablespoon chili powder
3   cups cooked brown rice
¼   cup minced fresh
      parsley
2   cups corn kernels
    Pinch of cayenne
1   teaspoon dried basil
1½ cups cooked pinto beans
      or 1 can
      (16 ounces)
8   ounces salt-free tomato
      sauce

Preheat oven to 350 degrees F.

~ ~

Hamburger substitute may be
used instead of the beans for a
traditional taste alternative.

Read the labels on bean cans,
you will be surprised at the
unwanted ingredients some
of them contain.

~ ~

This versatile filling can also be used to stuff tomatoes, egg-plant, or zucchini.

1. Cut tops from bell peppers (reserve tops). Clean inside of peppers, removing the membranes. If the peppers do not sit upright, cut a small slice from the bottom being careful not to cut into the pepper cavity.
2. Place peppers into a steamer and steam for 5 minutes. Drain inverted on paper towels.
3. Prepare a nonstick skillet by lightly coating surface with vegetable cooking spray or by using an oiled pastry brush. Chop pepper tops and along with the onions, garlic, and chile powder sauté until tender.
4. Combine remaining ingredients with ¼ cup of the tomato sauce. Stuff the peppers.
5. Place ¼ cup tomato sauce on bottom of baking dish and add enough water to completely cover bottom of pan. Place stuffed peppers upright into pan and top with remaining tomato sauce. Bake for 30 minutes.

Makes 6 Servings

341	Calories
14 g	Protein
70 g	Carbohydrates
3 g	Fat
7%	Calories from Fat
9 g	Fiber
176 mg	Sodium
0 mg	Cholesterol

Rinsing rice and pasta after cooking washes away a portion of the vitamins and minerals.

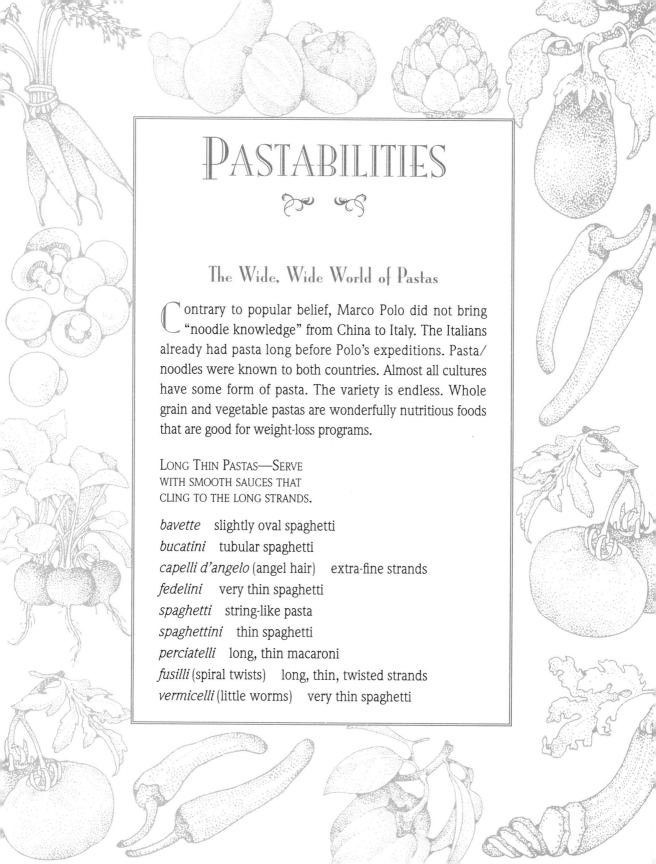

PASTABILITIES

❧ ❧

The Wide, Wide World of Pastas

Contrary to popular belief, Marco Polo did not bring "noodle knowledge" from China to Italy. The Italians already had pasta long before Polo's expeditions. Pasta/noodles were known to both countries. Almost all cultures have some form of pasta. The variety is endless. Whole grain and vegetable pastas are wonderfully nutritious foods that are good for weight-loss programs.

LONG THIN PASTAS—SERVE
WITH SMOOTH SAUCES THAT
CLING TO THE LONG STRANDS.

bavette   slightly oval spaghetti

bucatini   tubular spaghetti

capelli d'angelo (angel hair)   extra-fine strands

fedelini   very thin spaghetti

spaghetti   string-like pasta

spaghettini   thin spaghetti

perciatelli   long, thin macaroni

fusilli (spiral twists)   long, thin, twisted strands

vermicelli (little worms)   very thin spaghetti

SHORT TUBULAR—SERVE
WITH CHUNKY TOMATO OR
"CREAM" VEGETABLE SAUCES.

ditali (thimbles)   short macaroni tubes

ditalini (salad macaroni)   small ditalini tubes

elbows   macaroni tube pasta

manicotti   large, long tubes

manicotti rigati   large, long grooved tubes

rigatoni   large (1 ½-inch) ridged tubes

ziti (bridegrooms)   straight tubes in short lengths

penne (quill pens)   short tubes with diagonal cuts

mostaccioli (small mustaches)   2-inch-long tubes cut diagonally

rigatoni   large ridged tubes

RIBBONS—BEST SERVED
WITH RICH "CREAM" SAUCES.

linguine (little tongues)   slender, flat ribbons

fettuccelli   narrow form of fettuccine

fettuccine   ½-inch-wide ribbons

mafalda   wide with rippled edges

papardelle   wide, short ribbons

lasagna   widest ribbon with rippled edges

tagliatelli   similar to fettuccine, but wider

margherite   ribbons with twists and turns

FANCY SHAPES—GOOD WITH
CREAM OR TOMATO SAUCES.

conchigliette (small shells)   shaped like conch shells

stellette (stars)   little star-shaped pasta

orzo   a tiny rice-shaped pasta

gemeli (twins)   two short strands twisted together

rotini fusilli (spirals)   small corkscrews

radiatori   ½-inch pasta tubes with fluted edges

conchiglie   medium shells

farfalle   bowties

rotelle   wagon wheels

cavatappi   narrow shells with rippled surface

gnocchi   small seashell-shaped pasta dumplings (can also be made with potatoes)

orecchiette (ears)   1-inch cup-shaped pasta

I found Italy to be a vegetarian traveler's delight because of the wonderful pasta and vegetable dishes. In the Italian shops, the most commonly found pasta is dried (*pasta secca*), which is traditional in southern Italy. In northern Italy, fresh pasta (*pasta fresca*) is the pasta of choice.

Pasta is the most filling of the complex carbohydrates and a delicious, nutritious source of energy. When buying pasta look for vegetable and whole wheat varieties for extra nutrition. In health food stores, you can find pasta made from rice, quinoa, amaranth, spelt, corn, kamut, buckwheat, millet, and chickpeas, to name a few. Enjoy pasta; it is wonderful on weight-loss programs. It's not the pasta that's fattening, it's the sauce people normally put on pasta that's fattening.

- Every *pound* of pasta needs to cook in *4 quarts* of boiling water. Pasta loves to swim!
- Add long pasta in several batches, slowly pushing each batch into the boiling water as it softens.
- Short pasta can be added all at one time. Stir to separate pasta. Return to a boil and stir occasionally during cooking.
- Pasta should be *al dente*—tender but firm. Drain immediately.
- To make 1 cup of pasta, use 2 ounces uncooked.

No Time to Cook Pasta?

When cooking pasta, make extra servings for the freezer. Drain and cool cooked pasta; place in containers and freeze. At serving time just plunge frozen pasta in hot water.

QUICK NO-COOK PASTA TOPPERS

Fat-free or low-fat Italian dressing (½ cup per pound of pasta) tossed with or without:

Capers	Garlic	Soup
Peanut sauce	Scallions	Pimientos
Salsa	Fresh basil	Curry sauce
Ratatouille	Mayo	Caponata
Canned tomatoes	Reconstituted	Diced cucumbers
Thai sauce	mushrooms	Snow peas
Minced onions	Balsamic vinegar	Cooked legumes
Minced bell pepper	Peas	Asparagus spears
Sliced carrots	Chopped fresh	Diced fresh
Broccoli florets	spinach leaves	tomatoes
Dairy-free sour	Parmesan cheese	Nondairy cream
cream	alternative	cheese

The combinations are endless. You can find recipes for more sauces in the chapters called "Sauces/Marinades" and "Added Touches." You are limited only by your imagination.

When cooking pasta, throw
raw vegetables into the pot
and cook along with the pasta.

Recipes

"Burger" and Shells

Eggplant Pasta

Fettuccini Alfredo

Linguine de Cannellini

Linguine à la Greek

Pad Thai

Pasta Primavera

Pasta Pie

Pepper Pasta

Shiitake Bolognese

Speedy Ziti

Spinach Manicotti

Summer Pasta

Tangy Peppercorn
Soba

Vegetable Lasagna

"Burger" and Shells

꧁ ꧂

1 large onion, chopped
1 red bell pepper, chopped
2 cloves garlic, pressed
1 tube (14 ounces)
  Gimme Lean, beef
  flavor (Lightlife)
1/2 teaspoon dried oregano
1 can (28 ounces) crushed
  tomatoes
1 vegetable bouillon cube
  (Hugli)
2 tablespoons liquid
  aminos
1 tablespoon salt-free
  tomato paste
12 ounces pasta shells,
  cooked

No one will say "Where's the beef?" to this quick and tasty dish.

1. Prepare a nonstick skillet by lightly coating surface with vegetable cooking spray or by using an oiled pastry brush. Sauté the onion, bell pepper, and garlic until soft. Add burger and cook, breaking it up with the back of a wooden spoon.
2. When burger is firm, add remaining ingredients except cooked shells and simmer for 15 minutes.
3. Add cooked shells and toss to coat.

Makes 6 servings

Bell peppers (green peppers) are very high in vitamin C. Red bell peppers, compared to the green, contain more carotenes, potassium, and vitamin C, and have powerhouse beta-carotene. The green are good choices also, especially when eaten raw.

330	Calories
20 g	Protein
59 g	Carbohydrates
1 g	Fat
4%	Calories from Fat
5 g	Fiber
872 mg	Sodium
0 mg	Cholesterol

Eggplant Pasta

1   large onion, chopped
      (at least 2 cups)
1   bell pepper, chopped
3   cloves garlic, pressed
1   large eggplant, peeled
      and cut into $^1/_2$ to
      1-inch cubes
1   teaspoon dried oregano
1   bay leaf
$^1/_8$ teaspoon cayenne
1   tablespoon Vogue
      Instant Vege Base
1   large carrot, chopped
1   can (28 ounces) crushed
      tomatoes
1   pound pasta shells,
      cooked
2   tablespoons grated
      Parmesan cheese
      alternative for
      garnish

1. Prepare a nonstick skillet by lightly coating surface with vegetable cooking spray or by using an oiled pastry brush. Sauté onion, bell pepper, and garlic until soft.
2. While onions are cooking, place eggplant into a steamer and cook until tender, about 10 minutes.
3. Stir oregano, bay leaf, cayenne, and Vogue Instant Vege Base into the cooked onion mixture. Cook about 1 minute. Add carrot and tomatoes; cover and simmer for 30 minutes.
4. Add pasta and cheese to pan. Toss to coat.

Makes 6 servings

Gentlemen, did you know that consuming 10 ($^1/_2$ cup) servings of tomatoes a week has been shown to reduce prostate cancer by 45 percent? And the tomatoes can be used as an ingredient, cooked in pasta sauces or on pizzas.

345	Calories
12 g	Protein
70 g	Carbohydrates
2 g	Fat
5%	Calories from Fat
6 g	Fiber
420 mg	Sodium
0 mg	Cholesterol

Fettuccini Alfredo

❧ ❧

2	cups lite rice milk
2	tablespoons whole wheat flour
2	cloves garlic, minced
1	tablespoon Vogue Instant Vege Base
¼	cup Parmesan cheese substitute
8	ounces dry spinach fettucini, cooked, warm

1. In a medium saucepan combine a little rice milk with the flour to make a paste. Add remaining rice milk, garlic, and Vogue Instant Vege Base.
2. Stirring constantly over medium heat, bring to a boil. Reduce heat and simmer for 10 minutes, while still stirring.
3. In a warm bowl place the cooked pasta. Toss with the white sauce and cheese substitute.
4. Serve immediately.

Makes 4 Servings

The best things in life are free . . . at least this nutrient is: light.

It is very important for your well-being to be outside in indirect *sunlight (shade), without eye glasses or contact lens for at least 15 minutes a day. Without light, plants cannot survive and neither can you.*

270	Calories
9 g	Protein
52 g	Carbohydrates
3 g	Fat
10%	Calories from Fat
4 g	Fiber
171 mg	Sodium
48 mg	Cholesterol

The First Book of Vegetarian Cooking

Linguine de Cannellini

1   onion, chopped (about 1 1/2 cups)
3   cloves garlic, pressed
1   package (10.5 ounces) firm lite silken tofu, drained
2   cups cooked cannellini beans or 1 can (15 ounces), drained, reserve liquid
1/8   teaspoon nutmeg
1/4   cup dry sherry
1/4   teaspoon salt substitute
    Dash of white pepper
1/2   pound spinach linguine pasta, cooked

Tofu is a wonderful substitute for heavy cream. A great impersonator, it takes on the flavor of whatever it is cooked with.

1. Prepare a nonstick skillet by lightly coating surface with vegetable cooking spray or by using an oiled pastry brush. Sauté the onion and garlic until the onions are tender. Add a little water if the mixture is too dry.
2. Place tofu in a blender or food processor along with the liquid drained from the beans. Process until smooth and creamy.
3. Stir tofu mixture into onions.
4. Chop beans into pea-size pieces and add to the tofu and onions.
5. Add nutmeg, sherry, salt, and pepper and bring to a simmer. Cook for 10 minutes, stirring occasionally. If sauce seems too thick, add a little rice milk. Add cooked linguine to sauce and toss to coat.

Makes 4 servings

391	Calories
22 g	Protein
67 g	Carbohydrates
3 g	Fat
7%	Calories from Fat
9 g	Fiber
152 mg	Sodium
53 mg	Cholesterol

Linguine à la Greek

❧ ❧

½ pound cooked linguine
2 teaspoons extra virgin
  olive oil
1 package (10 ounces)
  frozen chopped
  spinach, cooked
8 ounces cooked garbanzo
  (chickpea) beans
¼ cup raisins
⅛ teaspoon cayenne
  pepper
½ teaspoon salt substitute
⅛ teaspoon fresh cracked
  pepper

In a large skillet or wok, over medium heat, toss linguine with olive oil to coat. Add remaining ingredients, toss well, and cook until thoroughly heated, about 5 minutes.

Makes 4 servings

222	Calories
9 g	Protein
38 g	Carbohydrates
5 g	Fat
20%	Calories from Fat
4 g	Fiber
331 mg	Sodium
0 mg	Cholesterol

The First Book of Vegetarian Cooking

Pad Thai

8 ounces uncooked Oriental noodles or linguine
1/4 pound bean sprouts
1/2 cup thinly sliced scallions
1/4 cup coarsely chopped peanuts for garnish
1 tablespoon chopped fresh parsley or cilantro for garnish

Peanut sauce

1/2 cup natural chunky peanut butter
1/4 cup lite rice milk
2 teaspoons reduced-sodium tamari sauce
1/4 cup frozen orange juice concentrate
2 teaspoons fresh lime juice
2 teaspoons honey
4 scallions thinly sliced (2 tablespoons)
1 teaspoon freshly grated ginger
1/8 teaspoon cayenne
1/8 teaspoon coconut extract

My favorite Thai dish.

1. Prepare pasta according to package directions. Just before draining, add sprouts to heat. Drain and keep warm.
2. In a saucepan, whisk peanut butter and milk. Add remaining sauce ingredients; mix well. Heat to a simmer.
3. Toss pasta with sauce and scallions.
4. Serve garnished with peanuts and parsley.

Makes 6 servings

336	Calories
12 g	Protein
42 g	Carbohydrates
15 g	Fat
39%	Calories from Fat
4 g	Fiber
188 mg	Sodium
0 mg	Cholesterol

Pasta Primavera

6   shallots, minced
2   cloves garlic, minced or
     pressed
3   zucchini, cut into small
     pieces
½   pound small broccoli
     florets
½   cup snow peas, stems
     and strings removed
¼   cup carrots, cut into
     small pieces
½   cup sliced mushrooms
¼   cup minced fresh
     flat-leaf parsley
2   teaspoons minced fresh
     basil
⅛   teaspoon cracked black
     pepper
¼   cup sweet marsala wine
1   pound farfalle (bowtie)
     pasta, cooked
2   teaspoons liquid aminos
¼   cup Parmesan cheese
     substitute

1. Prepare a nonstick skillet by lightly coating surface with vegetable cooking spray or by using an oiled pastry brush. Sauté shallots and garlic until soft. Add vegetables, cover and steam/cook for 5 minutes.
2. Add parsley, basil, pepper, and wine. Toss to coat. Cook until vegetables are done but still crisp, about 10 minutes.
3. Add cooked pasta, aminos, and cheese. Toss and serve.

Makes 8 servings

253 Calories
11 g Protein
49 g Carbohydrates
1 g Fat
5% Calories from Fat
5 g Fiber
96 mg Sodium
0 mg Cholesterol

The First Book of Vegetarian Cooking

Pasta Pie

Crust

1/3   cup soy milk

1   tablespoon egg replacer (Ener-G) whisked with 1/4 cup distilled water until foamy

2   tablespoons Parmesan cheese substitute

8   ounces linguine, cooked

Filling

1   large onion, chopped

1   bell pepper, chopped

2   cloves garlic, minced or pressed

1   cup shredded carrots

3   cups crushed tomatoes

2   tablespoons salt-free tomato paste

1 1/2   teaspoons dried basil

1   teaspoon dried oregano

1   package (10 ounces) Tofu Crumbles* (Marjon)

2   teaspoons liquid aminos

1/2   cup shredded mozzarella tofu cheese

Preheat oven to 350 degrees F.

If you have leftover pasta be sure to make this crust. You can freeze it until ready to use.

1. In large pan, mix soy milk with prepared egg replacer. Whisk in Parmesan substitute. Add cooked linguine and toss to coat.
2. Spread evenly over the bottom of a sprayed 9-inch springform pan (or similar pan). Bake for 20 minutes.
3. Prepare a nonstick skillet by lightly coating surface with vegetable cooking spray or by using an oiled pastry brush. Sauté onion, bell pepper, and garlic until tender. Add carrots and cook another minute or two.
4. Add tomatoes, tomato paste, basil, and oregano and simmer for 15 minutes.
5. Add crumbled tofu and liquid aminos and cook until heated through.
6. Spoon into filling and top with cheese. Bake for 10 to 15 minutes or until cheese is melted.
7. Remove ring from pan and cut pie into 8 wedges.

Makes 8 servings

*Tofu Crumbles are available in the produce section of most supermarkets.

176	Calories
10 g	Protein
29 g	Carbohydrates
3 g	Fat
13%	Calories from Fat
2 g	Fiber
284 mg	Sodium
0 mg	Cholesterol

Pepper Pasta

❧ ❧

1 tablespoon low-sodium tamari

2 purple onions, halved then cut into ¼-inch slices

2 bell peppers (1 red and 1 yellow), cut into 1-inch chunks

2 cloves garlic, pressed

⅛ cup capers

½ teaspoon extra virgin olive oil

⅓ cup chopped fresh basil

¼ teaspoon cracked pepper

¼ pound cooked penne or mostaccioli pasta
Grated Parmesan cheese alternative (optional)

Colorful as well as tasty.

1. To a large skillet or wok, add 1 tablespoon of tamari and 2 tablespoons water. Add onions, bell peppers, and garlic and sauté until onions are translucent.
2. Add capers, olive oil, basil, and cracked pepper. Toss to coat. Turn off heat and add cooked pasta. Toss again. Remove to warm serving platter. Sprinkle with cheese if desired.

Makes 2 servings

302	Calories
10 g	Protein
60 g	Carbohydrates
4 g	Fat
11%	Calories from Fat
6 g	Fiber
204 mg	Sodium
0 mg	Cholesterol

The First Book of Vegetarian Cooking

Shiitake Bolognese

8 ounces dried shiitake
      mushrooms
8 ounces button
      mushrooms
1 large onion, chopped
2 cloves garlic, minced
1 can (16 ounces) salt-free
      diced tomatoes
1 tablespoon tomato paste
1 tablespoon honey
$1/2$ tablespoon dried
      oregano
$1/2$ tablespoon dried basil
1 pound pasta, cooked
      (linguine or fettucini)

Shiitake mushrooms are steak-like in flavor and a nutritious addition to most any recipe.

1. Reconstitute shiitake mushrooms (page 371). Remove the stems and stem roots from the shiitake mushrooms. Discard. Chop the shiitake caps and button mushrooms. Set aside.
2. Prepare a nonstick skillet by lightly coating surface with vegetable cooking spray or by using an oiled pastry brush. Sauté the onion and garlic until tender, about 3 minutes. Add chopped mushrooms and sauté until all liquid has evaporated. Add tomatoes, tomato paste, honey, oregano, and basil.
3. Simmer until sauce thickens, about 15 minutes. Serve over warm pasta.

Serves 4

242	Calories
8 g	Protein
59 g	Carbohydrates
1 g	Fat
5%	Calories from Fat
9 g	Fiber
58 mg	Sodium
0 mg	Cholesterol

Speedy Ziti

8   ounces Jerusalem
        artichoke ziti*
½   cup fat-free mayonnaise
2   teaspoons Parmesan
        cheese substitute
1   cup thinly sliced
        scallions
    Freshly cracked pepper
    Salt substitute

1. Cook ziti according to package directions. Add mayonnaise and toss well.
2. Toss in remaining ingredients. Serve warm.

Makes 4 servings

*Other whole grain pastas may be substituted.

A good recipe to use your
leftover vegetables.

243	Calories
9 g	Protein
51 g	Carbohydrates
0 g	Fat
0%	Calories from Fat
2 g	Fiber
393 mg	Sodium
0 mg	Cholesterol

Spinach Manicotti

1 cup lite soy or rice milk
1 tablespoon arrowroot
1 tablespoon Vogue
    Instant Vege Base
1 teaspoon liquid aminos
    Pinch of nutmeg
1 package (10.5 ounces)
    extra firm, lite silken
    tofu, drained
1 package (10 ounces)
    frozen spinach,
    defrosted and
    squeezed dry
$\frac{1}{3}$ cup Parmesan cheese
    substitute
2 cloves garlic, minced or
    pressed
8 manicotti shells, cooked
2 ounces shredded lite
    mozzarella cheese
    substitute ($\frac{1}{2}$ cup)

Preheat oven to 350 degrees F.

1. In a small saucepan, combine milk, arrowroot, Vogue Instant Vege Base, liquid aminos, and nutmeg. Bring to a simmer and cook until thickened. Do not overcook arrowroot.
2. In a medium bowl, crumble drained tofu with a fork. Add spinach, Parmesan, and garlic. Mix well.
3. Stuff shells with tofu mixture. Spoon a little sauce over the bottom of a $13 \times 9 \times 2$-inch baking dish. Arrange shells to cover bottom of dish. Cover with the remaining sauce. Top with shredded mozzarella.
4. Cover dish and bake for 20 to 25 minutes. Uncover dish last 5 minutes of baking time.

Makes 4 servings

339	Calories
22 g	Protein
54 g	Carbohydrates
4 g	Fat
11%	Calories from Fat
3 g	Fiber
394 mg	Sodium
0 mg	Cholesterol

Summer Pasta

❧ ❧

2	pounds vine ripened tomatoes, peeled, seeded and cut into $\frac{1}{2}$-inch pieces
1	tablespoon extra virgin olive oil
3	tablespoons fresh lemon juice
2	tablespoons capers (optional)
3	tablespoons thinly sliced fresh basil
1	teaspoon fresh sage, minced
1	tablespoon fresh mint, minced
2	cloves garlic, pressed
3	tablespoons chopped Italian parsley
	Salt substitute
	Pepper
	Parmesan cheese substitute for garnish
1	pound penne pasta, cooked

Make this nutritious uncooked sauce when tomatoes are at their very best.

1. Combine all ingredients except pasta in a large bowl. Cover and marinate at room temperature for 30 minutes to allow flavors to mingle. Add pasta and toss.

Makes 4 servings

74	Calories
2 g	Protein
10 g	Carbohydrates
4 g	Fat
49%	Calories from Fat
3 g	Fiber
18 mg	Sodium
0 mg	Cholesterol

The First Book of Vegetarian Cooking

Tangy Peppercorn Soba

⁓ ⁓

⅓ cup minced shallots
½ cup dry white wine
2 teaspoons Dijon
 mustard
1½ teaspoons crushed green
 peppercorns
1½ cups rice or soy milk
8 ounces Japanese soba
 noodles (buckwheat
 noodles), uncooked
2 large tomatoes, diced
 and drained
 Parmesan cheese
 substitute (optional)

Soba, a Japanese buckwheat-flour noodle, is best when served al dente.

1. Prepare a nonstick skillet by lightly coating surface with vegetable cooking spray or by using an oiled pastry brush. Sauté the shallots until translucent. Add the wine, mustard, and peppercorns. Simmer until liquid has been reduced by half.
2. Add the rice milk and return to a simmer. Add soba noodles to pan and cook stirring for 5 minutes. The liquid should be almost completely absorbed. Remove from heat, cover, and rest for 5 minutes. Stir in diced tomato and cheese if desired.

Makes 4 servings.

196	Calories
7 g	Protein
40 g	Carbohydrates
2 g	Fat
8%	Calories from Fat
4 g	Fiber
204 mg	Sodium
0 mg	Cholesterol

Vegetable Lasagna

❧ ❧

1   package (10.5 ounces)
       extra-firm, lite silken
       tofu, drained
¼   cup lemon juice
2   tablespoons tahini
1   tablespoon miso
1   extra large onion,
       chopped (2 cups)
1   bell pepper, chopped
4   cloves garlic, pressed
⅛   teaspoon cayenne
1   teaspoon nutmeg
2   teaspoons oregano,
       dried
1   teaspoon basil, dried
½   pound fresh mush-
       rooms, sliced *or*
       1 ½ ounces dried
       shiitake mushrooms*
1   teaspoon kelp
⅓   cup chopped fresh
       parsley
1   can (28 ounces) crushed
       tomatoes
1   can (8 ounce) salt-free
       tomato sauce
1   package (1 pound)
       lasagna noodles,
       cooked

An old Sicilian tradition says good luck will come to those who eat lasagna on New Year's Day; any other noodle will bring bad luck.

1. Blend tofu, lemon juice, tahini, and miso in food processor or blender until smooth and creamy.
2. Prepare a nonstick skillet by lightly coating surface with vegetable cooking spray or by using an oiled pastry brush. Sauté the onion, bell pepper, and garlic until tender. Add cayenne, nutmeg, oregano, basil, and mushrooms and sauté for about 3 minutes. Stir in the kelp and parsley. Sauté for an additional 2 minutes. Remove from heat.
3. Combine processed tofu with the mushroom mixture.

*If using shiitake mushrooms, reconstitute (page 371), discard the stems, and slice the caps.

❧ ❧

If the jar of tahini has oil floating on the top, pour it off. You don't need the extra fat. Pour oil off all nut butters as well.
Fat makes you fat.

❧ ❧

The First Book of Vegetarian Cooking

6	zucchini, cooked and sliced
$^1/_2$	cup Parmesan cheese substitute
4	ounces shredded mozzarella soy cheese (1 cup)

Preheat oven to 350 degrees F.

4. Combine the crushed tomatoes with the tomato sauce. Spread one quarter of the tomato mixture over the bottom of a sprayed 13 × 9 × 2-inch baking dish. Place a layer of $^1/_3$ of the noodles over the tomatoes and a layer of $^1/_3$ of the tofu filling. Follow with a layer of $^1/_3$ of cooked zucchini then tomato sauce. Repeat layers ending with the tomato sauce. Sprinkle top with Parmesan.

5. Cover and bake 40 minutes. Uncover, top with the mozzarella and bake an additional 10 minutes. Allow to set for 20 minutes before cutting.

Makes 8 servings

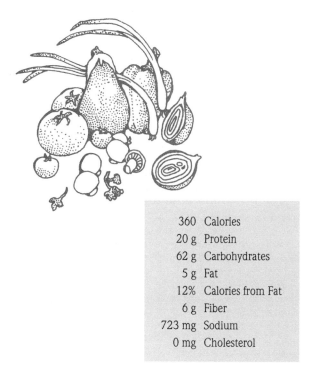

360	Calories
20 g	Protein
62 g	Carbohydrates
5 g	Fat
12%	Calories from Fat
6 g	Fiber
723 mg	Sodium
0 mg	Cholesterol

THRILLED TO PIZZAS

❧ ❧

Pizza—The All-American Food?

The origin of pizza is Italian, going back some 2,000 years to the city of Pompeii. When I was touring Pompeii I saw the forerunner of the modern pizza oven. To my untrained eye (I am not a pizza oven expert) the ovens haven't changed much in appearance in all those years.

Pizza is so popular, it is estimated Americans eat nearly 100 acres of pizza each day (57 square miles a year). That's a lot of pizza.

Pizza is not junk food if it is prepared properly. It can be a nutritional powerhouse. A whole wheat crust provides fiber and complex carbohydrates for energy. Tomato sauce and vegetable toppings provide vitamins and minerals. Add vegetarian pepperoni or beans for extra protein.

I enjoy pizza without the mozzarella cheese, using only Parmesan cheese substitute and crushed red pepper flakes as the topping over broccoli, onions, bell peppers, mushrooms (try different varieties). If you don't mind the extra fat, you can find lite soy mozzarella cheese that is a good substitute for the regular type.

Enjoy pizza without guilt. With lots of vegetables and a whole grain crust, you have a nutritious meal.

Recipes

Pizza Sauce

Cornmeal Pizza Dough

Pizza Dough

Pita Bread

Barbecue Pizza

Potato Pizza Dough

Eggplant Pizza

Pizza Margherita

Tex-Mex Pizza

Pizza Olé

Reuben Pizza

BLT Pizza

Pizza Sauce

6   cloves garlic, pressed or minced

2   pounds fresh tomatoes, diced or 1 can (28 ounces) crushed tomatoes

1   can (28 ounces) organic tomato purée

1 1/2   tablespoons dried basil

1 1/2   tablespoons dried oregano

1/2   teaspoon salt substitute

1/8   teaspoon cayenne

This recipe makes enough sauce for four large pizzas. I like to make extra and freeze individual portions for quick dinners.

Combine all ingredients in large saucepan. Simmer covered for 30 minutes, stirring often.

Makes sauce for 4 pizzas (or about 4 cups)

39	Calories
2 g	Protein
9 g	Carbohydrates
1 g	Fat
7%	Calories from Fat
2 g	Fiber
283 mg	Sodium
0 mg	Cholesterol

Cornmeal Pizza Dough

༺ ༻

1	package (¼ ounce) active dry yeast
¾	cup plus 2 tablespoons lukewarm distilled water (105 to 115 degrees F)
3	cups unbleached organic flour
⅓	cup fine cornmeal
1	teaspoon salt substitute

A hearty crust that goes well with vegetable and bean toppings.

1. In a small bowl, add yeast to the warm water. Stir to dissolve. Set aside for 10 minutes or until foamy on top.
2. In a large bowl, combine 2½ cups flour, cornmeal, and salt substitute. Make a well in the center. Pour yeast mixture into the mound center. With a fork, stirring in a circular motion, slowly stir the flour and cornmeal into the yeast mixture.
4. When a dough has formed, turn out onto a work surface, dusted with some of the remaining ½ cup flour.
5. Knead dough until smooth and elastic (about 10 minutes). Form into a ball and transfer to large bowl that has been sprayed with vegetable spray. Cover with cling wrap and place in warm area. Let dough double in size (1 to 2 hours).
6. Re-flour your work surface with the remaining ½ cup of flour. Turn dough out again and punch it down with your hand. Begin to press it into a 12-inch round (or desired shape), lifting, stretching and pulling.
7. Transfer dough to a baking sheet. Cover with dish towel and let rise again until almost double in size (about 20 minutes).
8. Dough can either be wrapped and frozen or topped and baked.

Makes 6 servings
(one 12-inch pizza)

246	Calories
7 g	Protein
47 g	Carbohydrates
3 g	Fat
11%	Calories from Fat
2 g	Fiber
357 mg	Sodium
0 mg	Cholesterol

The First Book of Vegetarian Cooking

Pizza Dough

႞ ႜ

1 cup warm distilled
water (105° to
115 degrees F)
1 teaspoon honey
1 package quick-rising
yeast
1 tablespoon olive oil
$1/2$ teaspoon salt substitute
1 cup whole wheat bread
flour
2 cups unbleached all-
purpose flour

Preheat oven to 450 degrees F.

1. In a large bowl combine the water and the honey. Sprinkle the yeast over the water. Let rest one minute. Stir yeast to dissolve. Set aside for 10 minutes or until mixture is foamy.
2. Stir in oil, salt, whole wheat flour, and $1 1/2$ cups of the all-purpose flour. Dough will be stiff. Gradually mix in the remaining $1/2$ cup flour.
3. On a lightly floured surface, knead the dough for 5 minutes, working in enough flour to make dough smooth and elastic.
4. Place dough in a bowl sprayed with vegetable oil. Turn dough over once exposing the oiled, smooth side. Cover bowl with a damp dish towel and place bowl in a warm, draft-free place until dough doubles in size, about 30 minutes.
5. Punch dough down and divide in half.
6. Dough can be rolled out into two pizzas or placed in plastic bags and frozen for later use.
7. To cook: Place rolled-out dough on sprayed baking sheet. Spray oil over top of dough. Bake at 450 degrees F for 10 minutes. Rest 10 minutes before adding topping. Reduce oven temperature to 400 degrees F and bake until crust is golden, about 10 minutes.

*Makes two 12-inch pizzas
(12 pieces)*

123	Calories
4 g	Protein
24 g	Carbohydrates
2 g	Fat
11%	Calories from Fat
2 g	Fiber
91 mg	Sodium
0 mg	Cholesterol

Pita Bread

꙾ ꙾

2 envelopes (¼ ounce each) dry yeast
1½ cups warm distilled water (105 to 115 degrees F)
2 cups unbleached organic flour
2 cups organic whole wheat flour

Preheat oven to 450 degrees F.

Pita bread makes a good crust for pizzas. Make up a big batch and freeze until needed.

1. In a large bowl, mix yeast with the warm water. Rest for 5 minutes. Stir again.
2. Stir in the whole wheat flour. Stir in unbleached flour ¼ cup at a time.
3. Turn out onto a lightly floured board and knead for 10 minutes. The dough will be smooth and elastic.
4. Spray a large bowl with vegetable spray and add dough. Turn dough over and cover with plastic and a dish towel. Let rise in a warm place for 1½ hours or until double in size.
5. Punch dough down and return to the floured board. Divide into 6 balls and roll each out to a 10-inch diameter.
6. Place on baking sheets and cover with dish towels. Let rise for 20 to 30 minutes.
7. Bake for 8 minutes. Cool pitas on racks.
8. Add desired toppings and bake at 400 degrees F for 10 minutes.

Makes 6 pitas (12 servings)

150	Calories
5 g	Protein
32 g	Carbohydrates
1 g	Fat
4%	Calories from Fat
3 g	Fiber
3 mg	Sodium
0 mg	Cholesterol

The First Book of Vegetarian Cooking

Barbecue Pizza

1   package (5.3 ounces)
        Burger 'n' Loaf,
        original
1 1/2   cups prepared barbecue
        sauce or homemade
        (page 252)
1/4   cup dehydrated
        chopped onion
1/8   cup date sugar
        Prepared pizza dough
        for 10 1/2 × 16-inch
        pan
4   ounces shredded fat-free
        soy cheese, Cheddar
        or Monterey Jack
        flavor

Preheat oven to 425 degrees F.

1. Prepared the burger according to package directions, omitting the oil. Cook burger in a large nonstick skillet that has been sprayed with non-aerosol cooking spray, breaking up burger with the edge of a wooden spoon into small (pea-size) pieces.
2. Add barbecue sauce, onion, and sugar to pan, stirring to combine.
3. Spread dough out on a sprayed 10 1/2 × 16-inch pan. Spray dough with cooking spray and bake for 7 minutes. Spread barbecue mixture over partially cooked pizza crust. Top with the shredded cheese and bake for 10 minutes or until crust is brown and cheese is melted.

Makes 4 Servings

537 Calories
23 g Protein
96 g Carbohydrates
9 g Fat
15% Calories from Fat
7 g Fiber
1239 mg Sodium
0 mg Cholesterol

Potato Pizza Dough

1   large (10-ounce) potato, unpeeled
1   package (¼ ounce) active dry yeast
¾   cup lukewarm distilled water (105 to 115 degrees F)
3   cups unbleached organic flour
1   teaspoon salt substitute

Here's another dough for your pizzas. This dough will provide a lovely crumbly texture.

1. Cook the potato in water to cover until soft (approximately 20 minutes). When done remove the skin and keep potato warm. Save water for soups.
2. In a small bowl, add yeast to the warm water. Stir to dissolve. Set aside for 10 minutes or until foamy on top.
3. Pass the potato through a ricer or shred into a large bowl. Form the riced potato into a mound with a well in the center. Pour yeast mixture into the mound. With a fork, stirring in a circular motion, slowly stir 2½ cups flour, salt, and potato into the yeast.
4. When a dough has formed, turn out onto a work surface that has been dusted with some of the remaining ½ cup flour.
5. Knead dough until smooth and elastic (about 10 minutes). Form into a ball and transfer to large bowl that has been sprayed with vegetable spray. Cover with cling wrap and place in warm area. Let dough double in size (1 to 2 hours).

The First Book of Vegetarian Cooking

6. Re-flour your work surface with the remaining ½ cup of flour. Turn dough out again, punch it down with your hand, and begin to press it into a 12-inch round (or desired shape), lifting, stretching and pulling.

7. Transfer dough to a baking sheet. Cover with dish towel and let rise again until almost double in size (about 20 minutes).

8. Dough can either be wrapped and frozen or topped and baked.

Makes 6 servings (one 12-inch pizza)

292	Calories
8 g	Protein
58 g	Carbohydrates
3 g	Fat
9%	Calories from Fat
2 g	Fiber
360 mg	Sodium
0 mg	Cholesterol

Eggplant Pizza

1   large eggplant, peeled, halved lengthwise and cut into ¼-inch slices
1   large onion, chopped
2   cloves garlic, minced
1   bell pepper, chopped
¼   cup balsamic vinegar
1   can (6 ounces) tomato sauce
1   teaspoon dried oregano
1   teaspoon dried basil
1   teaspoon dried parsley
     Pinch of cayenne
1   large prepared pizza dough *or* 2 8-inch, whole wheat pitas
2   tablespoons Parmesan cheese substitute
½   cup shredded soy mozzarella cheese

Preheat oven to 450 degrees F.

1. Cook eggplant on a ridged grill-griddle or grill pan that has been sprayed with non-aerosol vegetable spray. This will make appetizing score marks on the eggplant. Or, if no grill is available brown eggplant in a non-stick sprayed skillet. Cook until tender, about a couple of minutes per side. Set aside.
2. Prepare a nonstick skillet by lightly coating surface with vegetable cooking spray or by using an oiled pastry brush. Sauté the onion, garlic, and bell pepper for about 4 minutes or until onions are translucent.
3. Add vinegar, tomato sauce, and seasoning to onion mixture and cook until liquid is reduced and mixture is thick, about 10 minutes. Cool mixture.
4. Spray a large prepared pizza crust or two 8-inch whole wheat pitas with vegetable spray. Prebake pizza crust for 10 minutes.
5. Spread vegetable sauce over pizza crust or pitas. Top with Parmesan cheese substitute. Arrange eggplant slices over Parmesan and top with shredded mozzarella.
6. Bake for about 8 minutes or until cheese is melted and crust is browned.

Makes 4 servings

Eggplant, a member of the nightshade family, is native to India and has been grown for thousands of years. It is used in the prevention of atherosclerosis and convulsions and as an immunity enhancer. It also appears to block blood levels of cholesterol from rising when fatty foods have been eaten. Avoid nightshade vegetables if suffering from arthritis.

337	Calories
12 g	Protein
61 g	Carbohydrates
5 g	Fat
14%	Calories from Fat
4 g	Fiber
562 mg	Sodium
0 mg	Cholesterol

The First Book of Vegetarian Cooking

Pizza Margherita

❧ ❧

1	12-inch prepared pizza crust, unbaked
	Olive oil spray
2	large tomatoes, thinly sliced
	Salt substitute
	Freshly ground pepper
3	ounces shredded soy mozzarella cheese, low-fat or fat-free
30 to 35	fresh basil leaves, thinly sliced

Preheat oven to 425 degrees F.

1. Spray pizza crust with olive oil pan spray. Bake for 3 minutes.
2. Arrange tomato slices over crust. Top with salt substitute and pepper. Cover with mozzarella cheese substitute.
3. Bake for 10 minutes. Top with basil and cut into 4 slices.

Makes 3 to 4 servings

Basil (Ocimum basilicum) has been used successfully in the treatment of colds, flu, fever, stomach cramps, constipation, vomiting, headaches, and menstrual pains.

545	Calories
23 g	Protein
91 g	Carbohydrates
9 g	Fat
14%	Calories from Fat
4 g	Fiber
638 mg	Sodium
0 mg	Cholesterol

Tex–Mex Pizza

❧ ❧

1	extra-large whole wheat pita bread
8	ounces fat-free refried beans
½	onion, minced
½	bell pepper, minced
⅛	cup jalapeño peppers (jar style), drained and chopped
1	slice lite soy mozzarella style cheese, shredded

Preheat oven to 400 degrees F.

❧ ❧

For a change of taste top
with drained salsa.

❧ ❧

A snap to prepare.

1. Evenly cover pita with the refried beans.
2. Sprinkle beans with the onion and bell pepper. Top with the jalapeño peppers and cheese.
3. Bake for 10 minutes or until cheese melts.
4. Cut into wedges and serve warm.

Makes 2 servings

243	Calories
15 g	Protein
48 g	Carbohydrates
1 g	Fat
5%	Calories from Fat
9 g	Fiber
979 mg	Sodium
0 mg	Cholesterol

The First Book of Vegetarian Cooking

Pizza Olé

❧ ❧

1	large onion, thinly sliced
1	bell pepper, thinly sliced
2	cloves garlic, minced
4	ounces dried shiitake mushrooms, reconstituted (page 371) and sliced
1	teaspoon dried basil
1	teaspoon dried oregano
	Pinch of cayenne
2	cans (15 ounces each) pinto beans, drained
1	can (4 ounces) chopped green chiles
1	can (6 ounces) salt-free tomato sauce
$1/2$	teaspoon chili powder
1	cup cornmeal
$2/3$	cup cold distilled water
$2/3$	cup boiling water
2	tablespoons Parmesan cheese substitute
$1/2$	cup shredded lite mozzarella soy cheese

Preheat oven to 375 degrees F.

1. Prepare a nonstick skillet by lightly coating surface with vegetable cooking spray or by using an oiled pastry brush. Sauté onion, pepper, and garlic until onions are soft. Add mushrooms, basil, oregano, and cayenne. Cover and cook for 5 minutes. Remove from heat and add pintos, green chiles, and tomato sauce. Set aside.
2. Mix the chili powder and cornmeal together in a small saucepan. Add $2/3$ cup cold water. Gradually add boiling water, bring to a boil, reduce heat and cook, stirring constantly for 3 minutes or until mixture is thick.
3. Remove from heat and stir in 1 tablespoon Parmesan.
4. Spray a 9 × 13-inch baking pan with nonstick vegetable spray. With wet hands, spread cornmeal mixture out to edges of pan. Bake for 15 minutes.
5. Over the cooked cornmeal crust, sprinkle $1/2$ of the mozzarella and the remaining 1 tablespoon Parmesan. Top cheeses with bean mixture and top that with the remaining mozzarella.
6. Return to oven and cook for 15 minutes.

Makes 6 servings
(9 × 13-inch pizza)

277	Calories
12 g	Protein
56 g	Carbohydrates
1 g	Fat
4%	Calories from Fat
11 g	Fiber
356 mg	Sodium
0 mg	Cholesterol

Reuben Pizza

1   prebaked 12-inch pizza
      crust

1/4   cup fat-free Thousand
      Island dressing

2   cups sauerkraut, rinsed
      and squeezed dry

3   tablespoons Dijon
      mustard

4   ounces vegetarian
      corned beef (Heart
      and Soul), julienned

2   ounces shredded lite soy
      cheese, Swiss flavor

Preheat oven to 425 degrees F.

1. Spread dressing over cooked pizza crust. Follow with layers of sauerkraut, mustard, corned beef, and shredded cheese.
2. Bake on oven rack 8 to 10 minutes or until cheese melts.

Makes 3 servings

472	Calories
23 g	Protein
73 g	Carbohydrates
10 g	Fat
18%	Calories from Fat
5 g	Fiber
1988 mg	Sodium
0 mg	Cholesterol

BLT Pizza

2   large (plate-size) fat-free whole wheat pitas
¼   cup fat-free mayonnaise
2   tomatoes, sliced
¼   cup shredded mozzarella cheese-substitute
4   strips Stripples bacon substitute (Worthington), cooked crisp and chopped
2   cups shredded romaine lettuce for garnish

Preheat oven to 450 degrees F.

You can make your own pita crust if you prefer (see page 204).

1. Spread mayonnaise over pitas. Top with tomatoes and cheese. Bake 8 to 10 minutes or until cheese melts.
2. Top with chopped bacon and lettuce.

Makes 4 servings

148	Calories
7 g	Protein
22 g	Carbohydrates
4 g	Fat
23%	Calories from Fat
3 g	Fiber
534 mg	Sodium
0 mg	Cholesterol

PASS THE POTATOES

❧ ❧

Potatoes—what a wonderful, delicious, versatile food! They were first cultivated in 200 B.C. by the Incas of Peru. Besides eating them, the Incas used *papas* (potatoes) medicinally for everything from curing headaches to mending broken bones.

Europe first saw the potato 400 years ago and it immediately became the subject of lies, slander, and myths. Thought to be evil, the innocent potato was blamed for carrying many diseases. The French finally proved these accusations wrong, bringing the potato to its present popularity.

Even today, some people unjustly malign potatoes, excluding them from their diet because they think that potatoes are fattening. A plain potato is almost fat free! Because potatoes are a powerhouse of nutrition, most diet and nutritional programs include potatoes, finally giving them the place of honor they deserve.

Recipes

Tater Toppers

Bombay Potatoes

Stuffed Sweet Potatoes

Bubble and Squeak

Potato Vegetable Quiche

Empanadas

Frittata

Heavenly Hash

Mexican Potatoes

Potato Gnocchi

Shepherd's Pie

Tater Toppers

❧ ❧

A dinner in itself: a perfect baked potato accompanied by luscious, healthful toppings.

1. If not using an organic potato, wash with Veggie Bath (page xviii). Pierce potato several times with a fork. Bake at 400 degrees F for about 45 minutes (extra large ones may take 1 hour).
2. After cooking, prepare the potato for the topping by cutting a large deep X into the top and pushing the ends towards the center to open.

TOPPINGS

Dairy-free sour cream	Cooked beans or lentils
Parmesan cheese substitute	Bean dips
Sauerkraut	Stewed veggies
Scallions	Bacon bits (soy)
Salsa	Melted soy cheese
Salad dressing	Chili

The potato is a valuable food, nutritious and helpful in weight-loss programs.

One eight-ounce potato contains: 0.2g fat, 3.6g fiber, 4.7g protein, 14 mg sodium, 1.1% calories from fat, 179.2 calories, and 0 mg cholesterol.

Bombay Potatoes

1	pound potatoes, cooked and cut into 1-inch cubes
1	teaspoon cumin seeds
1	medium onion, chopped
2	cloves garlic, minced
2	teaspoons curry powder
1	vegetable bouillon cube

This dish goes well with Black
Lentil Curry (page 164),
a green vegetable or salad,
and naan bread.

I first tasted these potatoes while sampling different dishes at an Indian buffet. It was love at first bite. I rushed home and came up with this adaptation. Bell peppers or cauliflower are sometimes added.

1. Prepare a nonstick skillet by lightly coating surface with vegetable cooking spray or by using an oiled pastry brush. Sauté the cumin, onion, and garlic until onion starts to brown. About 10 minutes.
2. Add 1 to 1½ teaspoons of water to the curry powder to make a paste. Add to onion and cook for an additional 3 minutes. Add more water as needed.
3. Add the bouillon cube and ½ cup water to pan and stir until cube is dissolved. Add potatoes and toss. Cook for 5 minutes more, frequently turning the potatoes in the sauce.
4. Cook until all the liquid is absorbed.

Make 4 servings

144	Calories
3 g	Protein
32 g	Carbohydrates
1 g	Fat
5%	Calories from Fat
2 g	Fiber
11 mg	Sodium
0 mg	Cholesterol

The First Book of Vegetarian Cooking

Stuffed Sweet Potatoes

4   medium sweet potatoes
        (about 8 ounces
        each)
2   cups or 1 can (15
        ounces) navy beans
2   tablespoons pure honey
1   teaspoon dark and
        grainy mustard
1   teaspoon cinnamon
¼   cup chopped onion
1   tablespoon fat-free
        tomato paste
1   tablespoon vegetarian
        bacon bits

I love the beans used in this stuffing for lunch, spread between two slices of whole wheat bread with a thick slab of onion. For dinner, beans stuffed in a baked sweet potato and served with a salad is not only quick, easy, and delicious but nutritious as well.

1. Bake potatoes 40 to 45 minutes or until tender.
2. While potatoes are cooking, combine remaining ingredients in a saucepan and cook covered over low heat for 15 to 20 minutes.
3. Run a knife lengthwise through center of each potato, pushing ends towards each other to form a pocket for the filling.
4. Spoon stuffing into potatoes and serve warm.

Makes 4 servings

342	Calories
10 g	Protein
75 g	Carbohydrates
1 g	Fat
3%	Calories from Fat
9 g	Fiber
158 mg	Sodium
0 mg	Cholesterol

Bubble and Squeak

1   large onion, chopped
1 1/2 pounds potatoes,
       peeled, cooked, and
       mashed
1   teaspoon salt substitute
1/8 teaspoon freshly ground
       pepper
1   package (10 ounces)
       frozen brussels
       sprouts, cooked,
       drained well and
       chopped

This recipe comes to us from England and gets its name from the sounds coming from the skillet when cooking. I make this dish with the potatoes and brussels sprouts left over from holiday dinners.

1. Prepare a nonstick skillet by lightly coating surface with vegetable cooking spray or by using an oiled pastry brush; add onion and sauté until soft.
2. Season the potatoes with the salt and pepper; mix well. Add sprouts and combine.
3. Add potato-sprout mixture to pan with onions. Mix together. Press down with a spatula, flattening out to edges of pan.
4. Brown on both sides.

Makes 6 servings

104	Calories
3 g	Protein
23 g	Carbohydrates
1 g	Fat
5%	Calories from Fat
4 g	Fiber
370 mg	Sodium
0 mg	Cholesterol

The First Book of Vegetarian Cooking

Potato Vegetable Quiche

3 medium potatoes, cooked and mashed
1 onion, chopped (1 cup)
1 clove garlic, minced or pressed
1 medium cauliflower, broken into small florets
$1/2$ cup sliced fresh carrots
$1/2$ teaspoon dried leaf savory
Pinch of oregano
$1/4$ teaspoon salt substitute
Freshly ground pepper
1 cup low-fat shredded Cheddar flavor soy cheese
1 tablespoon egg replacer (Ener-G), whisked with $1/4$ cup distilled water
$1/4$ cup soy milk

Preheat oven to 375 degrees F.

1. Spread mashed potatoes over bottom and up sides of 9-inch pie plate. Set aside.
2. Prepare a nonstick skillet by lightly coating surface with vegetable cooking spray or by using an oiled pastry brush. Sauté onion and garlic until tender. Add cauliflower, carrots, savory, oregano, salt, and pepper. Cover and cook 10 minutes, stirring occasionally or until vegetables are tender.
3. Sprinkle $1/2$ cup of cheese over crust.
4. Arrange vegetables over cheese; top with remaining $1/2$ cup cheese.
5. In small bowl whisk egg replacer with soy milk; pour over pie.
6. Bake for 35 to 40 minutes.

Makes 4 to 6 servings

127	Calories
8 g	Protein
23 g	Carbohydrates
1 g	Fat
4%	Calories from Fat
4 g	Fiber
281 mg	Sodium
0 mg	Cholesterol

Empanadas

2½ pounds peeled potatoes,
    quartered
2   teaspoons Tex-Mex or
    Cajun spice (see
    page 379) or use
    salt substitute
2   tablespoons liquid
    aminos
1   tablespoon tamari
1   large onion, minced
    (about 2 cups)
½   red bell pepper, minced
2   large cloves garlic,
    pressed or minced
1   cup Meat of Wheat,
    sausage style
1   tablespoon salsa
2   tablespoons salt-free
    tomato paste
    Pinch of cayenne
1   cup whole grain bread
    crumbs

Preheat oven to 400 degrees F.

This adaptation of the Spanish meat turnovers is sure to please.

1. Place potatoes in a medium saucepan covered with water. Bring to a boil, reduce heat, cover and cook for 15 minutes or until fork-tender. Drain and return to pan. Mash with 1 teaspoon Tex-Mex seasoning and 1 tablespoon aminos. Set aside.

2. To a nonstick wok or skillet, add 2 tablespoons water and 1 tablespoon tamari. Heat to a simmer and add onion, bell pepper, and garlic. Cook until tender over low heat. Stir in Meat of Wheat, salsa, tomato paste, 1 tablespoon aminos, and cayenne and cook an additional minute.

3. Take ¼ cup mashed potatoes and place on a piece of wax paper. Flatten out with your hand into a 4-inch circle. Place a heaping teaspoon of filling into the center of circle, forming a compact mound. Bring up sides of wax paper with the potatoes, covering over the filling. Remove wax paper and form potato into an oval shape, pressing edges together. No filling should show.

4. In a small bowl, combine bread crumbs with 1 teaspoon Tex-Mex seasoning. Roll ovals into seasoned bread crumbs and place on a baking sheet. Bake for 20 minutes, turning over and bake an additional 10 minutes.

Makes 30

41	Calories
2 g	Protein
8 g	Carbohydrates
1 g	Fat
4%	Calories from Fat
1 g	Fiber
74 mg	Sodium
0 mg	Cholesterol

Frittata

1   large onion, chopped
1   green bell pepper,
      chopped
1   clove garlic, minced
¼   teaspoon thyme
      Pinch of cayenne
1   pound extra-firm tofu
      (water pack), drained
      and wrapped in a
      dish towel for 30
      minutes*
1   tablespoon egg replacer
      (Ener-G), whisked
      with ¼ cup distilled
      water
3   tablespoons unbleached
      organic flour
1   tablespoon baking
      powder
½   teaspoon turmeric
1   teaspoon Vogue Instant
      Vege Base
1   teaspoon liquid aminos
1   large potato, cooked,
      halved and cut into
      ¼-inch slices

Preheat oven to 400 degrees F.

A delicious brunch or dinner dish.

1. Prepare a nonstick skillet by lightly coating surface with vegetable cooking spray or by using an oiled pastry brush. Sauté onion, bell pepper, and garlic until tender. Stir in thyme and cayenne. Cook an additional minute. Transfer to an oil-sprayed, 10-inch deep-dish pie pan.
2. In a food processor, combine tofu, egg replacer, flour, baking powder, turmeric, Vogue Instant Vege Base, and aminos. Blend until smooth
3. Spread tofu mixture over onions and bell peppers.
4. Cover top with a single layer of potatoes and bake for 30 minutes or until potatoes are brown and tofu mixture is fluffy.

Makes 4 servings

*Wrapping tofu helps to remove moisture and firms up the texture.

241	Calories
18 g	Protein
22 g	Carbohydrates
9 g	Fat
35%	Calories from Fat
2 g	Fiber
282 mg	Sodium
0 mg	Cholesterol

Heavenly Hash (Bean Cakes)

1 large onion, chopped
2 cloves garlic, pressed
1/2 large bell pepper, chopped
16 ounces cooked kidney beans, drained and slightly mashed *or* 1 (16 ounce) can kidney beans, drained and mashed
1 1/2 pounds potatoes, cooked and mashed
2 tablespoons minced fresh parsley
1/4 teaspoon cayenne pepper
1 teaspoon liquid aminos

A simple but delicious recipe that is very low in fat and high in fiber and protein.

1. Prepare a nonstick skillet by lightly coating surface with vegetable cooking spray or by using an oiled pastry brush. Sauté onion, garlic, and bell pepper until tender. Transfer to a large bowl, add remaining ingredients, and combine.
2. Form mixture into patties and, using the same skillet, brown each side well and serve.

Makes 6 servings (12 to 14 cakes)

Variation: Add 1 cup drained corn kernels.

I make up a big batch of these (shaped like hamburger patties) and freeze in old coffee cans. Place wax paper between the patties so they won't stick together.

178	Calories
8 g	Protein
36 g	Carbohydrates
1 g	Fat
4%	Calories from Fat
4 g	Fiber
46 mg	Sodium
0 mg	Cholesterol

Mexican Potatoes

❦ ❦

3   pounds potatoes,
     peeled, cut into
     2-inch cubes

1   large onion (about 1
     pound), chopped
     roughly

1   clove garlic, pressed or
     minced

3   jalapeño peppers, finely
     minced

1   can (4 ounces) chopped
     green chiles

2   cups cooked pinto beans
     or 1 can (16 ounces)
     Salt substitute

Originally potatoes were cultivated by the Inca Indians high in the Andes of Peru and are still the mainstay of their diet. In the 16th century, they were taken to England by Sir Francis Drake. From there they traveled to Ireland and finally arrived in America in 1719.

1. Put potatoes in a saucepan with enough water to cover. Cook covered until fork tender, about 20 minutes. Drain and return to pan to keep warm. Save water for soups.
2. Prepare a nonstick skillet by lightly coating surface with vegetable cooking spray or by using an oiled pastry brush. Sauté the onion, garlic, and peppers until soft. Add chiles, beans and salt and heat.
3. Combine potatoes and onion mixture, tossing to coat.

Makes 6 servings

Onions are a member of the allium family and contain organo sulfur, a potent compound which researchers say helps to prevent cancer by enhancing detoxification.

---

268   Calories
9 g   Protein
58 g   Carbohydrates
1 g   Fat
2%   Calories from Fat
7 g   Fiber
24 mg   Sodium
0 mg   Cholesterol

Potato Gnocchi

2   pounds potatoes, peeled
          and quartered
1½   cups unbleached flour
1   teaspoon salt substitute
      Parmesan cheese
          substitute

I first tasted these delicious little dumplings (pronounced ny-OH-key) in Italy swimming in a heavenly delicate sauce. I find this reduced-fat version just as good.

1. Cook potatoes until very soft, about 20 minutes. Drain, add salt, and mash or pass through a potato ricer.
2. Place potatoes onto a floured mixing board. Knead in ¼ cup of flour at a time, adding enough to make a firm smooth dough. Rest dough for 15 minutes. With the palms of your hands, roll the dough into a ½- inch strip. Cut strip into ¾-inch pieces. Place each piece into the palm of your hand and roll your thumb into the middle of dough. They should look similar to shells.
3. Drop gnocchi, one by one, into boiling water and cook for 10 minutes (they will be tender and float to the surface). Drain and top with sauce and Parmesan cheese substitute.

Makes 6 servings

215	Calories
5 g	Protein
47 g	Carbohydrates
1 g	Fat
2%	Calories from Fat
3 g	Fiber
362 mg	Sodium
0 mg	Cholesterol

The First Book of Vegetarian Cooking

Shepherd's Pie

1 package (5.3 ounces)
    Burger 'n' Loaf,
    original
1 ½ pounds potatoes, peeled
    and quartered
1 large onion, chopped
3 cloves garlic, minced
1 tablespoon salt
    substitute
1 tablespoon potato starch
    Pinch of cayenne
½ cup distilled water
    Pinch of paprika

Preheat oven to 400 degrees F.

A traditional Yorkshire dish adapted for a healthier lifestyle. My husband is a Yorkshireman, and when I had him taste this dish, I held my breath. The results: he said "Right on," (English for umm, umm good!).

1. Prepare the burger according to package directions, omitting the oil.
2. In a medium pot, cover potatoes with water and bring to a boil. Reduce heat and cover. Cook until potatoes are tender, about 20 minutes.
3. While potatoes are cooking, prepare a nonstick skillet by lightly coating surface with vegetable cooking spray or by using an oiled pastry brush. Sauté the onion and garlic till tender. Add burger and cook while breaking apart with a wooden fork or edge of wooden spoon.
4. Mix potato starch and cayenne with water. Stir into burger mixture. Cook for an additional 1 minute. Place into a sprayed, deep-dish casserole.
5. When potatoes are done add salt substitute and mash. Spread over meat layer. Top with paprika. Bake for 20 minutes.

Makes 6 servings

208	Calories
7 g	Protein
42 g	Carbohydrates
3 g	Fat
13%	Calories from Fat
3 g	Fiber
1137 mg	Sodium
0 mg	Cholesterol

OTHER MAIN COURSES

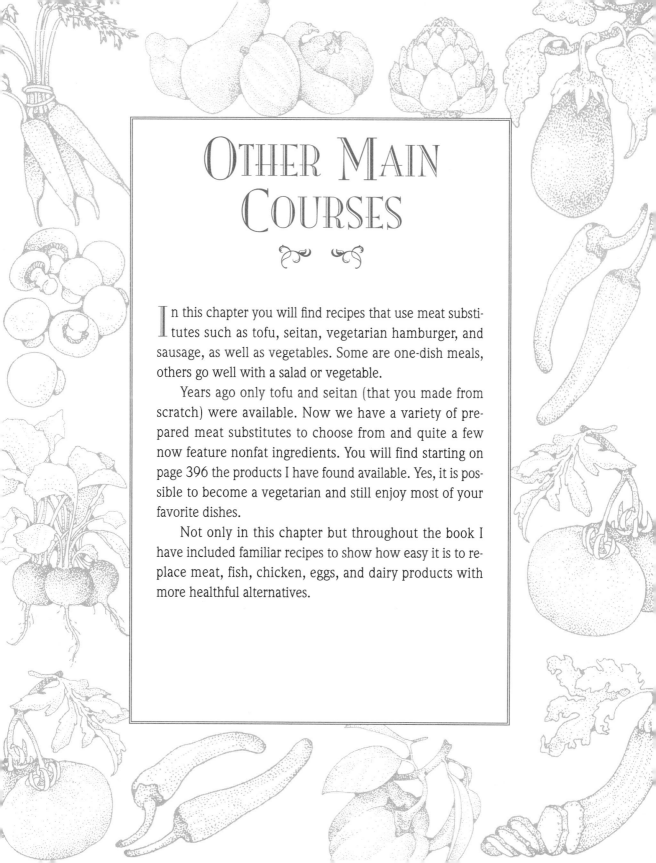

I n this chapter you will find recipes that use meat substitutes such as tofu, seitan, vegetarian hamburger, and sausage, as well as vegetables. Some are one-dish meals, others go well with a salad or vegetable.

Years ago only tofu and seitan (that you made from scratch) were available. Now we have a variety of prepared meat substitutes to choose from and quite a few now feature nonfat ingredients. You will find starting on page 396 the products I have found available. Yes, it is possible to become a vegetarian and still enjoy most of your favorite dishes.

Not only in this chapter but throughout the book I have included familiar recipes to show how easy it is to replace meat, fish, chicken, eggs, and dairy products with more healthful alternatives.

Recipes

❧ ❧

Barbecue Pie

Albondigas

"Beef" Stroganoff

French Toast

Grilled Tofu with Mango
Sauce

Chestnut and "Sausage"
Stuffing

Huevos Rancheros

Jerk Kebobs

Keema Matar

Mushroom à la King

"Pollo" Pubil

Quiche Lorraine

Reuben "Meat" Loaf

"Sausage, Cream Gravy,"
and Biscuits

"Turkey" Pot Pie

❧ ❧

Barbecue Pie

1¾ cups organic stone ground whole wheat flour

½ teaspoon baking soda

2 teaspoons baking powder

2 tablespoons soy margarine

¾ cup lite rice milk

2 teaspoons honey

12 ounces Meat of Wheat, chicken style, torn into bite-size pieces

1 cup barbecue sauce

1¼ cups shredded low-fat Cheddar soy cheese

Preheat oven to 400 degrees F.

1. Sift flour, baking soda, and baking powder into a large bowl. Cut margarine into flour until it disappears.
2. Whisk rice milk and honey together and stir into the flour mixture. The dough should be stiff.
3. Knead for about 3 or 4 minutes or until dough is no longer sticky.
4. Turn out onto a floured surface and roll out to a 8-inch circle. Cut into 2-inch circles (I use the rim of a jar). Set aside.
5. Place barbecue sauce into bowl. Add pieces of Meat of Wheat and toss to coat. Transfer to oiled/sprayed 9-inch pie dish, spreading over bottom of pan.
6. Surround pie mixture with biscuits and top with cheese.
7. Bake for 15 minutes.

Makes 4 to 6 servings

300	Calories
25 g	Protein
38 g	Carbohydrates
6 g	Fat
17%	Calories from Fat
5 g	Fiber
1036 mg	Sodium
0 mg	Cholesterol

Albondigas (Mexican "Meatballs")

Mexicans will never miss the meat in this delightful dish. Serve over pasta, noodles, or rice.

1	package (5.3 ounces) Burger 'n' Loaf, original
2	tablespoons flax seed-extract (page 365) including the seeds
2	slices whole grain bread, rinsed with distilled water and squeezed dry
1	can (4 ounces) diced chiles
1	clove garlic, pressed
½	cup minced onion
¼	cup minced fresh parsley
	Pinch of cayenne
1	teaspoon liquid aminos
½	teaspoon powered cumin
⅓	cup dried whole grain bread crumbs

Sauce

1	can (28 ounces) crushed tomatoes
1	tablespoon chili powder
1	can (4 ounces) diced green chiles
1	clove garlic, pressed or minced
½	cup minced onions
2	teaspoons liquid aminos

1. Prepare burger according to package directions, omitting the oil. Combine with flax seed extract, bread, chiles, garlic, onion, parsley, cayenne, 1 teaspoon aminos, cumin, and the bread crumbs. Mix with hands to completely combine. Form into walnut-size balls.
2. Prepare a nonstick skillet by lightly coating surface with vegetable cooking spray or by using an oiled pastry brush. Brown meatballs well on all sides. Cook until done (balls will be firm).
3. Prepare sauce while meatballs are browning. In a large saucepan combine the tomatoes, chili powder, green chiles, garlic, and onions. Cover and simmer for about 20 minutes. Add aminos after cooking.
4. When meatballs are browned, arrange on a large platter and top with sauce.

Makes about 35 balls

To speed up the browning process, place meatballs on a broiler-safe pan under the hot broiler to brown tops.

41	Calories
2 g	Protein
7 g	Carbohydrates
1 g	Fat
21%	Calories from Fat
1 g	Fiber
102 mg	Sodium
0 mg	Cholesterol

The First Book of Vegetarian Cooking

"Beef" Stroganoff

❧ ❧

1   medium onion, chopped
2   cloves garlic, minced
½   pound button
       mushrooms, sliced
       (about 2 cups)
1   package (10.5 ounces)
       firm, lite silken tofu,
       drained
1   cup lite rice milk
1   teaspoon Dijon mustard
       Fresh cracked pepper
8   ounces Meat of Wheat,
       Beyond Roast Beef
       (Ivy Foods), thinly
       sliced

A light vegan version of the cholesterol- and fat-laden traditional recipe. Delicious served over pasta.

1. Prepare a nonstick skillet by lightly coating surface with vegetable cooking spray or by using an oiled pastry brush. Sauté the onion and garlic until transparent. Add sliced mushrooms and cook over medium heat for 3 minutes.
2. Process tofu in a blender or food processor until smooth and creamy and lump-free. Add a little of the milk, if necessary, for blending. Add milk, mustard, and pepper and process.
3. Add contents to skillet and simmer for 10 to 15 minutes or until reduced by a third and the sauce is rich and creamy. Stir occasionally. Add the meat and cook an additional 3 minutes.
4. Serve over eggless noodles, rice, mashed potatoes, or pasta ribbons.

Makes 4 servings

165	Calories
21 g	Protein
15 g	Carbohydrates
3 g	Fat
16%	Calories from Fat
1 g	Fiber
306 mg	Sodium
0 mg	Cholesterol

French Toast

๛ ๙

3 bananas sliced (2 cups)
¾ cup lite rice or soy milk
1 teaspoon cinnamon
¼ teaspoon powdered
   orange peel
½ teaspoon vanilla
8 slices firm whole grain
   bread (Ezekiel 4:9
   brand bread)

Yes, it is possible to make French toast without eggs or milk and still have it taste good.

1. Place bananas, milk, cinnamon, peel, and vanilla into a food processor or blender and process until smooth.
2. Pour mixture into a flat dish.
3. Prepare a nonstick skillet by lightly coating surface with vegetable cooking spray or by using an oiled pastry brush. Dip bread into mixture, coating both sides. Shake off excess. Brown bread slices on both sides.
4. Serve warm topped with maple syrup, fruit spread or sprinkled with Darifree* powder.

Makes 8 slices

"Take wheat and barley, and beans and lentils, and millet and spelt; put them in a single vessel and make bread out of them."

—EZEKIEL 4:9

*See "Glossary"

118	Calories
4 g	Protein
26 g	Carbohydrates
1 g	Fat
10%	Calories from Fat
3 g	Fiber
149 mg	Sodium
0 mg	Cholesterol

Grilled Tofu with Mango Sauce

❧ ❧

1   cup rosé wine
1   tablespoon lite tamari
2   cloves garlic, minced or
    pressed
1   tablespoon honey
1   teaspoon grated fresh
    gingerroot
1   tablespoon dehydrated
    onion flakes
1   pound extra-firm water-
    pack tofu, drained
    and cut into 4 slices

Mango sauce
2   whole tomatoes, diced
2   whole mangos, peeled
    and chopped
1   jalapeño pepper, minced
2   tablespoons tomato
    paste
1/2 cup minced fresh
    cilantro

1. Combine all ingredients except tofu and sauce. Place in a shallow dish along with the sliced tofu. The marinade should completely cover the tofu.
2. Cover and refrigerate for at least 1 hour or overnight.
3. Combine all the sauce ingredients. Refrigerate until serving time.
4. Remove tofu from marinade and place into an nonstick skillet or a grill that has been lightly coated with vegetable oil. Brown tofu on both sides.
5. Serve grilled tofu topped with the mango sauce.

Makes 4 servings

Tofu for hot flashes? Tofu, a soybean product, is rich in natural estrogen which might explain why Japanese women, whose diets include many soybean products, report fewer incidents of hot flashes and other related menopausal symptoms.

256	Calories
18 g	Protein
27 g	Carbohydrates
10 g	Fat
34%	Calories from Fat
4 g	Fiber
100 mg	Sodium
0 mg	Cholesterol

Chestnut and "Sausage" Stuffing

❧ ❧

1   box (8 1/2 ounces) Not
So Sausage (Knox
Mountain Farm)

2   loaves (1 pound each)
whole grain bread,
cubed

1   pound chestnuts

1   large onion, chopped

8   stalks celery, chopped

2   packages (6 ounces
each) portabello
mushrooms, chopped

2   tablespoons Vogue
Instant Vege Base

1   teaspoon poultry
seasoning
Salt and fresh ground
pepper

Preheat oven to 350 degrees F.

1. Prepare Not So Sausage according to package directions, reserving the broth. Chop 1 1/2 cups of the prepared sausage and freeze remainder for future use.
2. Place cubed bread on cookie sheet and bake for 10 minutes.
3. With a paring knife cut a big, deep X on the flat sides of the chestnuts (this is to avoid an exploding chestnut). Place on baking sheet and bake for 15 to 20 minutes. When cool enough to handle, remove shells and skin. Chop.
4. Prepare a nonstick skillet by lightly coating surface with vegetable cooking spray or by using an oiled pastry brush. Sauté the onion and celery until tender. Add mushrooms and sauté a minute longer. Remove onion mixture to a large bowl.
5. Add chopped sausage, chestnuts, and bread cubes. Mix well.
6. Stir Vogue Instant Vege Base and salt and pepper into reserved broth and heat until dissolved. Add liquid to bread mixture using only enough to moisten bread crumbs, about 6 cups of liquid.
7. Place into large casserole dish (4-quart or larger), cover and bake for 45 minutes.

Makes 10 servings

The First Book of Vegetarian Cooking

Recent studies have shown the soy bean to almost be a miracle food. Soy is low in saturated fat, cholesterol-free, high in fiber, protein, iron, calcium, zinc, and B-vitamins, contains all the essential amino acids, and is packed with phytomins. Tofu is the only good source of isoflavones.

Soy foods help prevent heart disease, breast and prostate cancers, and osteoporosis. They also help relieve menopause systems and lower cholesterol. Soy products are almost the only source of genistein, which blocks the process in which new blood vessels grow and is needed to nourish malignant tumors.

How many soy foods should we consume for good health? Experts don't all agree on this point, but one of the top soy experts advises at least one serving of a soy food daily. Examples of one serving:

1 cup (8 ounces) soy milk
1/2 cup (2 to 3 ounces) tofu
1/2 cup rehydrated TVP

1/2 cup green soy beans
("sweet beans")
3 ounces soy burger

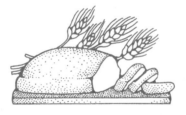

410	Calories
20 g	Protein
70 g	Carbohydrates
8 g	Fat
17%	Calories from Fat
11 g	Fiber
781 mg	Sodium
0 mg	Cholesterol

Huevos Rancheros

An eggless version of the Mexican favorite.

Sauce

1   large onion, chopped
1/2   bell pepper, chopped
2   cloves garlic, pressed
1   can (16 ounces) diced tomatoes, drained
1/4   cup minced fresh parsley
1   can (4 ounces) chopped green chiles, drained
1/4   teaspoon cumin powder
  Pinch of cayenne

1   pound extra-firm, water-packed tofu, drained and crumbled
1/4   teaspoon turmeric
1/4   teaspoon curry powder
1/4   teaspoon cumin seed
1   teaspoon onion powder
1   teaspoon liquid aminos
4   whole wheat fat-free tortillas, kept warm and moist

1. Prepare a nonstick skillet by lightly coating surface with vegetable cooking spray or by using an oiled pastry brush. Sauté onion, bell pepper, and garlic until tender.
2. To the skillet add the tomatoes, parsley, chiles, cumin powder, and cayenne. Stir and sauté for 5 minutes. Transfer to a bowl and cover to keep warm.
3. Respray skillet with cooking oil and add tofu, turmeric, curry powder, cumin seed, onion powder, and liquid aminos. Cook for 2 to 3 minutes stirring frequently.
4. Place one tortilla on each plate. Add one quarter of scrambled tofu into the center of each tortilla and roll up. Top with the sauce.

Makes 4 servings

265	Calories
20 g	Protein
26 g	Carbohydrates
10 g	Fat
33%	Calories from Fat
11 g	Fiber
452 mg	Sodium
0 mg	Cholesterol

The First Book of Vegetarian Cooking

Jerk Kebobs

1 recipe Jerk Sauce
Marinade, page 257
12 ounces seitan or tofu,
cut into one-inch
cubes
1 cup pineapple chunks
(1-inch cubes)
2 bell peppers, cut into
1-inch pieces
1 zucchini, cut into 1-inch
rounds
1 onion cut into 1-inch
chunks
1 pound cherry tomatoes
8 ounces whole button
mushrooms

Jerk sauce is traditionally Jamaican and usually very hot. This milder version really perks up the seitan in this dish. The sauce is a marinade and can be frozen and reused over and over again as long as no animal products come in contact with it.

1. Prepare Jerk Sauce Marinade, page 257.
2. In a glass bowl, pour marinade over seitan or tofu and refrigerate overnight.
2. On skewers, alternate fruits and vegetables with marinated seitan.
3. Cook on barbecue grill or broil in oven until vegetables are browned and tender, about 10 to 20 minutes.

Makes 4 servings

268	Calories
26 g	Protein
39 g	Carbohydrates
3 g	Fat
9%	Calories from Fat
5 g	Fiber
518 mg	Sodium
0 mg	Cholesterol

Keema Matar ("Beef" and Pea Curry)

꧁ ꧂

package (5.3 ounces)
    Burger 'n' Loaf,
    original
    teaspoon cumin seeds
1   teaspoon coriander
    seeds
1   piece (1 inch) fresh
    gingerroot
    Pinch of mace
    Pinch of nutmeg
1/2 teaspoon turmeric
1   teaspoon dried red
    chiles
1   large onion, chopped
2   cloves garlic, minced
2   tablespoons Vogue
    Instant Vege Base
1   cup distilled water
1   can (24 ounces) salt-free
    tomato sauce
2   whole cloves
1   bay leaf
3   cardamom seeds
2   cups frozen green peas

꧁ ꧂

Serve over rice or
with naan bread.

꧁ ꧂

A wonderful, hearty Indian vegetable curry.

1. Prepare the burger according to package directions, omitting the oil.
2. Grind cumin, coriander, gingerroot, mace, nutmeg, turmeric, and chiles into a smooth paste. A mortar and pestle works here if you happen to have one. If not, use the back of a spoon.
3. Prepare a nonstick skillet by lightly coating surface with vegetable cooking spray or by using an oiled pastry brush. Sauté the onions and garlic until soft. Add burger and cook, breaking up with the edge of a wooden spoon. When browned, add ground seasonings, cover, and cook over low heat for 10 minutes. Stir once or twice. Add a little water if mixture is too dry.
4. Mix together Vogue Instant Vege Base and water to make a broth. Add to the burger mixture along with the tomato sauce, cloves, bay leaf, and cardamom. Cover and simmer for 10 minutes, stirring occasionally.
5. Add peas, cover and simmer for an additional 5 minutes.

Makes 6 servings

189	Calories
18 g	Protein
27 g	Carbohydrates
4 g	Fat
19%	Calories from Fat
7 g	Fiber
461 mg	Sodium
0 mg	Cholesterol

The First Book of Vegetarian Cooking

Mushroom à la King

⤳ ⤳

2/3 cup sliced scallions
2 cloves garlic, minced
10 ounces button
     mushroom caps,
     sliced*
2 cups vegetable broth *or*
     2 tablespoons Vogue
     Instant Vege Base
     mixed with 2 cups
     distilled water
1 cup lite silken tofu
     (extra firm), drained
1/4 cup dry sherry
2/3 cup frozen peas, thawed
1/4 cup pimientos, drained
     Salt substitute
2 tablespoons kuzu or
     arrowroot, dissolved
     in 1/2 cup distilled
     water
4 slices whole grain bread,
     halved diagonally

Often à la king is served over toast but this sauce is also wonderful over rice or on a baked potato.

1. Prepare a nonstick skillet by lightly coating surface with vegetable cooking spray or by using an oiled pastry brush. Sauté scallions and garlic until soft; add mushrooms and cook an additional minute or two. Stir occasionally.
2. Process vegetable broth and the tofu in a blender. Blend until smooth. Add to the mushroom mix.
3. Add sherry, peas, pimientos, and salt substitute.
4. Stir in dissolved kuzu and cook only until thickened.
5. Ladle over toast halves.

Makes 4 Servings

⤳ ⤳

*Exotic mushrooms can be substituted for the button. Certain varieties may darken the color, but the flavor will be enhanced.

See page 98 for a homemade vegetable broth recipe.

⤳ ⤳

FLU BUSTERS

When I feel the first sign of flu, I place one dried shiitake mushroom (no other kind will work) in a cup and fill with nearly boiling water. Steep until the water turns yellow. Remove mushroom and drink mushroom tea with two cayenne pepper capsules. I do this three times a day until I feel improvement, and always follow with food to absorb the cayenne.

Shiitake mushrooms have been found to produce interferon in the body.

184	Calories
10 g	Protein
31 g	Carbohydrates
2 g	Fat
10%	Calories from Fat
4 g	Fiber
685 mg	Sodium
0 mg	Cholesterol

"Pollo" Pubil

❦ ❧

1 pound prepared seitan
   (page 376)

Marinade
1 large onion, chopped
2 cloves garlic, minced
¼ teaspoon cumin
5 whole peppercorns
4 tablespoons achiote*
   (annatto)
2 tablespoons Vogue
   Instant Vege Base
½ cup distilled water
1 cup sour orange juice

Onion Topping
2 large purple onions
⅓ cup distilled water
⅔ cup white vinegar
5 peppercorns
¼ teaspoon cumin
¼ teaspoon garlic powder
¼ teaspoon oregano

❦ ❧
Regular orange juice can
be used with the addition of
2 tablespoons of vinegar
❦ ❧

On a wonderful trip to the Yucatán, visiting Mayan ruins, I discovered this delicious dish. Originally, I understand, it was made with pork, but the restaurant where I first sampled it made it with chicken wrapped in a banana leaf (my prevegetarian days). This recipe is pretty close to that one.

1. Mix marinade ingredients and pour into a deep glass dish. Add seitan, cover and marinate overnight. Turn once.
2. Next day remove seitan from marinade. Marinade can be frozen for future use.
3. Prepare a nonstick skillet by lightly coating surface with vegetable cooking spray or by using an oiled pastry brush. Sauté onions until crisp-tender. Add remaining topping ingredients and cook until almost all the liquid is absorbed.
4. Add seitan to pan to warm and serve with onion topping.

*Achiote, the seed of the annatto tree, is available in the Spanish section of some supermarkets or in East Indian, Spanish, and Latin American markets. If you can't find it, use 2 tablespoons paprika and ½ teaspoon turmeric.

272	Calories
25 g	Protein
35 g	Carbohydrates
2 g	Fat
6%	Calories from Fat
5 g	Fiber
104 mg	Sodium
0 mg	Cholesterol

Quiche Lorraine

1 extra-large onion, thinly sliced
1 package (10.5 ounces) firm lite silken tofu, drained
1 cup rice milk
2 tablespoons flour
1/8 teaspoon nutmeg
Pinch of white pepper
1 teaspoon salt substitute
2 cups crushed baked tortilla chips
6 strips Stripples bacon substitute, cooked crisp and chopped
1 cup shredded Swiss cheese substitute

Preheat oven to 375 degrees F.

1. Prepare a nonstick skillet by lightly coating surface with vegetable cooking spray or by using an oiled pastry brush. Sauté the onion until soft.
2. Process tofu in a blender or food processor until creamy. Add milk, flour, nutmeg, pepper, and salt. Process again to incorporate.
3. Place crushed tortilla chips into the bottom of sprayed 10-inch, deep-dish pie pan. Add a layer of onion, bacon, and the cheese. Pour in tofu mixture.
4. Bake for 30 minutes or until firm.

Makes 8 servings

199	Calories
9 g	Protein
32 g	Carbohydrates
4 g	Fat
16%	Calories from Fat
2 g	Fiber
494 mg	Sodium
0 mg	Cholesterol

Reuben "Meat" Loaf

2   packages (5.3 ounces each) Burger 'n' Loaf, original
3   cloves garlic, minced
1   teaspoon caraway seeds
2   slices rye bread, moistened with distilled water and squeezed dry, torn into pieces
2   tablespoons dark and grainy mustard
1 1/2   cups rinsed sauerkraut, squeezed dry

Preheat oven to 375 degrees F.

For variety substitute mashed potatoes for the sauerkraut. Don't use butter or milk in the potatoes, just a little rice milk if potatoes are too dry.

I love to use leftovers from this recipe in sandwiches with Thousand Island dressing and mustard.

1. Prepare burger according to package directions, omitting the oil. Add garlic, caraway seeds, bread pieces, and mustard. Mix thoroughly with your hands.
2. On a piece of wax paper, form the mixture into a large rectangle.
3. Spread the sauerkraut over the rectangle, adding a little extra mustard.
4. Roll the loaf jelly-roll fashion. Place seam-side down into a loaf pan that has been lightly sprayed or oiled with vegetable spray.
5. Bake for 30 minutes.

Makes 8 servings

156	Calories
23 g	Protein
18 g	Carbohydrates
2 g	Fat
11%	Calories from Fat
7 g	Fiber
812 mg	Sodium
0 mg	Cholesterol

The First Book of Vegetarian Cooking

"Sausage, Cream Gravy," and Biscuits

Biscuits

1 ¾ cups organic stone-
       ground whole wheat
       flour
½   teaspoon baking soda
2   teaspoons baking
       powder
2   tablespoons soy
       margarine
¾   cup lite rice milk
2   teaspoons honey

"Sausage and Gravy"

1   medium onion, chopped
       (1 cup)
1   clove garlic, minced or
       pressed
1   package (14 ounces)
       Gimme Lean,
       sausage taste
1   cup firm, lite silken tofu,
       drained
1 ¼ cups lite rice milk
2   tablespoons arrowroot
       Pinch of cayenne

Preheat oven to 425 degrees F.

A comfort food that's good for breakfast, lunch, or dinner with all the bad stuff taken out.

1. To prepare biscuits, sift dry ingredients into a large bowl.
2. Cut margarine into flour until it disappears.
3. Whisk rice milk and honey together and stir into the flour mixture. The dough should be stiff.
4. Knead for about 3 or 4 minutes or until dough is no longer sticky.
5. Turn out onto a floured surface and roll out to a 8-inch circle. Cut into 2-inch circles (I use the floured rim of a jar).
6. Bake on an oiled/sprayed pie or cake pan for 15 minutes.
7. While biscuits are baking, prepare a nonstick skillet by lightly coating surface with vegetable cooking spray or by using an oiled pastry brush. Sauté onion and garlic until soft.
8. Add sausage, breaking into small pieces with the edge of a wooden spoon. Cook for about 10 minutes, stirring frequently.
9. Meanwhile, process tofu in a blender or food processor until smooth and creamy. Add milk, arrowroot, and cayenne and blend.
10. Add tofu mixture to sausage and cook until thick and thoroughly heated. Serve over biscuits.

*Makes 4 servings including
1 dozen biscuits*

298	Calories
19 g	Protein
41 g	Carbohydrates
6 g	Fat
19%	Calories from Fat
3 g	Fiber
921 mg	Sodium
0 mg	Cholesterol

"Turkey" Pot Pie
෨෧ ෨෧

Chestnut stuffing

1	loaf (1 pound) whole grain bread, cubed
½	pound chestnuts
1	large onion, chopped (1½ cups)
4	stalks celery, chopped
6	ounces portabello mushrooms, chopped
1	tablespoon Vogue Instant Vege Base
3	cups distilled water
½	teaspoon poultry seasoning
	Salt substitute and freshly ground pepper
1	box (1 pound) Meat of Wheat, chicken style, cut into ¾-inch lengthwise slices or prepared seitan
1	recipe Mushroom Gravy (page 370)
1	unbaked 10-inch whole grain pie shell
¼	cup rice milk

Preheat oven to 350 degrees F.

I made this dish as part of our Christmas dinner last year, and it was a hit with non-vegetarians as well as vegetarians.

1. Place cubed bread on cookie sheet and bake for 10 minutes.
2. With a paring knife cut a big, deep X on the flat sides of each chestnut (this is to avoid an exploding chestnut). Place on baking sheet and bake for 15 to 20 minutes. When cool enough to handle, remove shells and skin. Chop. Set oven temperature to 400 degrees F.
3. Prepare a nonstick skillet by lightly coating surface with vegetable cooking spray or by using an oiled pastry brush. Sauté the onion and celery until tender. Add mushrooms and sauté a minute longer. Remove onion mixture to a large bowl.
4. Add chestnuts and bread cubes. Mix well.

෨෧ ෨෧

Last year I decorated the pie by cutting out a pastry Christmas tree, balls and all, and applied it before baking. Your decoration could be adapted for any occasion.

෨෧ ෨෧

5. Stir Vogue Instant Vege Base into water and heat until dissolved. Add poultry seasoning, salt and pepper, and liquid to bread mixture using only enough to moisten bread crumbs.

6. Assemble the pie: With a pastry brush, paint each piece of seitan with gravy and place in the bottom of a sprayed 10-inch deep-dish pie plate.

7. Top with stuffing, completely covering seitan and spreading out to edge of pie dish.

8. Place pastry over stuffing; brush pastry with rice milk

9. Bake for 1 hour. Pastry should be golden.

Makes 8 to 10 servings

431	Calories
22 g	Protein
58 g	Carbohydrates
14 g	Fat
30%	Calories from Fat
8 g	Fiber
714 mg	Sodium
0 mg	Cholesterol

Sauces, Marinades, and Salad Dressings

❧ ❧

What's a salad without dressing? What's tofu or seitan without a marinade? What's pasta without a sauce? The answer is . . . bland.

This chapter features practically fat-free sauces, marinades, and salad dressings. I think you will find leaving out the fat does not affect the taste. Actually, if you taste oil directly from the bottle, I think you will find it tastes terrible. So, why add it? I remember one time I was doing a liver flush that included drinking a ½ cup of olive oil. It is not one of my favorite memories.

But, you say, olive oil is good for you. I say, it still can clog your arteries, contributing to heart disease not to mention obesity. So feel free to enjoy these recipes without guilt!

These recipes can double as marinades as well as sauces. Place in a glass dish with a cover, or pour into a sealable plastic bag. Turn marinated foods to cover with sauce. Marinate from one hour to overnight.

Recipes

Sauces and Marinades

Pizza Sauce

Barbecue Sauce

Shortcut Barbecue Sauce

Hot Mustard Sauce

Horseradish Sauce

Peanut Sauce

Jerk Sauce

Marinara Sauce

Pesto Sauce

Sweet and Sour Sauce

Pronto Plum Sauce

Teriyaki Sauce

Oriental Marinade

Italian Marinade

Easy Italian Marinade

Ginger Mustard Sauce

Salad Dressings

Orange Dressing

Poppy Dressing

Fat-Free Italian Dressing

Honey Mustard Dressing

Peanut Dressing

Caesar Dressing

Thousand Island Dressing

Sweet and Sour Dressing

Banana Dressing

Pizza Sauce

½ cup salt-free tomato
    paste
2 cups salt-free tomato
    sauce
½ teaspoon dried basil
½ teaspoon dried oregano
½ teaspoon garlic powder
½ teaspoon onion powder

Combine and simmer for 15 minutes.

Makes 2 ½ cups

14 Calories
1 g Protein
3 g Carbohydrates
1 g Fat
7% Calories from Fat
1 g Fiber
9 mg Sodium
0 mg Cholesterol

Barbecue Sauce

1   can (28 ounces) salt-free tomato purée
½   cup salt-free tomato paste
3   large shallots, chopped
1½   teaspoons Tabasco sauce
2   tablespoons vegetarian Worcestershire sauce
1   bay leaf
½   cup date sugar
2   teaspoons chili powder
¾   cup apple cider vinegar
1   teaspoon Liquid Smoke
½   teaspoon dry mustard
½   teaspoon paprika
¼   teaspoon garlic powder
1   vegetable bouillon cube
1   teaspoon crushed red pepper
2   tablespoons liquid aminos

Combine ingredients except aminos in a saucepan and simmer, covered for 1 hour. Remove from heat and add aminos.

Makes 4 cups

24	Calories
1 g	Protein
6 g	Carbohydrates
1 g	Fat
5%	Calories from Fat
1 g	Fiber
73 mg	Sodium
0 mg	Cholesterol

Shortcut Barbecue Sauce

½ cup fruit-sweetened
    ketchup
2 tablespoons honey
1 tablespoon Stir Krazy
    (Wizard's) vegetarian
    Worcestershire sauce
2 tablespoons natural
    apple cider vinegar
½ teaspoon chili powder

Whisk ingredients together.

Makes ¾ cup

39	Calories
0 g	Protein
11g	Carbohydrates
1 g	Fat
1%	Calories from Fat
0 g	Fiber
64 mg	Sodium
0 mg	Cholesterol

Hot Mustard Sauce

❧❧ ❧❧

¼ cup dry mustard
3 tablespoons cold
      distilled water

Combine until smooth. Let stand 10 minutes.

Makes about ½ cup

27   Calories
2g   Protein
1 g   Carbohydrates
2 g   Fat
60%   Calories from Fat
0 g   Fiber
0 mg   Sodium
0 mg   Cholesterol

The First Book of Vegetarian Cooking

Horseradish Sauce

1   cup lite silken tofu,
     drained
½ cup fat-free, dairy-free
     mayonnaise
2   tablespoons prepared
     horseradish

Whisk ingredients together.

Makes 1 ½ cups

12	Calories
1 g	Protein
2 g	Carbohydrates
1 g	Fat
6%	Calories from Fat
0 g	Fiber
130 mg	Sodium
0 mg	Cholesterol

Peanut Sauce

½ cup reduced-fat natural
   chunky peanut
   butter
¼ cup lite rice milk
2 teaspoons low-sodium
   tamari sauce
¼ cup frozen orange juice
   concentrate
2 teaspoons fresh lime
   juice
2 teaspoons honey
4 scallions, thinly sliced
   (2 tablespoons)
1 teaspoon freshly grated
   ginger
⅛ teaspoon cayenne
⅛ teaspoon coconut
   extract

In a saucepan, whisk peanut butter and milk. Add remaining sauce ingredients; mix well. Heat to a simmer.

Makes 1 ½ cups

43	Calories
1 g	Protein
4 g	Carbohydrates
3 g	Fat
57%	Calories from Fat
1 g	Fiber
48 mg	Sodium
0 mg	Cholesterol

The First Book of Vegetarian Cooking

Jerk Sauce

1   cup minced onion
½   cup minced bell pepper
2   tablespoons minced
           fresh ginger
2   cloves garlic, pressed
1   teaspoon minced
           Bonnet or Habañero
           chile pepper
¼   cup frozen orange juice
           concentrate
¼   cup honey
2   cups distilled water
½   cup low-sodium tamari
       Pinch of cayenne pepper
¼   teaspoon dried thyme
           leaf
½   teaspoon dried sage
½   teaspoon dried basil
       Pinch of fresh cracked
           pepper
¼   teaspoon cumin
¼   teaspoon nutmeg
½   teaspoon allspice

Whisk ingredients together in glass bowl.

Makes 4 cups

Use this sauce as a marinade
for Jerk Kebabs (page 239).

21	Calories
1 g	Protein
4 g	Carbohydrates
0 g	Fat
2%	Calories from Fat
0 g	Fiber
176 mg	Sodium
0 mg	Cholesterol

Marinara Sauce

1   cup chopped onion
¼   cup chopped celery
¼   cup chopped carrots
3   cloves garlic, minced
16   ounces diced tomatoes
     or 1 can (28 ounces)
     crushed tomatoes
¼   teaspoon dried basil
¼   teaspoon dried thyme
¼   teaspoon dried oregano
1   bay leaf
¼   cup red wine

Serve over cooked spaghetti or use as a pizza sauce.

1. Prepare a nonstick skillet by lightly coating surface with vegetable cooking spray or by using an oiled pastry brush. Sauté onion, celery, carrots, and garlic until tender.
2. Add remaining ingredients and simmer covered for 20 minutes.

Makes 6 servings

36	Calories
1 g	Protein
7 g	Carbohydrates
1 g	Fat
9 %	Calories from Fat
2 g	Fiber
13 mg	Sodium
0 mg	Cholesterol

The First Book of Vegetarian Cooking

Pesto Sauce

¼ cup lemon juice
¼ cup pine nuts
4 cloves garlic
1 ½ cups fresh basil leaves
¼ cup grated Parmesan
    cheese substitute

Process in blender or food processor until smooth.

Makes ½ cup

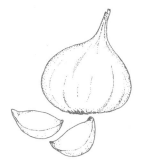

70	Calories
4 g	Protein
5 g	Carbohydrates
5 g	Fat
70%	Calories from Fat
1 g	Fiber
41 mg	Sodium
0 mg	Cholesterol

Sweet and Sour Sauce

❧ ❧

1 jar (10 ounces) sugarless
    apricot fruit spread
1 tablespoon Chinese hot
    mustard
1 tablespoon pure apple
    cider vinegar
1 tablespoon honey
¼ cup frozen apple juice
    concentrate, thawed
1 tablespoon teriyaki
    sauce
   Distilled water to thin
    (3 to 4 tablespoons)

Whisk ingredients together and serve.

Makes 1 ½ cups

98	Calories
0 g	Protein
24 g	Carbohydrates
1 g	Fat
1%	Calories from Fat
0 g	Fiber
59 mg	Sodium
0 mg	Cholesterol

The First Book of Vegetarian Cooking

Pronto Plum Sauce

½ cup sugarless all-fruit
    spread, grape or
    apricot flavor
1   tablespoon hot mustard
    sauce

Combine until smooth.

Makes ½ cup

99	Calories
0 g	Protein
24 g	Carbohydrates
1 g	Fat
2%	Calories from Fat
0 g	Fiber
0 mg	Sodium
0 mg	Cholesterol

Teriyaki Sauce

1   can (15 ounces) pine-
      apple chunks in
      own juice, drained
      (reserve juice)
1/3   cup low-sodium tamari
      sauce
1   clove garlic, pressed
3/4   teaspoon ground ginger

Whisk ingredients together. Add reserved juice a little at a time to achieve desired consistency.

Makes 1 3/4 cups

28	Calories
1 g	Protein
6 g	Carbohydrates
1 g	Fat
1%	Calories from Fat
0 g	Fiber
266 mg	Sodium
0 mg	Cholesterol

Oriental Marinade

½ cup rice vinegar
1 teaspoon sesame oil
¼ cup honey
2 cloves garlic, pressed or minced
2 tablespoons grated fresh gingerroot
¼ cup pineapple juice

Whisk ingredients together.

Makes 1 cup

45	Calories
0 g	Protein
10 g	Carbohydrates
1 g	Fat
12%	Calories from Fat
0 g	Fiber
2 mg	Sodium
0 mg	Cholesterol

Italian Marinade

⤞ ⤝

¼ cup balsamic vinegar
¼ cup minced shallots
1 clove garlic, minced or
   pressed
1 tablespoon dried
   oregano
⅛ teaspoon freshly ground
   pepper
1 teaspoon liquid aminos

Whisk ingredients together.

Makes ½ cup

20	Calories
0 g	Protein
5 g	Carbohydrates
0 g	Fat
0%	Calories from Fat
0 g	Fiber
150 mg	Sodium
0 mg	Cholesterol

Easy Italian Marinade

❧ ❧

1   bottle fat-free or low-fat
    Italian dressing

Grab a bottle of your favorite fat-free or lowfat Italian dressing. You will be amazed at the wonderful flavor it adds when used as a marinade. Try it! Here we used Marie's Fat-Free Italian Dressing.

See size of bottle for yield amount.

28   Calories
1 g Protein
6 g Carbohydrates
0 g Fat
4%   Calories from Fat
0 g Fiber
59 mg Sodium
0 mg Cholesterol

Ginger Mustard Sauce

❧ ❧

½ cup orange juice
2 tablespoons low-sodium
    tamari sauce
1 tablespoon Dijon
    mustard
1 teaspoon ginger
1 teaspoon date sugar

Combine all ingredients in a saucepan and heat to dissolve date sugar. Blend ingredients.

Makes ½ cup

36	Calories
2 g	Protein
6 g	Carbohydrates
1 g	Fat
14%	Calories from Fat
0 g	Fiber
451 mg	Sodium
0 mg	Cholesterol

The First Book of Vegetarian Cooking

Orange Dressing

½ cup minced onions
2 cloves garlic, pressed
¼ cup white balsamic
    vinegar
2 tablespoons Ume plum
    vinegar
½ cup orange juice

Whisk all ingredients together.

Makes 1 cup

25	Calories
0 g	Protein
6 g	Carbohydrates
0 g	Fat
0%	Calories from Fat
0 g	Fiber
202 mg	Sodium
0 mg	Cholesterol

Poppy Dressing

1   tablespoon grainy
      mustard
1   tablespoon honey
1   tablespoon fresh lemon
      juice
½   cup lite soy or rice milk
1   teaspoon poppy seeds
¼   teaspoon grated orange
      zest

1. In a small bowl combine the mustard and honey.
2. Whisk in remaining ingredients.

Makes ³/₄ cup

29	Calories
1 g	Protein
4 g	Carbohydrates
1 g	Fat
37%	Calories from Fat
0 g	Fiber
50 mg	Sodium
0 mg	Cholesterol

Fat-Free Italian Dressing

೨৽ ৵ও

1 cup distilled water
¼ cup raw, unfiltered organic apple cider vinegar
¼ teaspoon powdered barley malt sweetener (Dr. Bronner's)
1 teaspoon garlic powder
½ teaspoon onion powder
½ teaspoon dried oregano
1 teaspoon Parmesan cheese substitute
½ teaspoon xanthan gum*
1 tablespoon dehydrated mixed vegetable bits

1. In a blender or food processor, combine water, vinegar, sweetener, garlic powder, onion powder, oregano, and Parmesan cheese substitute.
2. Slowly add xanthan gum and process for 1 minute. Add mixed vegetables.
3. Bottle and refrigerate at least one hour to allow flavors to mingle.

Makes 1 ¾ cups

*Can be found in health food stores.

3	Calories
0 g	Protein
1 g	Carbohydrates
0 g	Fat
0%	Calories from Fat
0 g	Fiber
1 mg	Sodium
0 mg	Cholesterol

Honey Mustard Dressing

1   package (10.5 ounces)
      firm, lite silken tofu
3   tablespoons Dijon
      mustard
1 ½   tablespoons balsamic
      vinegar
1   tablespoon honey

1. Wrap tofu in several thicknesses of a clean kitchen towel for 30 minutes.
2. Cut drained tofu into cubes and place in a food processor or blender with remaining ingredients. Process until smooth and creamy.
3. Chill until serving time. Surround dip with an array of fresh vegetables.

Makes about 1 ½ cups

16	Calories
1 g	Protein
2 g	Carbohydrates
1 g	Fat
33%	Calories from Fat
0 g	Fiber
101 mg	Sodium
0 mg	Cholesterol

The First Book of Vegetarian Cooking

Peanut Dressing

¼ cup reduced-fat natural
    chunky peanut
    butter
⅛ cup lite rice milk
1 teaspoon low-sodium
    tamari sauce
2 tablespoons frozen
    orange juice
    concentrate
1 teaspoon fresh lime
1 teaspoon honey
2 scallions, thinly sliced
    (1 tablespoon)
½ teaspoon freshly grated
    ginger
⅛ teaspoon cayenne
   Dash of coconut extract
    (scant ⅛ teaspoon)

Whisk ingredients together.

Makes ¾ cup

84	Calories
3 g	Protein
7 g	Carbohydrates
5 g	Fat
58%	Calories from Fat
1 g	Fiber
95 mg	Sodium
0 mg	Cholesterol

Caesar Dressing

1   clove garlic, pressed
¼   cup fat-free, dairy-free
       mayonnaise
¼   cup fat-free Italian
       dressing
       Freshly cracked pepper
2   tablespoons grated
       Parmesan cheese
       substitute

Whisk ingredients together.

Makes ⅔ cup

28	Calories
0 g	Protein
6 g	Carbohydrates
1 g	Fat
3%	Calories from Fat
0 g	Fiber
270 mg	Sodium
0 mg	Cholesterol

Thousand Island Dressing

※ ※

1   cup fat-free mayonnaise
⅓   cup sugar-free relish
¼   cup fruit-sweetened
        ketchup

※ ※

I use this recipe on Reuben
pizzas and sandwiches.

※ ※

To make a healthful dressing, the ingredients should be free of fat, sugar, and dairy products. The health food store will have these items or you can make your own using the recipes in "Added Touches."

Combine ingredients and store in refrigerator in a recycled glass jar.

Makes 1 ½ cups

20	Calories
0 g	Protein
5 g	Carbohydrates
0 g	Fat
0%	Calories from Fat
0 g	Fiber
338 mg	Sodium
0 mg	Cholesterol

Sweet and Sour Dressing

❧ ❧

2   tablespoons orange juice
1   tablespoon honey
4   tablespoons natural
       apple cider vinegar
2   tablespoons Dijon
       mustard
1   teaspoon low-sodium
       tamari

Whisk ingredients together.

Makes ¾ cup

24	Calories
1 g	Protein
4 g	Carbohydrates
1 g	Fat
25%	Calories from Fat
0 g	Fiber
174 mg	Sodium
0 mg	Cholesterol

Banana Dressing

1	banana (4 ounces), peeled and quartered
¼	cup distilled water
2	tablespoons balsamic vinegar
1	tablespoon Dijon mustard
1	tablespoon honey
1	teaspoon powdered cumin
1	teaspoon liquid aminos
⅛	teaspoon freshly cracked pepper

A tangy dressing for lettuce or fruits.

1. Process ingredients in blender or food processor until smooth.
2. Refrigerate 1 hour.

Makes one cup

31	Calories
0 g	Protein
7 g	Carbohydrates
1 g	Fat
12%	Calories from Fat
0 g	Fiber
81 mg	Sodium
0 mg	Cholesterol

LIQUID ASSETS

W hen we first think of beverages, we associate drinks with entertaining. True, since the beginning of time that is how we greeted a guest—with a welcoming drink. As Don Quixote said, "I drink upon occasion and sometimes I drink upon no occasion!" I don't suppose he was talking about water although drinking water (distilled, that is) is very important to our health, lubricating and maintaining our internal systems. Sometimes we want something a little more imaginative.

This chapter contains a collection of beverages that will satisfy everyday tastes and will allow you to make elegant offerings for your guests.

Recipes

Banana Drink

Café Om

Burgundy Kir

"Eggnog"

Grape Expectations

Glögg

Lemonade

Hot Carob Drink

Masala Tea

Piña Colada Cooler

"Champagne"

Pineapple Blush

Sangria

Sangria Blanca

Apricot Smoothie

Blueberry Smoothie

Spiced Tea

Carob-Coconut Frappé

Spiced Apple Punch

Banana Drink

4   ripe frozen bananas
6   ounces orange juice
       concentrate
3   cups frozen strawberries
2   cups soy milk

A low-calorie solution for that sweet tooth. Try this drink for a nutritious breakfast or an afternoon energy boost.

Mix together in blender until creamy.

Makes 6 to 8 servings.

When bananas become overripe don't throw them away—peel, wrap, and freeze them for future use.

BANANAS

Bananas are believed to be our oldest fruit and possibly the most nutritious. They are high in fiber, potassium, and vitamin A as well as other vitamins and minerals. Bananas are excellent for infants and young children, and adults can enjoy bananas knowing they are low in fat and will satisfy the appetite. Bananas are ripe and most digestible when no green is present on the skin.

140	Calories
4 g	Protein
29 g	Carbohydrates
2 g	Fat
13%	Calories from Fat
3 g	Fiber
11 mg	Sodium
0 mg	Cholesterol

Café Om

❧ ❧

4	cups distilled water
6	tablespoons grain coffee substitute
$1/8$	teaspoon freshly ground nutmeg
2	tablespoons carob powder
$1/4$	teaspoon vanilla
4	tablespoons Tia Maria liqueur
	Soy or rice milk and honey

A satisfying after-dinner drink.

1. Pour water in a saucepan. Stir in coffee substitute and nutmeg. Bring to a boil.
2. Remove $1/4$ cup of the hot coffee from the saucepan and add the carob powder. Stir until dissolved. Return carob mixture to the coffee in the saucepan and bring to a boil again.
3. Remove from heat and add the vanilla and the Tia Maria.
4. Serve with milk and honey to taste.

Serves 4

Drinking too much caffeine can cause osteoporosis by blocking calcium absorption in the body. The caffeine in two to three cups of coffee can draw 30 milligrams of calcium from your bones. Coffee is not the only culprit:

Colas—35 to 47 mg *Hot cocoa—4 mg*
Cappuccino—61 mg *Decaf coffee—2 to 8 mg*
Tea—25 to 110 mg *Expresso—100 mg*

81	Calories
0 g	Protein
15 g	Carbohydrates
1 g	Fat
3%	Calories from Fat
0 g	Fiber
17 mg	Sodium
0 mg	Cholesterol

The First Book of Vegetarian Cooking

Burgundy Kir

1   bottle Burgundy
½   cup crème de cassis

Most Kir recipes call for a fruity white wine, which is delicious, but try Burgundy for a wonderful change.

Combine ingredients and serve with or without ice.

Makes 8 servings

93	Calories
0 g	Protein
4 g	Carbohydrates
0 g	Fat
0%	Calories from Fat
0 g	Fiber
6 mg	Sodium
0 mg	Cholesterol

"Eggnog"

1   package (10.5 ounces)
     firm, lite silken tofu,
     drained
16   ounces (2 cups) lite rice
     milk
1 1/2 teaspoons vanilla
1/3 cup honey
1/4 teaspoon turmeric
     (for color)
1/2 cup brandy or bourbon
     (optional)
     Freshly ground nutmeg
     for garnish

*A nondairy eggnog for the holidays that can be served with or
without the alcohol.*

1. Combine ingredients (except nutmeg) in blender or food
   processor. It might be necessary to make two batches depending on the capacity of the machine.
2. Chill and serve garnished with nutmeg.

Makes 8 servings or 6 cups

91	Calories
3 g	Protein
18 g	Carbohydrates
1 g	Fat
9%	Calories from Fat
0 g	Fiber
27 mg	Sodium
0 mg	Cholesterol

Grape Expectations

1 quart organic grape juice
2 oranges, juiced
1 lemon, juiced
1 quart carbonated water
1 orange, thinly sliced for
    garnish

A wine-less sangria.

Combine ingredients and chill.

Makes 2 1/2 quarts

A high percentage of grapes in one's diet has been linked to low cancer incidence. Grapes are a good source of magnesium, are cleansing to the liver, and aid kidney function.

74	Calories
1 g	Protein
18 g	Carbohydrates
1 g	Fat
1%	Calories from Fat
0 g	Fiber
33 mg	Sodium
0 mg	Cholesterol

Glögg

ๆ๛ ๛฿

1½ cups distilled water
½ cup raisins
1 teaspoon cardamom
     seeds, crushed
2 teaspoons whole cloves
1 cinnamon stick
1 bottle (750 ml) dry red
     wine
¼ cup honey
   Almonds and raisins for
     garnish

Light the fireplace and serve this Swedish favorite.

1. In a medium saucepan, combine water, raisins, cardamom, cloves, and cinnamon stick, simmer for 30 minutes. Strain and return spiced liquid to pan. Add wine and honey and bring to a simmer, stirring until honey is dissolved.
2. Serve in a heated pitcher or warmed individual mugs. Garnish with almonds and raisins.

Makes 8 cups

ๆ๛ ๛฿

White wine or blush can be
substituted for the red.

ๆ๛ ๛฿

98	Calories
0 g	Protein
10 g	Carbohydrates
0 g	Fat
0%	Calories from Fat
0 g	Fiber
8 mg	Sodium
0 mg	Cholesterol

The First Book of Vegetarian Cooking

Lemonade

ஒ~ ~ஒ

1   cup fresh lemon juice
     (about 6 lemons)
$1/3$ cup honey
4   cups distilled water
     Ice cubes
     Fresh mint for garnish

An old-fashioned refresher.

1. Blend lemon juice and honey together. Add water and stir.
2. Serve chilled with sprigs of mint in each glass.

Makes 6 cups

DECORATIVE ICE CUBES

Place small pieces of melon balls, fresh mint sprigs,
lemon or orange peels, raspberries, strawberries,
or any other small pieces of fruit into ice cube trays.
Fill with distilled water and freeze. Place one or two
cubes into each glass.

58	Calories
0 g	Protein
15 g	Carbohydrates
0 g	Fat
0%	Calories from Fat
0 g	Fiber
6 mg	Sodium
0 mg	Cholesterol

Hot Carob Drink

❦ ❦

1¼ cups soy milk
1   tablespoon carob
      powder
2   teaspoons honey
      Dash of vanilla
½   teaspoon cinnamon

Blend ingredients together. Heat and serve.

Enough for 1 large mug

120	Calories
5 g	Protein
24 g	Carbohydrates
3 g	Fat
24%	Calories from Fat
0 g	Fiber
30 mg	Sodium
0 mg	Cholesterol

The First Book of Vegetarian Cooking

Masala Tea

3 cups distilled water
1 piece (¹⁄₂-inch) ginger-root, unpeeled and chopped
¹⁄₂ teaspoon crushed cardamom pods
¹⁄₂ cinnamon stick
2 whole peppercorns
2 whole cloves
2 bags green tea
  Soy milk
  Honey

A favorite tea in India.

1. In a medium saucepan, bring water, ginger, cardamom, cinnamon, peppercorns, and cloves to a simmer. Cook covered for 20 minutes.
2. Remove from heat and strain into warmed teapot. Add tea bags; cover and steep for 5 minutes.
3. Add milk and honey to taste.

Makes 3 cups

Green tea has been making headlines lately. Because it is lightly processed, it retains many of its phytochemicals like catechins. Studies show this plant nutrient can lower cholesterol, helping to prevent atherosclerosis and can inhibit the growth of cancerous tumors. This tea also kills the bacteria in the mouth that is responsible for tooth decay. Green tea does contain caffeine, but half the amount in coffee.

1	Calorie
0 g	Protein
0 g	Carbohydrates
0 g	Fat
0%	Calories from Fat
0 g	Fiber
10 mg	Sodium
0 mg	Cholesterol

Piña Colada Cooler

1   cup low-fat cream of
     coconut
2   cups pineapple juice
5   cups ice

A nonalcoholic version of a familiar favorite.

In a blender, combine ingredients until smooth. This can be made in batches.

Makes 8 servings

COCONUT

Coconut has been a source of food for over 3,000 years. It has been estimated that over a quarter of a million people use coconut in some form each day. There is an old saying: "He who plants a coconut tree plants vessels and clothing, food and drink, a habitation for himself, and a heritage for his children." Coconut milk compares to mother's milk in its chemical balance, it is quite a complete protein food when taken in its natural form. Although high in fat and calories, it is also high in carbohydrates, calcium, phosphorus, iron, thiamin, riboflavin, niacin, and ascorbic acid.

53	Calories
0 g	Protein
10 g	Carbohydrates
1 g	Fat
4%	Calories from Fat
0 g	Fiber
2 mg	Sodium
0 mg	Cholesterol

"Champagne"

1 bottle (33.8 ounces)
    ginger ale, chilled
1 bottle (33.8 ounces)
    carbonated water,
    chilled
3 cups white grape juice,
    chilled
    One half strawberry per
    glass for garnish

Combine ingredients in a large pitcher and pour into chilled wine glasses.

Makes 10 cups

83	Calories
1 g	Protein
21 g	Carbohydrates
1 g	Fat
1%	Calories from Fat
0 g	Fiber
30 mg	Sodium
0 mg	Cholesterol

Pineapple Blush

꽃 꽃

2   cups blush wine, chilled
2   cups naturally sweet-
      ened, chilled
      cranberry juice
1   can (6 ounces) frozen
      pineapple juice
      concentrate

Pineapples were originally cultivated in the West Indies. No one seems to know how the fruit got to Hawaii. This is a refreshing cooler high in vitamin C. The pineapple helps digest proteins and is alkaline in nature.

1. Stir ingredients together until concentrate is dissolved.
2. Serve in chilled wine glasses.

Makes 8 servings

Cranberries have long been known as a treatment for urinary infections. They are also therapeutic for rectal disturbances. Due to their acid content they should not be eaten too frequently.

129	Calories
0 g	Protein
23 g	Carbohydrates
0 g	Fat
0%	Calories from Fat
0 g	Fiber
5 mg	Sodium
0 mg	Cholesterol

The First Book of Vegetarian Cooking

Sangria

1   bottle dry red wine
½   cup cointreau
2   cups fresh orange juice
¼   cup honey

Serve in a clear glass pitcher filled with ice and garnished with orange slices.

Combine ingredients and chill.

Makes 8 servings

165	Calories
1 g	Protein
21 g	Carbohydrates
1 g	Fat
1%	Calories from Fat
0 g	Fiber
10 mg	Sodium
0 mg	Cholesterol

Sangria Blanca

¼ cup honey
½ cup fresh lemon juice
   (about 3 lemons)
1 bottle (750 ml) dry
   white wine
½ cup orange juice
¼ cup cointreau (optional)
1 cup distilled water
   Lemon and orange slices
      for garnish

For a taste treat give your guests a choice between regular red sangria and this white version.

1. In a large glass pitcher, blend honey and lemon juice. Stir in remaining ingredients. Float lemon and orange slices on top.
2. Chill until ready to serve.

Makes 6 cups

141	Calories
0 g	Protein
16 g	Carbohydrates
0 g	Fat
0%	Calories from Fat
0 g	Fiber
10 mg	Sodium
0 mg	Cholesterol

The First Book of Vegetarian Cooking

Apricot Smoothie

❧　☙

1	cup apricot nectar
1	cup pineapple juice
$1/2$	cup soy milk or almond milk
1	teaspoon bee pollen

In a blender, process until smooth and creamy.

Makes 2 drinks

❧　☙

Smoothies—nourishing
and refreshing drinks.

❧　☙

BEE POLLEN

Ancient Egyptians, Persians, Chinese, even Hippocrates, the father of modern medicine, believed bee pollen contributed to long life and eternal youth; no wonder—it contains 22 amino acids, 27 mineral salts, all the vitamins, minerals, fructose, glucose, lecithin, hormones, carbohydrates, all the essential fatty acids, rutin, bioflavonoids, and over 5,000 enzymes, and coenzymes. Truly a wonder food and perhaps a wonder medicine.

Bee pollen has proved successful to the hay fever sufferer. Using pollen collected within a ten mile radius of your home will help build an immunity to the local offending pollen.

In my case, this pollen is not available. My local apiarist assures me the use of local "wildflower" honey will have the same effect and suggested a tablespoon a day.

159	Calories
2 g	Protein
37 g	Carbohydrates
1 g	Fat
5%	Calories from Fat
1 g	Fiber
9 mg	Sodium
0 mg	Cholesterol

Blueberry Smoothie

~ ~

3	cups soy milk
1	cup fresh or frozen blueberries (do not thaw)
1	very ripe banana
3	teaspoons raw honey

Process in blender for 3 minutes.

Makes 1 quart

96	Calories
3 g	Protein
18 g	Carbohydrates
2 g	Fat
20%	Calories from Fat
1 g	Fiber
14 mg	Sodium
0 mg	Cholesterol

The First Book of Vegetarian Cooking

Spiced Tea

2 cups boiling distilled water
½ cinnamon stick
2 whole cloves
2 whole allspice
1 sprig of mint
  Honey

Serve iced in the summer with a sprig of mint. In the winter, serve hot with a cinnamon stick.

1. In saucepan of boiling water, add cinnamon stick, cloves, and allspice. Boil 1 minute. Stir in mint. Remove from heat.
2. Cover and steep for 5 minutes.
3. Strain and serve with honey to taste.

Makes 2 cups

3	Calories
0 g	Protein
1 g	Carbohydrates
0 g	Fat
0%	Calories from Fat
0 g	Fiber
7 mg	Sodium
0 mg	Cholesterol

Carob-Coconut Frappé

2 tablespoons carob powder

3 tablespoons warm distilled water

2½ cups lite coconut milk

1 tablespoon raw honey

1. Dissolve carob powder in the water. Place all ingredients in blender and process at medium speed for 2 minutes.
2. Fill five wine glasses qith crushed ice. Pour frappé over ice.

Makes 2½ cups or 5 servings

92	Calories
1 g	Protein
11 g	Carbohydrates
1 g	Fat
6%	Calories from Fat
0 g	Fiber
9 mg	Sodium
0 mg	Cholesterol

The First Book of Vegetarian Cooking

Spiced Apple Punch

1 quart organic apple juice
2 tablespoons Spice Hunter's Witching Brew Mulling Spice,* wrapped in cheese cloth or placed in a tea infuser.

This brew can also be prepared with red wine, apple cider, cranberry juice, or any fruit nectar.

1. Simmer 2 cups of the apple juice with spice bag for 15 to 20 minutes.
2. Remove spice bag. Add remaining 2 cups juice and serve.

Makes one quart

Make as a sun tea and serve chilled.

*Available at most health food stores or see mail-order directory.

CINNAMON

Cinnamon has long been a common ingredient in folklore remedies. Recent studies have indicated cinnamon as an antiseptic, astringent, stomach-distress reliever, and fungicide. It also has ulcer fighting properties and may even stimulate the brain.

90	Calories
0 g	Protein
22 g	Carbohydrates
1 g	Fat
2%	Calories from Fat
0 g	Fiber
10 mg	Sodium
0 mg	Cholesterol

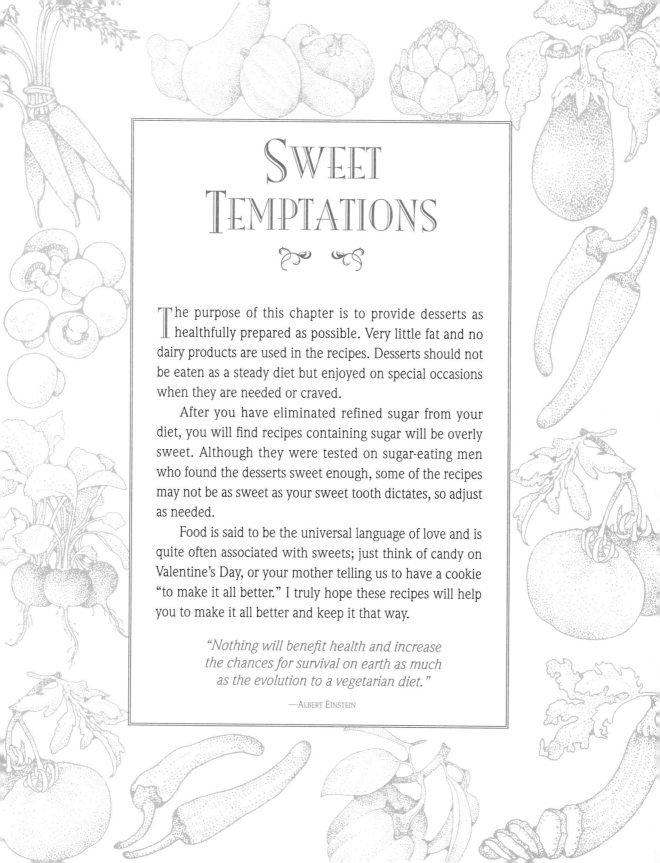

Sweet Temptations

The purpose of this chapter is to provide desserts as healthfully prepared as possible. Very little fat and no dairy products are used in the recipes. Desserts should not be eaten as a steady diet but enjoyed on special occasions when they are needed or craved.

After you have eliminated refined sugar from your diet, you will find recipes containing sugar will be overly sweet. Although they were tested on sugar-eating men who found the desserts sweet enough, some of the recipes may not be as sweet as your sweet tooth dictates, so adjust as needed.

Food is said to be the universal language of love and is quite often associated with sweets; just think of candy on Valentine's Day, or your mother telling us to have a cookie "to make it all better." I truly hope these recipes will help you to make it all better and keep it that way.

"Nothing will benefit health and increase the chances for survival on earth as much as the evolution to a vegetarian diet."

—ALBERT EINSTEIN

Recipes

❧ ❧

Rum Balls	Creamy Dreamy Fudge
Energy Squares	Orange Sponge Cake
Nutty Nuggets	Carrot Cake
Apricot Nuggets	Dirt Cake
Carob Chip Cookies	Banana Nut Muffins
Peanut Butter Cookies	Pumpkin Muffins
Coconut Macaroons	Raspberry Shortcake
Amaretto Cheesecake	Sherry Trifle
Apple Tart	Vanilla Custard
Baked Bananas	Stuffed Dates
"Chocolate" Nut Mousse	Peanut Butter Carob Pie
Banana Pineapple Pudding	Pumpkin Pecan Pie
Brownies	Fresh Peach Pie
Caramels	Key Lime Pie
Carrot Halvah	Fruit Pie Crust
Cherries Jubilee	Banana Pie Crust
	Peanut Butter Crust

❧ ❧

Rum Balls

❧ ❧

1 tablespoon carob powder

1 tablespoon powdered grain coffee (a coffee substitute)

1 package (6¾ ounces) Darifree powder (reserving ⅓ cup)

14 whole graham crackers, crushed

3 tablespoons honey

¼ cup rum

1 cup chopped pecans

A Christmas favorite that's good any time of the year.

1. Combine carob, coffee, Darifree, and graham crackers.
2. Blend in honey. Add rum and cream ingredients together until well blended. The batter will be stiff. Blend in nuts.
3. Knead batter into 1-inch balls. Roll balls into the reserved Darifree, shaking off excess.

Makes about 3 dozen

❧ ❧

For Bourbon Balls, substitute bourbon for the rum.

❧ ❧

63	Calories
1 g	Protein
9 g	Carbohydrates
3 g	Fat
36%	Calories from Fat
0 g	Fiber
47 mg	Sodium
0 mg	Cholesterol

Energy Squares

1 cup raisins
2 tablespoons bee pollen
1 cup mixed dried fruit
½ cup protein powder
½ cup chopped nuts
½ cup sunflower seeds
¼ cup orange juice

An easy and quick-to-make high energy snack for a mid-afternoon lift or lunchbox dessert.

1. In a food processor or blender, blend raisins, bee pollen, fruit, protein powder, and nuts.
2. Place mixture into a mixing bowl and add seeds and juice. If too dry, add a little more juice (just enough to moisten). If too moist, add more protein powder. Mix well.
3. Line an 8-inch square pan with wax paper. Press mixture into pan. Cover and let rest several hours. Cut into squares. Store in refrigerator.

Makes 20 squares

105	Calories
6 g	Protein
14 g	Carbohydrates
4 g	Fat
37%	Calories from Fat
1 g	Fiber
38 mg	Sodium
0 mg	Cholesterol

Nutty Nuggets

1 cup organic peanut
butter,* creamy style
1/3 cup Darifree powdered
milk substitute (use
powder only)
2 tablespoons honey
1/2 cup carob morsels
(Chatfield's Carob
and Compliments),
chopped
1/4 cup sunflower seeds,
chopped
1/3 cup pecan meal

Watch out, these can become habit-forming.

1. Blend peanut butter with Darifree powder. The mixture should be stiff but manageable.
2. Mix in honey, carob chips, and seeds.
3. When well blended, knead dough into bite-size (1-inch) balls. Roll balls into pecan meal, shaking off excess. Chill.

Makes 35 to 40 nuggets

*All peanut butters are not created equal. The oil that rises to the top of the jar should be poured off. Who needs that extra oil! This will make some peanut butters drier than others depending upon the brand and might necessitate the addition of some water to the recipe.

49	Calories
2 g	Protein
4 g	Carbohydrates
3 g	Fat
61%	Calories from Fat
0 g	Fiber
29 mg	Sodium
0 mg	Cholesterol

Apricot Nuggets

1 cup dried apricots,
  unsulfured
1 cup almonds or walnuts
½ cup unsweetened grated
  coconut
2 tablespoons raw wheat
  germ
2 tablespoons bee pollen
¼ cup orange juice
  concentrate

One of my husband's favorite desserts.

1. In a food processor, add apricots and ½ cup of the nuts; process until chopped.
2. In a medium bowl, combine the apricot mixture with the remaining ingredients, reserving the ½ cup of unchopped nuts.
3. Finely process the ½ cup of nuts.
4. Form the mixture into firm walnut-size balls and roll in the processed nuts.

Makes 1 ½ dozen nuggets

101	Calories
3 g	Protein
11 g	Carbohydrates
6 g	Fat
52%	Calories from Fat
2 g	Fiber
3 mg	Sodium
0 mg	Cholesterol

The First Book of Vegetarian Cooking

Carob Chip Cookies

1 cup whole wheat flour
1 cup unbleached white flour
2 teaspoons baking powder (aluminum-free)
½ teaspoon salt substitute
1 cup organic peanut butter
¼ cup unsweetened apple sauce
1 cup Fruit Source, granular
1 tablespoon egg replacer, whisked with ¼ cup distilled water
⅓ cup lite soy milk
1 teaspoon vanilla
½ cup chopped peanuts
1 cup carob morsels, naturally sweetened

Preheat oven to 350 degrees F.

Have lots of these waiting for after-school snacks.

1. In a medium bowl, sift flours, baking powder, and salt substitute. Set aside.
2. In a large bowl, mix peanut butter with the applesauce.
3. Add Fruit Source to the peanut butter mixture. Mix well. The mixture will be stiff.
4. Add the egg replacer mixture, soy milk, and vanilla to the peanut butter mixture. Mix well.
5. Add flour mixture and blend well. Stir in the peanuts and carob chips.
6. Form 2-inch patties by hand and flatten slightly. Place cookie patties on oiled cookie sheet and bake for 12 to 15 minutes.

Makes 25 to 30 cookies

122	Calories
3 g	Protein
17 g	Carbohydrates
5 g	Fat
35%	Calories from Fat
1 g	Fiber
70 mg	Sodium
1 mg	Cholesterol

Peanut Butter Cookies

1 cup unbleached white flour
1 cup whole wheat flour
2 teaspoons baking powder
½ teaspoon salt substitute
2 tablespoons sunflower oil
1 cup crunchy peanut butter
½ cup honey
½ cup liquid Fruit Source
1 ½ teaspoons egg replacer, whisked with 2 tablespoons distilled water
1 teaspoon vanilla extract
⅓ cup lite soy milk

Preheat oven to 350 degrees F.

Children as well as adults like these in their lunch box.

1. Sift flours, baking powder, and salt substitute together and set aside.
2. In a large mixing bowl, mix remaining ingredients together. Mix well and let rest for 30 minutes (the mixture will be sticky).
3. Shape into balls and flatten with fork. Place on cookie sheet and bake for 12 to 15 minutes. Do not overbake.

Makes 2 dozen

144	Calories
4 g	Protein
19 g	Carbohydrates
7 g	Fat
41%	Calories from Fat
1 g	Fiber
78 mg	Sodium
0 mg	Cholesterol

The First Book of Vegetarian Cooking

Coconut Macaroons

3 ½ cups oatmeal, quick-cooking style
1 cup Fruit Source sweetener (granular)
¾ cup Wonder Slim, or other fat substitute
½ cup honey or light maple syrup
1 tablespoon egg replacer, whisked with ¼ cup distilled water
¼ cup amaranth flour
½ cup unsweetened shredded coconut
½ teaspoon salt substitute
2 teaspoons coconut extract
1 teaspoon vanilla extract

Preheat oven to 350 degrees F.

Here is a wheat-free version that should be started the day before serving.

Day 1

1. In a large bowl, combine oatmeal and Fruit Source.
2. In a small saucepan, mix the Wonder Slim with the honey. Heat slowly for 3 to 4 minutes, stirring often. Pour this mixture over the oatmeal and Fruit Source. Combine well. Cover and let sit overnight at room temperature.

Day 2

1. To the above mixture, add the egg replacer, flour, coconut, salt substitute, extract, and vanilla and mix well.
2. Drop rounded teaspoonfuls of batter onto an oiled cookie sheet.
3. Bake for 15 minutes.

Makes about 3 ½ dozen

72 Calories
1 g Protein
14 g Carbohydrates
1 g Fat
15% Calories from Fat
1 g Fiber
2 mg Sodium
0 mg Cholesterol

Amaretto Cheesecake

꙳ ꙳

3   packages (10.5 ounces each) firm, silken tofu, drained
½   cup soy milk
1   cup honey
2 ½ tablespoons tahini (raw, not toasted)
1 ½ teaspoons fresh grated lemon peel
1   teaspoon vanilla extract
1   tablespoon white miso
1   tablespoon umeboshi plum sauce
2   tablespoons agar-agar flakes
1   tablespoon amaretto liqueur
7   graham crackers, crumbled (naturally sweetened and fat free, if available)

Preheat oven to 350 degrees F.

1. In a blender or food processor blend the tofu and the milk until smooth and creamy. Add remaining ingredients, except the graham crackers, and blend to combine.
2. Line the bottom of an oiled/sprayed 9-inch springform pan with the crumbled graham crackers. Make sure there is enough for a thin layer on the bottom of the pan.
3. Slowly pour filling over the graham cracker crust. Bake for about 60 minutes or until the top has browned.
4. Release sides of pan when cool. Refrigerate until ready to serve. This pie can be served with or without a topping. If desired, top with fruit or "Fudge Sauce" (page 355).

Makes 8 to 12 servings

꙳ ꙳

An easy way to crumble cookies and crackers is to put them in a large sealable bag and roll until fine.

꙳ ꙳

168	Calories
7 g	Protein
30 g	Carbohydrates
3 g	Fat
16%	Calories from Fat
1 g	Fiber
99 mg	Sodium
0 mg	Cholesterol

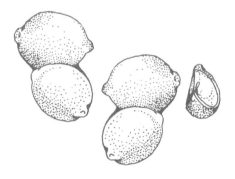

Apple Tart

1 1/2 cups unsweetened applesauce, thick and chunky style
1/2 cup honey
1 tablespoon vanilla extract
1 teaspoon grated lemon rind
1 9-inch fruit pie crust (page 335)
3 Granny Smith apples, peeled and sliced thin
1/2 cup all-fruit apricot preserves (no sugar added)

Preheat oven to 375 degrees F.

1. In a saucepan, simmer the applesauce, honey, vanilla, and lemon rind for 15 to 20 minutes, or until the mixture thickens.
2. Pour mixture into pie crust and place sliced apples on top.
3. In a blender, liquefy the preserves; transfer to a saucepan and heat until hot.
4. With a pastry brush, brush the preserves onto the apples. Bake for 30 minutes. Cool and serve.

Makes 8 servings (one 9-inch pie)

This can be topped with Whipped "Cream" (page 349).

APPLES

Throughout recorded history, apples have been used as a food and a medicine. They are high in carbohydrates and calcium and are a good source of protein, iron, vitamin A, thiamin, riboflavin, and ascorbic acid. Apples are the best known source of vitamin B_2, which promotes digestion and growth.

Apples are an effective blood purifier and are helpful in the treatment of hardening of the arteries and are believed to be a good heart medicine (lowering blood cholesterol and lowering blood pressure), a blood sugar stabilizer, virus fighter, and will also aid in the elimination process of the body.

All fruits are more nutritional when eaten raw. Desserts containing apples should never be placed or cooked in aluminum.

Grated apple is a perfect food for babies who are ready to begin a solid diet, and a glass of fresh apple juice is very therapeutic and refreshing. An apple a day keeps the doctor away!

271	Calories
2 g	Protein
68 g	Carbohydrates
1 g	Fat
2%	Calories from Fat
5 g	Fiber
69 mg	Sodium
0 mg	Cholesterol

Baked Bananas

༄ ༀ

4 medium unpeeled
   bananas
4 teaspoons honey
1 lime, quartered

Preheat oven to 350 degrees F.

Don't eat breakfast? Never fear, just grab a piece of fruit. Fresh fruit, eaten alone in the morning, is very cleansing to the system.

1. Line a baking dish with parchment paper. Arrange bananas (unpeeled) in the dish, spacing evenly.
2. Bake 20 to 30 minutes. The bananas will feel soft when done. Cool 5 minutes.
3. Cut bananas lengthwise through the skin and open partially; drizzle one teaspoon of honey onto each banana and squeeze a lime wedge over the honey.
4. Serve immediately.

Serves 4

For centuries, the banana has been used for healing purposes. Every part of the banana has been used, from the peel for curing warts, migraines, burns, rashes, boils, and cancerous sores, to the pulp for cures of diarrhea, stomach ulcers, and diverticulitis.

The oil of the banana can be difficult for some people to digest. Use only ripe bananas that are lightly speckled with no visible green and chew slowly to aid digestion.

128	Calories
1 g	Protein
33 g	Carbohydrates
1 g	Fat
4%	Calories from Fat
2 g	Fiber
1 mg	Sodium
0 mg	Cholesterol

"Chocolate" Nut Mousse

%&ℰ

²/₃ cup dairy-free, naturally
   sweetened carob
   chips
3 tablespoons honey
2 packages (10.5 ounces
   each) firm, lite silken
   tofu, drained
2 teaspoons vanilla
   flavoring
¹/₂ cup chopped pecans

Rich and delicious.

1. Melt carob chips with 1 tablespoon honey in the top of a double boiler.
2. In a blender or food processor, blend tofu, 2 tablespoons honey, and vanilla till smooth and creamy.
3. Add tofu mixture to carob chips and cook until well blended and carob is completely melted. Mix in the nuts.
4. Spoon into 6 custard cups. Chill.

Makes 6 servings

234	Calories
11 g	Protein
22 g	Carbohydrates
12 g	Fat
47%	Calories from Fat
1 g	Fiber
93 mg	Sodium
2 mg	Cholesterol

Banana Pineapple Pudding

❧ ❦

1 package (10.5 ounces) extra-firm, lite silken tofu, drained

1 package (1.2 ounces) banana soy protein powder (Spiru-tein High Protein Energy Meal)

¼ teaspoon powdered barley malt sweetener (Dr. Bronner's)

1 can crushed pineapple, in its own juice, drained

¼ cup chopped nuts

A pudding that's good for you? Yes!!

1. In a blender or food processor, blend tofu until it is smooth and creamy, scraping down sides as needed.
2. Add protein powder and sweetener; process to combine. Add a little pineapple juice if too dry.
3. Remove to bowl; stir in can of pineapple and nuts.
4. Spoon into 4 custard cups and chill for 1 hour.

Makes 4 servings

❧ ❦

Spiru-tein makes a variety of flavors that can be substituted for banana for a change of taste.

❧ ❦

165	Calories
15 g	Protein
17 g	Carbohydrates
6 g	Fat
32%	Calories from Fat
1 g	Fiber
72 mg	Sodium
0 mg	Cholesterol

The First Book of Vegetarian Cooking

Brownies

> 🙢 🙠

1 cup granular Fruit
    Source sweetener
3/4 cup date sugar
3/4 cup carob powder
1 1/4 cups whole grain or-
    ganic pastry flour
1/4 teaspoon salt substitute
1 1/2 teaspoons egg
    replacer, whisked
    with 2 tablespoons
    distilled water
1 teaspoon vanilla
1/2 cup prune butter
    (page 375)
1/2 cup plain dairy-free
    yogurt
1/2 cup chopped walnuts

Preheat oven to 350 degrees F.

These will satisfy that chocolate urge.

1. Mix all ingredients in a medium bowl. Mixture will be stiff.
2. Spoon into an 8-inch square pan. Smooth out evenly.
3. Bake for 35 minutes.

Makes 16 pieces

160	Calories
2 g	Protein
37 g	Carbohydrates
3 g	Fat
15%	Calories from Fat
2 g	Fiber
18 mg	Sodium
0 mg	Cholesterol

Caramels

꙳ ꙳

2 cups Darifree powder
¼ cup rice milk
½ cup barley malt
   sweetener (liquid)
¼ teaspoon powdered
   barley malt sweet-
   ener (Dr. Bronner's)
1 package (12 ounces)
   dairy-free carob
   morsels (Chatfield's
   Carob and
   Compliments)
1 cup Condensed "Milk"
   (page 356)
½ cup natural peanut
   butter
1 teaspoon vanilla
½ cup chopped walnuts

I was experimenting one day when to my complete surprise these delicious caramels were the end result.

1. Whisk Darifree powder with rice milk. Add barley malt sweeteners. Mix well.
2. In a double boiler, melt carob morsels over boiling water.
3. Stir Darifree mixture and peanut butter into the melted carob morsels. Mix well. Add vanilla and nuts.
4. Spray a 9-inch pan and spoon caramel mixture into pan. With vegetable sprayed hands, flatten mixture out to edges of pan.
5. Refrigerate for 30 minutes. Remove from pan and cut into serving pieces. Serve at room temperature.

Makes 42 pieces

The First Book of Vegetarian Cooking

HONEY

A food fit for the gods.

Honey contains over 25 different sugars, each one having a different function in human metabolism. Honey is a unique food. It is a living, organic, instant, energy-building food containing all the essential minerals necessary for life: seven vitamins of the B complex, amino acids, minerals, enzymes, and other vital factors.

Honey fortifies the heart, re-creates vigor, helps digestion, and reinforces the memory. Honey has been found to heal wounds where other methods have failed. Many health practitioners are using honey in the treatment of difficult wounds.

If possible, always eat local honey. Honey contains very small doses of pollen, which sometimes can help immunize the allergy sufferer. My apiarist suggests 1 tablespoon daily, using only local "wildflower" honey. I suffer from hay fever, so each morning I prepare a mixture containing 16 ounces of distilled water, 1 tablespoon wildflower honey, and 2 tablespoons of natural apple cider vinegar and drink it throughout the day.

95	Calories
2 g	Protein
16 g	Carbohydrates
3 g	Fat
27%	Calories from Fat
0 g	Fiber
80 mg	Sodium
1 mg	Cholesterol

Carrot Halvah

2	cups grated carrots, firmly packed (the pulp left from juicing carrots can be used)
3	cups lite soy milk
1/3	cup honey
1/2	cup slivered almonds
1/2	cup raisins
1/4	teaspoon ground cardamom
1	teaspoon vanilla
1	tablespoon light maple syrup

An adaptation of the classic Indian dessert. Cardamom is a spice native to India that is made from the crushed pods of a ginger-like plant. It gives the dessert its pungent eucalyptus scent and flavor.

1. In a medium saucepan, bring the carrots and milk to a boil. Reduce heat and simmer until all the milk is absorbed, about 1 1/2 hours. Stir frequently.
2. Add honey, almonds, raisins, cardamom, and vanilla. Stir to blend and cook for another minute or two.
3. Spoon mixture into 6 custard cups and drizzle maple syrup on top.

Makes 6 servings

When juicing vegetables, always try to use the leftover pulp. By discarding this precious substance you loose most of the fiber and, new studies show, half the vitamins and phytomins.

251	Calories
7 g	Protein
35 g	Carbohydrates
11 g	Fat
40%	Calories from Fat
5 g	Fiber
32 mg	Sodium
0 mg	Cholesterol

Cherries Jubilee

1 can (1 lb. 14 oz.) pitted Bing cherries (no sugar added)
2 teaspoons arrowroot, dissolved in 2 teaspoons distilled water
¼ cup brown rice syrup
½ cup fresh orange juice
1 teaspoon grated orange peel
1 quart vanilla non-dairy "ice cream"
3 tablespoons brandy or cognac

A healthier version of an elegant dessert.

1. Drain cherry juice into in a 1-quart saucepan. Set cherries aside. Add arrowroot slurry, brown rice syrup, orange juice, and orange peel. Bring to a boil and simmer 3 minutes. Remove from heat and gently stir in cherries.
2. At serving time, spoon ice cream into individual serving dishes. Slightly heat brandy or cognac. Pour cherry mixture into a chafing dish, add brandy or cognac and ignite. Spoon over ice cream.

Makes 6 servings

Six to eight cherries a day might keep gout pain away. Cherries are a good source of magnesium (the natural painkiller) and potassium. For centuries, the Japanese have treated joint pain with a syrup made from cherry juice.

319	Calories
4 g	Protein
59 g	Carbohydrates
7 g	Fat
19%	Calories from Fat
3 g	Fiber
68 mg	Sodium
0 mg	Cholesterol

Creamy Dreamy Fudge

༺ ༻

1 cup Darifree powder
1 cup finely chopped, moist, pitted dates (about 28 dates)
1 cup finely chopped apple
½ cup carob powder
½ cup organic peanut butter
½ cup grated pecans

1. In a wide bowl, combine Darifree, dates, apple, carob, and peanut butter using a wooden spoon.
2. Form into walnut-size balls. The mixture will be sticky.
3. Roll the fudge balls in the grated pecans and chill.

Makes 2 dozen

༺ ༻

To keep mixture from sticking to your hands, place a few drops of oil in the palms of your hands and rub together to coat. Repeat as necessary.

༺ ༻

49 Calories
1 g Protein
8 g Carbohydrates
2 g Fat
42% Calories from Fat
1 g Fiber
27 mg Sodium
0 mg Cholesterol

Orange Sponge Cake

1 cup whole wheat flour
1 cup unbleached white
    flour, organic
1 cup Fruit Source,
    granular
1 tablespoon baking
    powder
1 tablespoon egg
    replacer, whisked
    with ¼ cup
    distilled water
¼ cup unsweetened
    natural applesauce
1 cup distilled water
½ cup frozen sour orange
    juice concentrate
1 teaspoon vanilla

Preheat oven to 375 degrees F.

Serve plain or double this recipe and top with vanilla icing or fudge sauce for a company pleaser.

1. Mix dry and wet ingredients separately. Combine the two and beat for 2 to 3 minutes.
2. Pour into an oiled 8-inch cake pan and bake at 375 degrees F for 40 minutes or until middle of cake is firm to touch.
3. Cool.

Makes one 8-inch layer cake, serves 8

255	Calories
5 g	Protein
56 g	Carbohydrates
2 g	Fat
7%	Calories from Fat
3 g	Fiber
128 mg	Sodium
0 mg	Cholesterol

Carrot Cake

1 cup Fruit Source
    sweetener (granular)
1 ¾ cups distilled water
1 cup raisins
2 cups grated carrots
1 tablespoon olive oil
1 teaspoon ground cloves
1 teaspoon cinnamon
½ teaspoon nutmeg
1 teaspoon vanilla
1 cup chopped pecans
1 ¼ cups organic whole
    grain pastry flour or
    whole wheat flour
1 cup plus 2 tablespoons
    unbleached organic
    white flour
2 teaspoons baking
    powder
1 teaspoon baking soda
½ teaspoon salt substitute

Start this recipe the day before serving.

1. Combine Fruit Source, water, raisins, carrots, oil, cloves, cinnamon, nutmeg, and vanilla in a medium saucepan. Bring to a boil. Reduce heat and simmer for 5 minutes.
2. Cover pan and rest overnight.
3. Next day, preheat oven to 275 degrees F. In a medium bowl, combine pecans, flours, baking powder, baking soda, and salt substitute. Add the rested carrot mixture and mix until blended.
4. Spoon into an oiled 9 × 3-inch tube pan and bake 1 hour 30 minutes or until toothpick inserted into center comes out clean. Cool in pan.

Makes one 9 × 3-inch tube cake

200	Calories
3 g	Protein
35 g	Carbohydrates
6 g	Fat
28%	Calories from Fat
2 g	Fiber
117 mg	Sodium
0 mg	Cholesterol

Dirt Cake

1 stick (½ cup) soy margarine
1 ¼ cups Darifree powder
8 ounces dairy-free cream cheese
3 packages (1 ounce each) instant vanilla pudding mix
2 cups soy or rice milk
12 ounces nondairy whipped topping
3 packages (8 ounces each) Creme Supremes*, crushed
Artificial flowers, etc. for garnish

An easy way to crush cookies is to place cookies in a large sealable bag and roll with a rolling pin until crushed.

The original Dirt Cake recipe is filled with undesirable and fattening ingredients. I worked and worked on it and came up with this substitute recipe. Go easy, it is still very rich. Served in a clay flowerpot, it looks as if the "dirt" is just waiting to be planted or decorated to match any theme.

1. In a bowl, cream together soy margarine, Darifree, and cream cheese substitute. Add pudding mix, soy milk, and whipped topping to butter mixture.
2. Line an 8-inch clay flower pot with cling film; alternate layers of crushed cookies and pudding mixture ending with a cookie layer.
3. Chill until serving time. Decorate with flowers, miniature animals, toys, etc.

Makes 16 servings

*Available at health food stores.

246	Calories
4 g	Protein
44 g	Carbohydrates
8 g	Fat
27%	Calories from Fat
2 g	Fiber
170 mg	Sodium
0 mg	Cholesterol

Banana Nut Muffins

1 cup oat bran
1 cup wheat bran
¼ cup wheat germ
¼ teaspoon powdered barley malt sweetener (Dr. Bronner's)
1 tablespoon baking powder
¼ cup chopped nuts
1 tablespoon egg replacer, whisked with ¼ cup distilled water
2 tablespoons unsweetened natural apple sauce
1 cup (about 2 to 3) very ripe mashed bananas
1 cup lite soy or rice milk

Preheat oven to 400 degrees F.

Nutritious as well as filling and they taste good too.

1. Mix dry and wet ingredients separately. Mix together.
2. Spoon mixture into an oiled or sprayed 12-cup muffin tin.
3. Bake for 20 minutes. Cool and refrigerate.

Makes 12 muffins

88	Calories
3 g	Protein
18 g	Carbohydrates
3 g	Fat
29%	Calories from Fat
4 g	Fiber
93 mg	Sodium
0 mg	Cholesterol

The First Book of Vegetarian Cooking

Pumpkin Muffins

1   cup oat bran
1   cup wheat bran
¼   cup wheat germ
1   tablespoon baking
     powder
¼   cup chopped walnuts
½   teaspoon powdered
     barley malt sweet-
     ener (Dr. Bronner's)
1   teaspoon pumpkin pie
     spice
2   tablespoons raisins
1   cup canned pumpkin
1   cup light soy or rice
     milk
3   tablespoons prune
     "butter" (page 375)
1   tablespoon egg replacer,
     whisked with ¼ cup
     distilled water
1   teaspoon natural maple
     flavor

Preheat oven to 400 degrees F.

A tasty muffin without any added fat and low in calories with vitamin A, beta-carotene, and fiber.

1. Mix the dry and wet ingredients separately. Combine and blend.
2. Spoon batter into an oiled 12-cup muffin tin. Bake for 20 minutes. Cool and refrigerate.

Makes 12 muffins

84	Calories
3 g	Protein
18 g	Carbohydrates
3 g	Fat
30%	Calories from Fat
4 g	Fiber
94 mg	Sodium
0 mg	Cholesterol

Raspberry Shortcake

4 cups fresh raspberries, rinsed and drained
¾ cup brown rice syrup
½ cup whole wheat flour
1 ½ cups unbleached flour
¼ cup Fruit Source sweetener (granular)
2 ½ teaspoons baking powder
¼ teaspoon salt
¼ cup safflower oil margarine
⅔ cup soy milk, creamy original
1 tablespoon ice water
¼ teaspoon apple cider vinegar
1 recipe Whipped "Cream" (page 349)

Preheat oven to 400 degrees F.

To make strawberry shortcake or peach shortcake follow same instructions, substituting fruit.

A summertime favorite.

1. Oil and flour an 8-inch round cake pan.
2. Place raspberries in a large bowl. Add rice syrup and mix gently with a wooden spoon. Set aside.
3. Sift together flours, Fruit Source, baking powder, and salt into large mixing bowl. Cut in margarine with pastry blender until mixture resembles coarse flakes. Add soy milk. Combine water and vinegar and add to mixture. Stir mixture with a fork until completely moistened. Do not beat or overwork the mixture. Scrape dough onto lightly floured board; knead very briefly only twice. Pat dough onto bottom of prepared pan. Bake on center rack of oven until golden brown, about 25 minutes.
4. Cool shortcake in pan about 10 minutes.
5. Remove shortcake from pan. Split into two layers with long serrated knife. Set bottom half, cut-side up, on serving plate and spoon on about ⅔ of the raspberries. Set top half of cake (cut-side down) on top of raspberries.
6. Just before serving prepare whipped cream. Spread cream over cake. Spoon remaining raspberries over cream. Serve immediately.

Makes 6 to 8 servings

308	Calories
5 g	Protein
55 g	Carbohydrates
8 g	Fat
25%	Calories from Fat
3 g	Fiber
183 mg	Sodium
0 mg	Cholesterol

Sherry Trifle

1   single 8-inch layer sponge cake*, torn into 2-inch pieces

1/3   cup sherry

1/2   jar sugarless strawberry preserves

2   cans (16 ounces each) fruit cocktail (in its own juices), drained

2   cups dairy-free vanilla custard*

1   large banana, sliced

1   cup whipped "cream"*

1/2   cup slivered almonds

1/4   cup grated coconut

1/2   pint sliced strawberries

A slimmed-down version of an English classic, which can easily become a tradition in your home.

1. Cover the bottom of a trifle bowl (or a large, high sided, clear glass dish) with the cake. Pour the sherry evenly over cake.
2. Spread the strawberry preserves over the marinated cake. Follow with layers of fruit cocktail, custard, and banana. Cover with wax paper and refrigerate until ready to serve.
3. Just before serving, top with whipped cream, almonds, coconut, and sliced strawberries.

Makes 12 servings

*Can use purchased or see pages 321, 349, and 328.

316	Calories
8 g	Protein
51 g	Carbohydrates
9 g	Fat
25%	Calories from Fat
2 g	Fiber
101 mg	Sodium
39 mg	Cholesterol

Vanilla Custard

2   cups soy milk
1   teaspoon vanilla
½   teaspoon powdered
     barley malt
     sweetener
     (Dr. Bronner's)
⅛   teaspoon turmeric
2   tablespoons agar-agar
     flakes

The basic ingredient for an English sherry trifle.

1. Put all ingredients into a saucepan and, stirring constantly, bring to a boil. Reduce heat and simmer for 5 minutes.
2. Pour into 5 custard cups. Cool and chill until firm.

Makes 5 servings

63	Calories
4 g	Protein
8 g	Carbohydrates
2 g	Fat
29%	Calories from Fat
1 g	Fiber
52 mg	Sodium
0 mg	Cholesterol

Stuffed Dates

2 teaspoons grain coffee powder (Cafix)
2 teaspoons distilled water (or as needed for spreading consistency)
½ cup natural peanut butter
16 ounces pitted dates
¼ cup Darifree powder

A novel combination for a wonderful taste.

1. Mix coffee powder with water. Add to peanut butter and mix.
2. Cut dates to make a pocket. Stuff with mixture. Close, removing excess, and roll in Darifree powder.

Makes about 60

35	Calories
1 g	Protein
6 g	Carbohydrates
1 g	Fat
30%	Calories from Fat
1 g	Fiber
13 mg	Sodium
0 mg	Cholesterol

Peanut Butter Carob Pie

꿍 ꩜

10 ounces naturally
  sweetened carob
  chips
3 tablespoons honey or
  light maple syrup
2 packages (10.5 ounces
  each) firm silken
  tofu, drained
½ cup peanut butter
1 peanut butter pie crust
  (page 337)

꿍 ꩜

This can be topped with
"whipped cream" (page 349)

Freshly ground peanut butter
contains no additives.

꿍 ꩜

Peanut butter and "chocolate" make a great combination.

1. In a small double-boiler, melt the carob chips. Add honey and stir until smooth. Keep warm.
2. Process tofu and peanut butter in a blender until smooth. Whisk into the carob-honey mixture until creamy.
3. Pour filling into the pie shell.
4. Chill until firm.

Makes 12 slices

333	Calories
14 g	Protein
32 g	Carbohydrates
18 g	Fat
50%	Calories from Fat
3 g	Fiber
206 mg	Sodium
2 mg	Cholesterol

The First Book of Vegetarian Cooking

Pumpkin Pecan Pie

2   packages (10.5 ounces each) firm, silken tofu, drained
²/₃   cup honey
1 ³/₄   cups pumpkin
2   teaspoons ground cinnamon
1   teaspoon ground nutmeg
1 ¹/₂   teaspoons pumpkin pie spice
¹/₄   teaspoon salt substitute
1   unbaked 9-inch deep-dish pie crust
1   cup chopped pecans

Preheat oven to 400 degrees F.

Pumpkin is an excellent source of fiber, and vitamin A, and beta-carotene.

1. In a blender, process tofu until smooth and creamy.
2. Add honey, pumpkin, spices, and salt. Blend.
3. Pour into the pie shell and sprinkle the pecans over the top. Bake for 1 hour or until a toothpick inserted into the center comes out almost clean.
4. Cool and serve.

Makes 8 servings.

Pie can be topped
with Whipped "Cream."
(page 349)

407	Calories
8 g	Protein
42 g	Carbohydrates
25 g	Fat
55%	Calories from Fat
2 g	Fiber
150 mg	Sodium
0 mg	Cholesterol

Fresh Peach Pie

Crust
3/4 cup whole wheat pastry flour
3/4 cup unbleached white flour
1/4 cup soy margarine
1/8 teaspoon salt substitute
2 teaspoons fresh lemon juice
1/2 cup ice water

Glaze
1 1/4 cups peach nectar
1/2 cup sugarless peach jam

Filling
8 medium-size fresh peaches, peeled and sliced
2 tablespoons fresh lemon juice
3/4 cup granular Fruit Source sweetener
1/8 teaspoon freshly grated nutmeg
3 tablespoons arrowroot

A dessert that brings sweet memories of summer.

1. For the crust, mix the flours, and cut in margarine with pastry cutter until it forms a crumbly meal.
2. Stir salt substitute and lemon juice into ice water. Add to flour mixture. Mix very lightly, only to bind the dough. Chill dough for 1 hour before using.
3. Roll out half the dough on a floured surface. Transfer the dough to a 9-inch pie pan.
4. Combine glaze ingredients and cook over medium heat until reduced to 1/2 cup. Strain and cool. Brush bottom and sides of pastry with the glaze.
5. Combine filling ingredients, and add to bottom pastry.
6. Preheat oven to 425 degrees F. Roll out remaining pie crust into a 10-inch round. Cut 1/2-inch strips of dough. Arrange in lattice design atop filling, pressing ends into edge of bottom crust. Fold pastry overhang up over lattice ends and crimp decoratively.
7. Cut strip of foil 2 to 3 inches wide and 30 inches long and cover edge of crust.

The First Book of Vegetarian Cooking

8. Bake for 20 minutes. Remove foil and continue baking until golden brown, about 30 additional minutes.
9. Cool slightly. Serve warm.

Makes one 9-inch pie

PEACHES

Peaches are ancient fruits that have been referred to as the "Persian apple." They are high in vitamins A and C, calcium, and phosphorus. The body assimilates peaches very easily because they are easy to digest. A good quality peach is not always easy to find as they do not sweeten after being picked because there is no reserve of starch. If a peach is picked green or immature it will have a tough, rubbery texture. At the market, do not buy if the color is weak and the skins are shriveled. When using canned peaches, always discard the juice they are canned in and rinse the peaches with distilled water.

310	Calories
3 g	Protein
64 g	Carbohydrates
5 g	Fat
16%	Calories from Fat
2 g	Fiber
59 mg	Sodium
0 mg	Cholesterol

Key Lime Pie

1 cup soy milk
4 tablespoons agar-agar flakes
2 packages (10.5 ounces each) firm, lite silken tofu, drained
2/3 cup honey or liquid Fruit Source sweetener
1/2 teaspoon powdered barley malt sweetener (Dr. Bronner's)
1/2 tablespoon vanilla
1/2 cup Key lime juice
   Rind of one lemon, grated
2 tablespoons liquid lecithin
1 baked 9-inch deep-dish pie crust

Kool Whip

1 1/2 cups distilled water
2 tablespoons agar-agar flakes
3/4 cup Darifree powder
1/4 cup Devan granular brown rice sweetener
1 teaspoon vanilla
1/8 teaspoon course ground kosher salt
2 tablespoons safflower oil

If lime juice is not available, you can turn this recipe into a lemon pie by substituting fresh lemon juice for the lime.

1. Pour soy milk into saucepan. Sprinkle agar-agar flakes over milk. Do not stir. Bring to a simmer and cook for 5 minutes. Stir occasionally after mixture comes to a simmer. Set aside.

2. In a food processor or blender, process the tofu until smooth and creamy. Add the honey, sweetener, vanilla, lime juice, and lemon rind; process. Add the lecithin and the agar-agar mixture, briefly process again.

3. Pour mixture into the baked pie shell. Refrigerate for 1 hour or until filling is firm.

4. To make meringue, bring water and agar to a boil; reduce heat and simmer for 5 minutes or until flakes are dissolved. Remove from heat and cool for 1/2 hour.

5. To blender, add agar-agar mixture, Darifree, sweetener, vanilla and salt. Process until smooth.

6. While machine is still running, slowly add oil (don't clean blender, you will use it again).

7. Chill mixture for 1 1/2 hours or until cold. Return to blender and process until smooth.

8. Top pie just before serving.

Makes one 9-inch deep-dish pie; topping makes makes 2 cups (32 1-tablespoon servings with topping)

415	Calories
8 g	Protein
57 g	Carbohydrates
18 g	Fat
38%	Calories from Fat
2 g	Fiber
261 g	Sodium
0 mg	Cholesterol

Fruit Pie Crust

1 cup pitted dates
1 teaspoon fresh lemon
   zest
3/4 cup Grape Nuts cereal
1/2 teaspoon ground
   cinnamon

A quick and tasty crust for pies that require no baking.

1. Process ingredients in food processor until crumbly and sticking together.
2. In a 9-inch pie tin with moistened fingers, press mixture to edges of pan.

Makes one 9-inch pie crust

In many countries, cinnamon is traditionally used to treat fever, diarrhea, menstrual problems, and post-partum bleeding and is also used as a digestive aid. In the United States, most of the cinnamon we use is actually cassia. True cinnamon grows in Sri Lanka and on the Malabar coast of India. True cinnamon can sometimes be found in Mexican grocery stores. Its light yellowish-brown bark will be soft enough to crumble in your hands.

106	Calories
2 g	Protein
26 g	Carbohydrates
1 g	Fat
3%	Calories from Fat
3 g	Fiber
67 mg	Sodium
0 mg	Cholesterol

Banana Pie Crust

❧ ❧

1   ripe banana
     Dash of lemon juice
$1/2$ cup raw coconut
$1/4$ cup oat bran
$1/4$ cup fresh wheat germ
$1/4$ cup chopped dates

This makes a delicious and different pie crust.

Combine all ingredients and press into a 9-inch pie pan. Use only with a filling that does not require cooking.

Makes one 9-inch pie shell

Wheat germ is an excellent source of vitamin E. A recent British study had astonishing results indicating 400 to 800 IUs of vitamin E daily will reduce heart attacks by 75%! Eating foods rich in vitamin E such as dark green leafy vegetables, whole grains, nuts, seeds, and legumes seems like a good idea.

66	Calories
2 g	Protein
12 g	Carbohydrates
2 g	Fat
31%	Calories from Fat
2 g	Fiber
2 mg	Sodium
0 mg	Cholesterol

Peanut Butter Crust

½ cup natural peanut butter
¼ cup Fruit Source, granular
½ cup raw wheat germ
½ cup oat bran

A pie crust that does not require cooking and can double as a crumbled topping.

Combine all ingredients and press into a 10-inch pie pan.

Makes one 10-inch pie shell

Use only with fillings that do not require cooking.

158	Calories
7 g	Protein
17 g	Carbohydrates
9 g	Fat
52%	Calories from Fat
3 g	Fiber
78 mg	Sodium
0 mg	Cholesterol

GARNISHES

❧ ❧

Visual appeal is very important in satisfying the senses. We eat with our eyes. Have you ever turned food down because you didn't like the way it looked?

Whenever possible, garnish with edible fresh greens. I have a potted herb garden on my patio with different and interesting herbs. I find potted plants work better for me, this way my cats can't use the smaller pots to sleep in or worse! The herbs thrive under a screen and get only the morning sun. Fresh herbs used as a garnish can give the nutritional boost we can all use.

Don't save your garnishes for company, liven up all your dishes. A garnish can be very simple, like a sprig of parsley or a very elegant carved vegetable flower. All will add more appeal to the dish.

Recipes

❧   ☙

Lemon Rose

Tomato Rose

Radish Rose

Scallion Mum

Asparagus Bundles

Carrot Curls

Olive Rings

Colored Garnishes

Edible Garnishes

Natural Containers

Frozen Wine Bucket

❧   ☙

Lemon Rose

Take one lemon and cut across the bottom (do not sever) and continue cutting a strip in a spiral fashion. At the end of the spiral, taper the end to a point. Remove fruit from peel and curl peel into a rose shape.

Tomato Rose

Starting at the top of the tomato with a sharp paring knife, cut a continuous ¾-inch wide strip all the way around the tomato. Rewind skin in a coil, starting with a tight turn and with each successive turn, fan out slightly. You can either use the top or the bottom of the rose.

Radish Rose

Cut a thin slice from the top and bottom of a large radish. With a sharp paring knife, cut 4 to 6 slices starting at the top and working downward to the base (do not cut through the base). Place radish in a bowl of ice water and refrigerate until petals open, about 1 hour.

Scallion Mum

Remove the root and cut off a 3-inch piece from each scallion. With a sharp paring knife cut long slits lengthwise, slicing all the way through, leaving ½-inch at the top uncut. The more cuts made, the fluffier the mum. Place in ice water until ready to use, at least 15 minutes. At serving time gently shove a halved almond down into the center of each flower.

Asparagus Bundles

Blanch a 7-inch piece of the green part of a leek for 10 minutes in boiling water. Cut into ¼-inch wide strips. Tie around asparagus bundles. Use chives to bundle smaller vegetables.

Carrot Curls

Make lengthwise strips of carrot using a vegetable peeler. Curl strips in tight circles and secure with a toothpick. Place in ice water and refrigerate. Before serving, remove toothpicks.

Olive Rings

Peel carrots and celery. Cut into ¼-inch wide by 2 ½ to 3-inch long sticks. Cut pitted olives into 2 or 3 circles and place vegetable sticks through the olives.

Colored Garnishes

Garnishes can be colored by placing in beet, carrot, purple onion, or spinach juice.

Edible Garnishes

Fresh flowers or herbs are a beautiful addition to any food. When selecting garnishes make sure they are free of pesticides and fertilizers.

HERBS

Chives	Parsley	Tarragon
Cilantro	Rosemary	Thyme
Dill	Sage	Watercress

The First Book of Vegetarian Cooking

FLOWERS

Carnations	Pansies	Strawberry leaves
Geraniums	Primrose	Violets
Nasturtiums	Roses	

Swish herbs and flowers gently in warm distilled water to cleanse. Blot dry with a paper towel. Store in a plastic bag in the refrigerator until ready to use.

Natural Containers

Slice off the tops of tomatoes or bell peppers (red, green, or yellow are fine). If they do not sit up properly, take a small slice from the bottom. Hollow out and fill with sauces, spreads, or dips.

For individual containers, use large cooked mushrooms, cherry tomatoes, or any small vegetable.

Frozen Wine Bucket

Make sure you have freezer space for this artistic presentation. At serving time position your chilled wine bottle in the center of this "ice bucket" and place on a garnished serving platter to catch any melting ice.

Large round plastic container (10 to 20 cups, looks do not matter, this just forms the ice)

Red and white grapes with leaves, fresh or plastic

Bags of ice, cubed or pieces

Empty wine bottle (use same size bottle that you will be serving), fill with small rocks or dried beans

Flowers

1. Position bottle in the center of the plastic container. Put a layer of ice cubes around the bottle. Arrange grapes and grape leaves around the bottle. Secure their position with ice. Container should be full. Add water almost to top of container.
2. Place in freezer and freeze until firm.
3. To unmold: pour beans or rocks out of bottle and fill with warm water. Remove bottle. Dip plastic container in hot water for several seconds. Unmold and place in freezer until serving time.

The First Book of Vegetarian Cooking

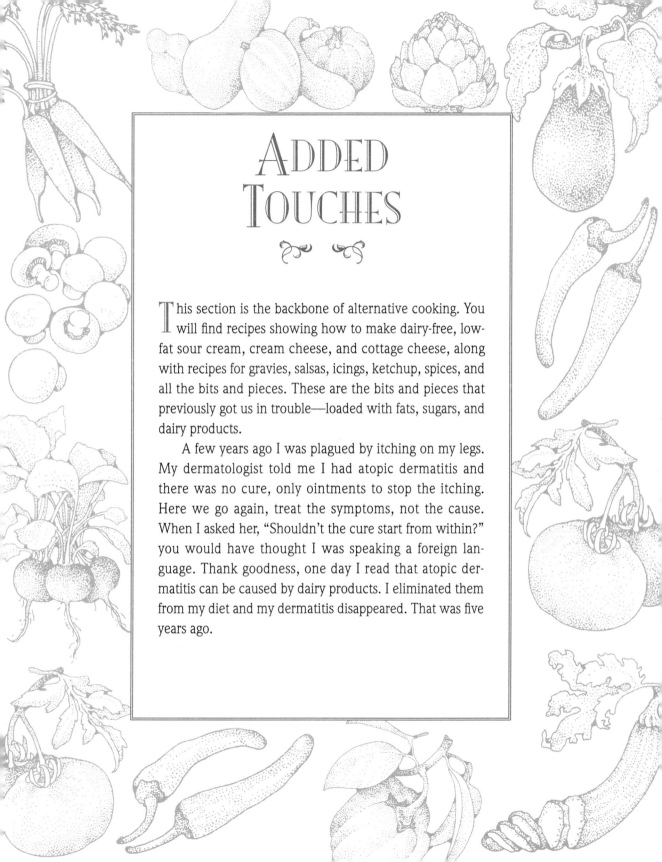

ADDED TOUCHES

❧ ❧

This section is the backbone of alternative cooking. You will find recipes showing how to make dairy-free, low-fat sour cream, cream cheese, and cottage cheese, along with recipes for gravies, salsas, icings, ketchup, spices, and all the bits and pieces. These are the bits and pieces that previously got us in trouble—loaded with fats, sugars, and dairy products.

A few years ago I was plagued by itching on my legs. My dermatologist told me I had atopic dermatitis and there was no cure, only ointments to stop the itching. Here we go again, treat the symptoms, not the cause. When I asked her, "Shouldn't the cure start from within?" you would have thought I was speaking a foreign language. Thank goodness, one day I read that atopic dermatitis can be caused by dairy products. I eliminated them from my diet and my dermatitis disappeared. That was five years ago.

Recipes

Agar-Agar	Gravy
Vanilla Icing	Ketchup
Whipped "Cream"	Mushroom Gravy
Lite Maple Syrup	Mushroom Reconstituting
Kool Whip	Organic Fruit Zest
"Yogurt"	Papaya Capers
Applesauce	Polenta
"Chocolate" Icing	Prune Butter
Fudge Sauce	Seitan Preparation
Condensed "Milk"	Relish
Organic Rice Milk	Cajun Spice
Cottage "Cheese"	Herb "Salt"
"Cream Cheese"	Tex-Mex Seasoning
Croutons	Sweet and Sour Corn Relish
Dairyless Sour Cream	TVP Reconstituting
Reconstituting Dried Chile Peppers	Tangy Fruit Salsa
Fat-Free Mayonnaise	Melon Salsa
"Feta Cheese"	Thick and Chunky Salsa
Flax Seed Extract	Thousand Island Dressing
Flax Meal Paste	Tomatoes
Fruit Sauce	Yuba Reconstituting

Agar-Agar

To prepare agar-agar

1 tablespoon agar-agar
    flakes
1 cup distilled water
    (fruit juice can
    be substituted)

This vegetarian substitute for gelatin (which is derived from animals) has been used for thousands of years. It is a gel made from nature's sea vegetables (seaweed). It is tasteless and odorless, and is used in soups, sauces, pie fillings, puddings, parfaits, "yogurt" (page 352), and other dessert recipes.

Add flakes to the liquid and bring to a boil. Reduce heat and simmer for 5 minutes or until all the flakes are dissolved. Cool slightly before adding to recipe.

**Alternate method
(when less thickness
is required)**

2 tablespoons agar-agar
3 cups liquid

Soak flakes in liquid for 5 minutes.

Vanilla Icing

8 ounces dairy-free cream cheese (or page 359)
¼ cup honey
1 teaspoon vanilla

Add different flavors and nuts to extend this recipe.

1. Combine cream cheese with honey. Beat in vanilla.
2. Spread on cooled cake or cupcakes.

Makes icing for 1 cake or 12 cupcakes

55	Calories
3 g	Protein
6 g	Carbohydrates
2 g	Fat
39%	Calories from Fat
0 g	Fiber
69 mg	Sodium
0 mg	Cholesterol

The First Book of Vegetarian Cooking

Whipped "Cream"

1 package (10.5 ounces) lite silken firm tofu, drained well
2 tablespoons lite maple syrup
1 teaspoon vanilla extract
1 teaspoon freshly grated orange peel
   Dash of nutmeg

Make sure the tofu is very fresh for this great whipped cream substitute.

1. Process all ingredients in blender until smooth and creamy.
2. Chill for at least ½ hour before serving.

Makes 1 cup

18	Calories
1 g	Protein
1 g	Carbohydrates
1 g	Fat
62%	Calories from Fat
0 g	Fiber
0 mg	Sodium
0 mg	Cholesterol

Lite Maple Syrup

❧ ❧

1   cup pure maple syrup
1⅓ cups distilled water
1½ tablespoon kuzu or
       arrowroot

A tasty and thick light syrup.

1. Bring maple syrup and 1 cup water to a simmer. Remove from heat.
2. Mix the remaining ⅓ cup water with the kuzu or arrowroot until dissolved. Whisk into the maple syrup mixture.
3. Return the pan to the heat and simmer for 5 minutes to thicken. Stir frequently.

Makes 2 cups

25	Calories
0 g	Protein
7 g	Carbohydrates
0 g	Fat
0%	Calories from Fat
0 g	Fiber
1 mg	Sodium
0 mg	Cholesterol

The First Book of Vegetarian Cooking

Kool Whip

1½ cups distilled water
2 tablespoons agar-agar flakes
¾ cup Darifree powder
¼ cup Devan granular brown rice sweetener
1 teaspoon vanilla
⅛ teaspoon course ground kosher salt
2 tablespoons safflower oil

1. Bring water and agar to a boil; reduce heat and simmer for 5 minutes or until flakes are dissolved. Remove from heat and cool for ½ hour.
2. To blender add agar-agar mixture, Darifree, sweetener, vanilla and salt. Process until smooth.
3. While machine is still running slowly, add oil (don't clean blender, you will use it again).
4. Chill mixture for 1½ hours or until cold. Return to blender and process until smooth.
5. Return to refrigerator until ready to use.

Makes 2 cups (32 1-tablespoon servings)

26	Calories
0 g	Protein
4 g	Carbohydrates
1 g	Fat
28%	Calories from Fat
0 g	Fiber
21 mg	Sodium
0 mg	Cholesterol

"Yogurt"

※ ❧

1	package (10.5 ounces) extra firm, lite silken tofu
1	tablespoon honey
¼	teaspoon salt
½	teaspoon vanilla

A non-dairy substitute for yogurt.

1. Process all ingredients in a blender or food processor until smooth and creamy.
2. Cover and refrigerate.

Makes 2 one-cup servings

※ ❧

Add fresh fruit and cereal
for a nutritious snack
or breakfast.

※ ❧

97	Calories
11 g	Protein
10 g	Carbohydrates
2 g	Fat
16%	Calories from Fat
0 g	Fiber
281 mg	Sodium
0 mg	Cholesterol

The First Book of Vegetarian Cooking

Applesauce

8   large apples, any variety except Red Delicious
¾   cup water
¾   cup Fruit Source liquid sweetener *or*
     ¼ teaspoon stevia powder
¼   teaspoon freshly ground nutmeg
     Pinch of cinnamon
1   teaspoon grated lemon peel

Serve warm for a real old-fashioned taste—delicious and nutritious. Children love applesauce in their lunch box along with a healthy cookie for dessert.

1. Peel and core apples; cut into slices. Place in a large saucepan (not aluminum). Add water and simmer until apples are tender (stirring apples with a wooden spoon) about 30 minutes.
2. This will produce a chunky sauce. For a smooth sauce put through a food mill or a sieve
3. Add sweetener, spices, and lemon peel. Mix well.

Makes about 6 cups

204	Calories
0 g	Protein
53 g	Carbohydrates
1 g	Fat
3%	Calories from Fat
4 g	Fiber
1 mg	Sodium
0 mg	Cholesterol

"Chocolate" Icing

❧ ❦

⅓	cup dairy-free carob chips (naturally sweetened)
1	recipe "Cream Cheese" (page 359)
½	teaspoon vanilla
1	tablespoon honey (or to taste)

A nice creamy topping.

1. Melt carob chips in a double boiler. Cool slightly and add to cream cheese.
2. Whisk all ingredients together. Chill until ready to use.

Makes 1 cup

43	Calories
2 g	Protein
4 g	Carbohydrates
3 g	Fat
52%	Calories from Fat
0 g	Fiber
51 mg	Sodium
0 mg	Cholesterol

The First Book of Vegetarian Cooking

Fudge Sauce

½ cup carob powder
¾ cup powdered coffee
   substitute
¾ cup liquid Fruit Source
¼ cup organic peanut
   butter, smooth style
½ cup distilled water
1 teaspoon vanilla extract
2 tablespoons liquid
   lecithin

Very nice served over cake or fresh fruit.

1. In a blender, process all ingredients except lecithin until smooth. Pour into a saucepan and heat.
2. Whisk the liquid lecithin into the heated carob mixture. Continue whisking until smooth.
3. Cool before using. Sauce thickens as it cools.

Makes 1 ½ cups

53	Calories
1 g	Protein
9 g	Carbohydrates
2 g	Fat
40%	Calories from Fat
0 g	Fiber
16 mg	Sodium
0 mg	Cholesterol

Condensed "Milk"

❧ ❧

1 ½ cups Darifree powder
½ cup rice milk
¼ cup honey
1 teaspoon vanilla
¼ teaspoon powdered
    barley malt
    sweetener
    (Dr. Bronner's)

For your recipes that call for condensed milk, here's a substitute that is good for you and will save some calories.

1. In a saucepan, whisk together the Darifree powder and rice milk until smooth.
2. Whisk in honey, vanilla, and barley malt powder. Cook over low heat, whisking constantly, for 5 minutes.
3. Cool. Whisk again. Cover and refrigerate for up to a week.

Makes about 2 cups

66	Calories
0 g	Protein
16 g	Carbohydrates
1 g	Fat
1%	Calories from Fat
0 g	Fiber
60 mg	Sodium
0 mg	Cholesterol

The First Book of Vegetarian Cooking

Organic Rice Milk

4 cups distilled water
1 cup cooked organic
   brown rice
½ teaspoon vanilla
   (optional)

If you prefer to make your own, here's your recipe.

1. Place all ingredients into blender jar and process until smooth.
2. Let sit for 30 minutes. Pour off the milk. Save sediment for soups.

Makes 4 cups

13	Calories
0 g	Protein
3 g	Carbohydrates
1 g	Fat
7%	Calories from Fat
0 g	Fiber
8 mg	Sodium
0 mg	Cholesterol

Cottage "Cheese"

ಶಾ ಳ

1   pound firm tofu, drained
1   tablespoon raw,
        unfiltered apple
        cider vinegar
2   tablespoons fresh lemon
        juice
2   tablespoons minced
        onion
1   tablespoon minced
        chives
1   teaspoon minced dill
1/2 teaspoon salt substitute

An excellent substitute for the dairy product. Try it in lasagna and other recipes calling for cottage cheese.

1. In a medium bowl, mash one half of the tofu with a fork. Set aside.
2. Process remaining tofu and remaining ingredients in a blender or food processor until smooth.
3. Add blended tofu to bowl with crumbled tofu. Mix lightly.
4. Refrigerate in a sealed glass jar until ready to use.

Makes 2 cups

104	Calories
7 g	Protein
2 g	Carbohydrates
8 g	Fat
68%	Calories from Fat
0 g	Fiber
268 mg	Sodium
0 mg	Cholesterol

The First Book of Vegetarian Cooking

"Cream Cheese"
❧ ❦

1 package (10.5 ounces) frozen (or fresh) firm silken lite tofu, thawed
2 teaspoons fresh lemon juice
1 teaspoon liquid lecithin
1/2 teaspoon tahini
1/4 teaspoon honey
1/4 teaspoon coarse kosher salt

This lowfat substitute can be used in recipes requiring cream cheese. I keep a supply of tofu frozen for use in certain recipes where a firmer texture is required.

1. Drain thawed tofu, wrap in a clean kitchen towel, and refrigerate overnight. In the morning, squeeze any excess water from tofu.
2. Process the tofu along with lemon juice and lecithin in a blender or food processor until smooth and creamy.
3. Add tahini, honey, and salt and blend.

Makes about 1/2 cup

23	Calories
3 g	Protein
1 g	Carbohydrates
1 g	Fat
45%	Calories from Fat
0 g	Fiber
10 mg	Sodium
0 mg	Cholesterol

Croutons

1 small (8 ounce) bag cubed herb stuffing
2 teaspoons garlic powder
1 teaspoon onion powder
1 tablespoon dried parsley flakes
1 tablespoon Parmesan cheese substitute
Non-aerosol olive oil spray

An ideal topping for soups and salads. These are the only croutons I use at home. The supermarket varieties are loaded with fat.

1. Place bread cubes into a plastic sealable bag. Spray with oil and add seasonings. Seal bag and shake to coat.
2. Store in the refrigerator.

Makes sixteen ¼-cup servings

You can make your own croutons with cubed stale bread. Make sure the bread is completely dried out before using.

24	Calories
1 g	Protein
4 g	Carbohydrates
1 g	Fat
19%	Calories from Fat
0 g	Fiber
41 mg	Sodium
0 mg	Cholesterol

The First Book of Vegetarian Cooking

Dairyless Sour Cream

1   package (10.5 ounces) firm, lite silken tofu, drained
2   tablespoons tahini
¼   cup pure apple cider vinegar
2   teaspoons honey
¼   teaspoon coarse kosher salt
1   teaspoon umeboshi vinegar (ume plum vinegar)

Sour cream is a popular ingredient in many recipes. Here's a lowfat, dairyless version.

1. Slice tofu lengthwise and wrap in a clean dish towel for 30 minutes.
2. In a food processor or blender, process tofu until smooth and creamy.
3. Add remaining ingredients and process. Chill.

Makes about 1 ½ cups

15	Calories
1 g	Protein
1 g	Carbohydrates
1 g	Fat
48%	Calories from Fat
0 g	Fiber
33 mg	Sodium
0 mg	Cholesterol

Reconstituting Dried Chile Peppers

The longer you cook chile peppers, the milder they become, losing some of their flavor as well. I remember the time, returning from a trip to Mexico, I tried to duplicate a molé sauce I had fallen in love with. I even brought the peppers home with me along with the recipe in Spanish (which I don't translate too well). The recipe was very long and complicated. To make a long story short, I overcooked the peppers, they became bitter, and the sauce was ruined.

1. Heat chile peppers in a skillet until they become pliable. *Be careful not to burn them or they will be bitter.*
2. Remove seeds and veins.
3. Soak in distilled water for about 30 minutes.

Fat-Free Mayonnaise

𝒫𝓌 ℯ𝒸

1   package (10.5 ounces)
     firm, lite silken tofu
1   teaspoon Dijon mustard
¼   teaspoon dry mustard
2   teaspoons fresh lemon
     juice
2   teaspoons umeboshi
     vinegar* (apple cider
     can be substituted)
2   teaspoons honey
¼   teaspoon onion powder
¼   teaspoon garlic powder
     Pinch of annatto seed or
     turmeric (for color)
¼   teaspoon xanthan gum*

𝒫𝓌 ℯ𝒸

For herb mayonnaise, add
1 tablespoon each of fresh
minced parsley and basil
before adding the
xanthan gum.

𝒫𝓌 ℯ𝒸

A healthful alternative to fat- and calorie-laden mayonnaise. When I make this mayonnaise, I usually drain and wrap the tofu in a dish towel and refrigerate the day before preparing.

1. Drain tofu and wrap in a clean kitchen towel for about an hour.
2. Cube tofu and process in blender or food processor until creamy, scraping sides as needed.
3. Add remaining ingredients (excluding xanthan gum) and process until smooth. While machine is running, blend in the xanthan gum.
4. Store in a small recycled jar and refrigerate to allow flavors to mingle.

Makes 1 cup

*Can be found in most health food stores.

13	Calories
1 g	Protein
1 g	Carbohydrates
1 g	Fat
20%	Calories from Fat
0 g	Fiber
42 mg	Sodium
0 mg	Cholesterol

"Feta Cheese"

❦   ❧

1   pound extra firm tofu,
    drained
1   tablespoon organic apple
    cider vinegar
2   tablespoons fresh lemon
    juice
2   tablespoons minced
    onion
2   teaspoons dill weed
½   teaspoon coarse kosher
    salt

This can be used in Greek salads or in most recipes requiring feta cheese.

1. Process half the tofu and remaining ingredients in a blender or food processor until smooth and creamy. Transfer to bowl.
2. Mash the remaining tofu with a fork; combine with blender tofu.

Makes 2 cups

81	Calories
8 g	Protein
2 g	Carbohydrates
5 g	Fat
50%	Calories from Fat
0 g	Fiber
134 mg	Sodium
0 mg	Cholesterol

Flax Seed Extract

1   cup distilled water
¼   cup flax seeds

2 tablespoons = 1 egg white

The liquid extracted from
flax seeds contain only
soluble fiber and no fat.

This recipe may be strained or unstrained depending on the usage.

1. Mix water and flax seeds. Let seeds absorb the water for about 30 minutes. Stir occasionally.
2. Pour through strainer, stirring the seeds well to remove liquid. The liquid should be the consistency of egg whites. Reserve seeds for future use.

Makes ½ cup strained or 1 ¼ cups unstrained

FLAX SEED EGG REPLACER

Use either of the flax recipes as a substitute for egg whites in baking or in any recipe requiring egg whites. Will not work for soufflés, sorry to say. Both recipes can be stored in the refrigerator for up to two weeks. You can buy flax seeds and flax seed powder at your local health food store.

Flax Meal Paste

1 tablespoon flax seed powder

3 tablespoons distilled water

Combine powder and water.

Substitute for 1 egg

Flax seed fiber is nature's richest source of lignans, which dramatically reduce the risk of breast and colon cancers.

This vegetarian source of omega-3 fatty acids is essential in preventing cancer and heart disease as well as reducing joint pain from arthritis and helping with skin problems like eczema. New studies show daily consumption of ground flax seed in cereal or juices can lower cholesterol and help failing kidneys of people with lupus.

This truly might be nature's perfect dietary fiber.

Fruit Sauce

1   cup strawberries
3   tablespoons lite maple
        syrup
½   teaspoon freshly ground
        nutmeg
½   teaspoon grated lemon
        peel
1   tablespoon arrowroot

1. In a blender, purée all the ingredients until smooth and creamy.
2. In a small saucepan, simmer the sauce only until it thickens, 5 minutes.
3. Cool before serving.

Makes 1 cup

7	Calories
0 g	Protein
2 g	Carbohydrates
1 g	Fat
7%	Calories from Fat
0 g	Fiber
0 mg	Sodium
0 mg	Cholesterol

Gravy

༄ ༄

1   bag (10 ounces) frozen
      cauliflower
2   cups distilled water
2   tablespoons Vogue
      Instant Vege Base, *or*
      3 bouillon cubes

A favorite with people on a weight-loss program.

1. Cook all ingredients in covered saucepan until tender; cool slightly; drain (reserve liquid).
2. Transfer to a blender or food processor and blend until smooth. Add additional liquid as needed for desired consistency.

Makes 4 to 6 servings

17	Calories
1 g	Protein
3 g	Carbohydrates
1 g	Fat
22%	Calories from Fat
1 g	Fiber
108 mg	Sodium
0 mg	Cholesterol

The First Book of Vegetarian Cooking

Ketchup

❧ ❧

1 large onion, chopped
1 can (14 ounces) plum
  tomatoes
½ cup apple cider vinegar
½ cup frozen apple juice
  concentrate
3 tablespoons salt-free
  tomato paste
1 teaspoon chili powder
1 teaspoon ground
  coriander
1 teaspoon minced fresh
  cilantro
  Salt substitute
  Pepper

A fruit-sweetened, homemade ketchup using natural ingredients.

1. Prepare a nonstick skillet by lightly coating surface with vegetable cooking spray or by using an oiled pastry brush. Sauté the onion until soft. Add tomatoes and vinegar. Bring to a boil.
2. Add apple juice, reduce to a simmer, and cook for 30 minutes. Add tomato paste, chili powder, coriander, and cilantro.
3. Transfer to blender or food processor and purée until smooth. Add salt substitute and pepper to taste.
4. Pour into a recycled ketchup or salad dressing bottles and store in the refrigerator for up to 2 weeks.

Makes 4 cups

7	Calories
0 g	Protein
2 g	Carbohydrates
1 g	Fat
7%	Calories from Fat
0 g	Fiber
14 mg	Sodium
0 mg	Cholesterol

Mushroom Gravy

1/2	cup chopped onion
1	ounce shiitake mushrooms, reconstituted (page 371), stems removed
1	cup liquid from soaking mushrooms
2	tablespoons chicken flavored bouillon or soup mix
7	drops Liquid Smoke (Wright's)
1/4	cup whole wheat flour
1	cup light soy milk
2	tablespoons liquid aminos

When I became a vegetarian the hardest thing I had to learn was to make a good gravy. I think you will find this one good over mashed potatoes, meatless loafs, dumplings, Neatballs (page 10), or prepared seitan.

1. Prepare a nonstick skillet by lightly coating surface with vegetable cooking spray or by using an oiled pastry brush. Sauté onion until soft. Add mushrooms and their liquid; simmer for 2 minutes.
2. Stir in bouillon, Liquid Smoke and flour whisked with soy milk. Bring to a simmer and cook for a couple of minutes or until desired consistency.
3. Stir in liquid aminos at serving time.

Makes 2 cups

Other mushrooms can be substituted for the shiitakes, like fresh portabellos.

62	Calories
3 g	Protein
11 g	Carbohydrates
1 g	Fat
15%	Calories from Fat
1 g	Fiber
1049 mg	Sodium
0 mg	Cholesterol

The First Book of Vegetarian Cooking

Mushroom Reconstituting

Dried mushrooms
Enough distilled water
to cover

Dried mushrooms are a handy item to keep in your refrigerator. They not only are delicious in recipes, they have another use— for centuries they have been used in healing many diseases throughout the world.

1. Place mushrooms in a heatproof bowl. Heat water to almost boiling and pour over mushrooms.
2. Cover and allow to steep for 20 minutes.

Button mushrooms (the most widely used in the United States) have few proven healing benefits. They contain hydrazides, which are said to cause cancer. Hydrazides are destroyed by cooking. So always cook button mushrooms.

Organic Fruit Zest

Organic lemons or
oranges

Preheat oven to 250 degrees F.

A spoonful of fruit zest added to recipes gives an added dimension.

1. Wash and dry fruit. Peel the rind with a potato peeler (do not include white pulp).
2. Place the peel on a baking sheet and bake for 30 minutes or until crisp.
3. Pulverize into a fine powder in a food processor or a cleaned coffee grinder.
4. Store in the refrigerator in a glass jar.

Each orange makes 1 to 2 tablespoons,
each lemon makes 2 teapoons

Papaya Capers

1   Papaya, halved
     A mixture of ½ balsamic
     vinegar and ½ pure
     apple cider vinegar
     as needed to cover
     seeds, about 1 cup

Enjoy papaya plain,
cut-up in a salad, or
puréed in a marinade
or a salad dressing.

Use these peppery papaya seeds as you would capers, in salads, garnishes, or any recipe calling for capers.

1. Scoop seeds from the papaya, separating the seeds from the pulp. Rinse and drain on a paper towel.
2. Place the seeds into a recycled glass jar and add as much vinegar as it takes to cover the seeds. Cover with jar lid and store in the refrigerator.

Polenta

ᏸᎥ Ꭱᏸ

1   cup fine grain yellow
      cornmeal
3¼ cups distilled water
2   tablespoons Vogue
      Instant Vege Base
¼   teaspoon salt substitute

Used extensively in Italian and Mexican foods.

1. Combine cornmeal with 1 ¼ cups water.
2. In large saucepan, bring Vogue Instant Vege Base, salt, and remaining 2 cups water to a boil. Add cornmeal paste, stirring
   constantly with a wooden spoon. Bring to a boil, reduce heat
   and simmer, stirring frequently, for about 10 minutes. If any
   lumps occur, smash with spoon to dissolve.
3. When done, the polenta will be very thick and will start to
   pull away from the sides of the pan.

Makes about 3 cups (6 servings)

92	Calories
2 g	Protein
19 g	Carbohydrates
1 g	Fat
7%	Calories from Fat
1 g	Fiber
196 mg	Sodium
0 mg	Cholesterol

Prune Butter

1 cup pitted prunes
¾ cup distilled water

Keep a jar of prune butter in the refrigerator to be used in place of fat in baked goods.

Purée in food processor or blender.

Makes 1 ½ cups

Seitan Preparation

To prepare seitan from mix

1   box (12 ounces) seitan quick mix (Arrowhead Mills)

9 ½ cups distilled water

½   cup tamari sauce

Prepared seitan can be frozen for a month or so or refrigerated for about a week. The cooking broth can be reused and is good in gravies.

I remember the first time I tasted seitan. Of all places, it was on an airplane. I have had a lot of vegetarian meals on airplanes and this was by far the best—I couldn't believe it wasn't meat.

Seitan is a meat substitute made from whole wheat flour and a good source of protein. Developed by Japanese warrior monks, it is very close to meat in texture and taste, as well as being very versatile. At some health food stores, you will find seitan already prepared in the refrigerated section, or the mix can be purchased dry in boxes. One 12 ounce box makes 1 ¼ pounds raw seitan.

1. In a bowl, stir seitan mix with 1 ½ cups water. Knead until mixed well and elastic; about 5 minutes.
2. Turn out on cutting board or cookie sheet. Roll and pull dough into a 2 ½-inch thick roll. Rest for 5 minutes.
3. Flatten dough out and stretch and pull into an irregular shape about ½ inch thick. Cut into 8 irregular pieces.

The First Book of Vegetarian Cooking

4. In a large saucepan (4 quart), place 8 cups of water with the tamari. Add seitan and bring to a boil. Reduce heat, cover, and simmer for 2 hours. The longer seitan is cooked, the softer it gets. Do not overcook.
5. The seitan is now ready for a marinade, if desired (see "Sauces, Marinades, and Salad Dresings"). It is often ground and used as "hamburger."

Makes 1 1/2 pounds or 8 servings

57	Calories
11 g	Protein
2 g	Carbohydrates
1 g	Fat
12%	Calories from Fat
0 g	Fiber
284 mg	Sodium
0 mg	Cholesterol

Relish

2   cups onions, minced
2   cups red and green bell
     peppers, minced
1 ½ cups celery, minced
4   cups tomatoes, peeled
     and chopped
1   cup honey
½   cup Fruit Source,
     granular
1   cup pure apple cider
     vinegar
1   tablespoon mustard seed
1   teaspoon celery seed
1   teaspoon salt substitute

Natural relish is so good on hot dogs (meatless, of course) but it can be expensive at health food stores. This version is very tasty and will save you some money. You will have enough leftover for the freezer or gifts for friends.

1. In a oiled Dutch oven or large saucepan, sauté the onions, peppers, and celery until soft, about 10 minutes.
2. Add remaining ingredients and simmer for 3 hours.
3. Cool, bottle, and refrigerate.

Makes 5 cups

To peel tomatoes, submerge them in boiling water for one minute. Peel skins as soon as tomatoes are cool enough to handle.

32 Calories
0 g Protein
8 g Carbohydrates
1 g Fat
4% Calories from Fat
0 g Fiber
6 mg Sodium
0 mg Cholesterol

Cajun Spice

1 tablespoon kelp granules
1 teaspoon garlic powder
1 teaspoon chili powder
1 teaspoon powdered
    lemon peel
2 tablespoons paprika
$1/2$ teaspoon cayenne
$1\,1/2$ teaspoons onion powder
$1\,1/4$ teaspoons dried thyme
$3/4$ teaspoon dried oregano
$1/2$ teaspoon ground bay
    leaves

Mix ingredients and store in spice jar.

Makes $1/4$ cup

SPICES

A coffee grinder provides an inexpensive and efficient way to grind your own herbs and spices. Hide it so no one uses it for coffee.

Herb "Salt"

1   tablespoon garlic
       powder
1   teaspoon onion powder
1   teaspoon ground thyme
1   teaspoon ground basil
1   teaspoon dried
       marjoram
1   teaspoon dried savory
1   teaspoon ground mace
1   teaspoon powdered sage
       Pinch of cayenne

A salt substitute that goes well with soups and vegetables.

1. Place all ingredients into a glass jar with a lid and shake until blended.
2. Store in the refrigerator.

Makes about $1/4$ cup

The First Book of Vegetarian Cooking

Tex-Mex Seasoning

1 tablespoon ground
   cumin
1 tablespoon paprika
2 teaspoons chili powder
1 teaspoon garlic powder
1 teaspoon onion powder
1 teaspoon unbleached
   flour
¼ teaspoon powdered
   oregano
¼ teaspoon cayenne

1. Combine ingredients and mix well.
2. Store in glass jar, covered tightly.

Makes ½ cup

Sweet and Sour Corn Relish

½ cup cooked corn
1 English cucumber, peeled and chopped
1 tablespoon minced onion
1 tablespoon minced bell pepper
3 tablespoons minced fresh cilantro
½ cup rice vinegar
2½ tablespoons honey

Corn is a nutritious food, just ask Mexicans and American Indians.

Combine all ingredients and refrigerate until serving time.

Makes 3 cups

Corn is one of the easiest foods to digest and is high in roughage and carbohydrates, there are only 178 calories per 1 cooked cup. Corn is a good source of iron, zinc, and potassium, and is low in sodium.

6	Calories
0 g	Protein
2 g	Carbohydrates
1 g	Fat
4%	Calories from Fat
0 g	Fiber
5 mg	Sodium
0 mg	Cholesterol

The First Book of Vegetarian Cooking

TVP Reconstituting

1 cup TVP*, chunk style (approx. 1 inch)
1 tablespoon Vogue Instant Vege Base or 1 bouillon cube
1 tablespoon onion flakes
1 tablespoon liquid aminos
1 tablespoon ketchup
½ teaspoon garlic powder
1 tablespoon balsamic vinegar
2 cups boiling distilled water

TVP (textured vegetable protein) is a healthful lowfat alternative to meat and poultry.

1. Combine all ingredients in a small saucepan and bring to a boil while stirring. Cover and simmer for 25 minutes.
2. Drain, reserving the liquid for use in sauces.

Makes 4 servings

*See "Glossary."

73	Calories
11 g	Protein
7 g	Carbohydrates
1 g	Fat
3%	Calories from Fat
3 g	Fiber
32 mg	Sodium
0 mg	Cholesterol

Tangy Fruit Salsa

2 cups seeded, chopped
    watermelon
1 cup chopped fresh
    pineapple
1 cup chopped onion
¼ cup minced cilantro
1 cup frozen orange juice
    concentrate
1 tablespoon Cajun spice

Combine all ingredients. Cover and refrigerate for 1 hour before serving.

Makes about 4 cups

24	Calories
1 g	Protein
6 g	Carbohydrates
1 g	Fat
6%	Calories from Fat
0 g	Fiber
22 mg	Sodium
0 mg	Cholesterol

The First Book of Vegetarian Cooking

Melon Salsa

1   cup chopped water-
        melon
½   cup chopped honeydew
        melon
¼   cup raisins
2   tablespoons minced
        fresh cilantro
¼   cup white balsamic
        vinegar
1   tablespoon honey
     Pinch of cayenne

Combine, chill, and serve.

Makes 2 cups

21	Calories
0 g	Protein
5 g	Carbohydrates
1 g	Fat
3%	Calories from Fat
0 g	Fiber
2 mg	Sodium
0 mg	Cholesterol

Thick and Chunky Salsa

1 ½ cups crushed tomatoes
¾ cup chopped onion
¼ cup pure unfiltered
   apple cider vinegar
2 jalapeño peppers*,
   seeded, deveined,
   and finely minced
   (1 tablespoon)
1 large clove garlic,
   pressed or minced
¼ cup minced bell pepper
½ teaspoon ground cumin
1 tablespoon chopped
   fresh cilantro
2 teaspoons liquid aminos

A quick and easy salsa. Adjust the amount of jalapeño pepper to taste.

Combine all ingredients and store in refrigerator in a recycled glass jar.

Makes about 2 cups

*Wear rubber gloves when handling hot peppers.

9	Calories
1 g	Protein
2 g	Carbohydrates
1 g	Fat
8%	Calories from Fat
0 g	Fiber
63 mg	Sodium
0 mg	Cholesterol

Thousand Island Dressing

1   cup fat-free mayonnaise
⅓   cup sugar-free relish
¼   cup fruit-sweetened
       ketchup

*I use this recipe on Reuben
pizzas and sandwiches.*

To make a healthful dressing, the ingredients should be free of fat, sugar, and dairy products. The health food store will have these items or you can make your own using the recipes in "Added Touches."

Combine ingredients and store in refrigerator in a recycled glass jar.

Makes 1 ½ cups

20	Calories
0 g	Protein
5 g	Carbohydrates
0 g	Fat
0%	Calories from Fat
0 g	Fiber
338 mg	Sodium
0 mg	Cholesterol

Tomatoes

For 1 cup
canned tomatoes

1 ⅓ cups coarsely chopped
fresh tomatoes

For 1 cup
tomato sauce

1   cup stewed tomatoes,
      blended *or*

1   cup tomato purée *or*

¾   cup tomato paste plus
      ¼ cup water

If your health food store does not carry organic canned tomatoes, prepare your own with fresh organic tomatoes or fresh tomatoes that have had their Veggie Bath (see "Glossary").

Simmer tomatoes for 10 minutes.

Yield

Canned (cups)	=	ounces	=	Fresh Tomatoes (cups)
1		8		1 ⅓
1 ½		12		2
2		16		2 ⅔
2 ½		20		3 ⅓
3		24		4

Tomatoes contain a compound called lycopene, which is thought to reduce the risk of cancer. People with low lycopene blood levels are considered a higher risk for pancreatic cancer. Watermelon and apricots also contain this compound.

Yuba Reconstituting

Yuba sheets
Distilled water

Yuba is a Japanese delicacy made from the film that develops when heating soy milk. It is used in dishes where a skin, much the same as chicken skin, is desired. It can be found in health food stores and Asian markets.

1. In a flat shallow dish, soak yuba in water for five minutes. It will be white, soft, and fragile.
2. Wrap yuba sheets around food; using a pastry brush, cover surface with olive oil or melted margarine. Bake according to recipe directions.

Ingredient Exchange

"Alternative cooking" substitutions for a more healthful lifestyle.

Recipes

Baking Powder
Brown Sugar
Buttermilk
Cheese
Chocolate
Cocoa
Confectioners' Sugar
Condensed Milk
Cornstarch
Cottage Cheese
Cream
Cream Cheese
Eggs

Eggs, scrambled
Fat
Honey
Meats
Milk
Ricotta Cheese
Salt
Sour Cream
Sugar
Tartar Sauce
Tomatoes, Organic
Worcestershire Sauce

Baking Powder Substitute

❧ ❧

Combine

2 tablespoons baking soda
4 tablespoons arrowroot
4 tablespoons cream of tartar

Makes $^2/_3$ cup

Brown Sugar Substitute

❧ ❧

Use any one of the following:

1 cup date sugar *or*
1 cup molasses *or*
¾ cup honey (reduce the liquid in recipe by ¼ cup)

Equivalent to 1 cup brown sugar

Buttermilk Substitute

❧ ❧

Combine

1 cup soy or rice milk
1 tablespoon vinegar

Makes 1 cup

Cheese

❧ ❧

Nondairy cheeses are available in health food stores. Some cheeses
contain casein, which is a dairy product.

Chocolate Substitute

Combine

1 ½   tablespoons carob powder
1 ½   tablespoons powdered grain coffee substitute
1   tablespoon water

Makes the equivalent of a 1-ounce square of chocolate

Cocoa Substitute

Combine

½   cup carob powder
½   cup powdered grain coffee substitute

Makes 1 cup

Confectioners' Sugar Substitute

Use Darifree powder in uncooked recipes.

Condensed Milk

See page 356.

Cornstarch Substitute

Use either of the following:

1   tablespoon arrowroot *or*
1   tablespoon kuzu (kudzu)

Equivalent to 1 tablespoon cornstarch

Cottage Cheese Substitute

See page 358.

Cream Substitute

Use either of the following:

1   teaspoon tahini plus ¼ cup water, whisked together *or*
¼   cup tofu processed in a blender or food processor with enough water added for desired consistency.

Makes equivalent of ¼ cup cream

Cream Cheese Substitute

Health food stores carry nondairy cream cheese. Tofutti is one brand I have used and like. Or see page 359.

Ingredient Exchange

Egg Substitutes

*Use the healthiest alternative, flax seed extract/paste (page 365)
or use one of the following:*

Substitute I

1	teaspoon arrowroot
¼	teaspoon baking powder
⅓	cup warm distilled water

Whisk ingredients together and microwave for 2 to 3 minutes or
until the consistency is that of a beaten egg white.

Substitute II

1	tablespoon Egg Replacer powder (Ener-G)
¼	cup distilled water

Whisk ingredients till frothy.

Makes the equivalent of 1 egg white

Eggs, Scrambled

1	pound tofu, drained (any lite tofu)
¼	teaspoon turmeric
¼	teaspoon curry powder
¼	teaspoon cumin
1	teaspoon onion powder
	Pinch of cayenne

Mash tofu with a fork, cook over low heat for 4 minutes with
remaining ingredients.

Makes 4 servings

Fat Substitutes (In Baking)

Use either of the following:
¼   cup apple sauce *or*
¼   cup all natural apple butter *or*
¼   cup prune butter (page 375)

Equivalent of ¼ cup oil

Honey Substitutes

Use any of the following:
1 ¼ cups Fruit Source *or*
1 ⅓ cups rice syrup *or*
¾   cup maple syrup

Equivalent of 1 cup honey

Meat Analogs (Substitutes)

Some brands available are very good and some not so good (another reason I've indicated brand names in my recipes). The industry has really come a long way in providing palatable meat substitutes that have good texture and are, just recently, lowfat or fat-free. I have tried to use a variety in my recipes to acquaint you with what is out there. Sometimes they are incidental to the recipe. I have listed what is available at most health food stores.

Ingredient Exchange

Bacon

- Heartline Meatless Meats: Canadian bacon (lite available), pepperoni (lite available) and Italian sausage (Lumen Foods)
- Stripples (Worthington)
- Fakin' Bacon' Bits (Lightlife)
- Morningstar (Worthington)
- Canadian Veggie Bacon (Yves Fine Foods)
- Veggie Pepperoni (Yves Fine Foods)

Beef

- Meat of Wheat, Beyond Roast Beef (Ivy Foods)
- Meat of Wheat, Hearty Original (Ivy Foods)
- Heartline Meatless Meats: fillet, Mexican, teriyaki—lite line available (Lumen Foods)
- Marinated seitan—savory, barbecue, or teriyaki flavor (various brands)
- TVP (textured vegetable protein), chunks
- Grilled portabello mushrooms—have a meat texture
- Seitan steaks made from package mixes
- Fajita Strips (White Wave)

Chicken

- Meat of Wheat, chicken style (Ivy Foods)
- Beyond Chicken Patties (Ivy Foods)
- ChikStiks (Worthington)

- Heartline Meatless Meats, chicken fillet, lite available (Lumen Foods)
- Marinated tofu and tempeh (various brands)

Cold Cuts
~ ~

- Trim Slice, various flavors (Heart & Soul)
- Meatless slices, various flavors (Worthington)
- Yves Veggie Deli Slices (Yves Fine Cuisine)
- Smart Deli Slices (Lightlife)
- Sandwich Slices (White Wave)

Ham
~ ~

- Heartline Meatless Meats, California ham (Lumen Foods)

Hamburger
~ ~

- Burger 'n' Loaf mix (Midland Harvest)
- Meat of Wheat, burger (Ivy Foods)
- Gimme Lean, beef style (Lightlife)
- Natural Touch, vegan burger (Worthington)
- Better Than Burger? mix (Sovex)
- Heartline Meatless Meats, minced or ground beef, lite available (Lumen Foods)
- Tofu Crumbles (Marjon Specialty Foods)

Ingredient Exchange

- Yves Veggie Burger Burgers and Garden Vegetable Patties (Yves Fine Cuisine)
- Morningstar (Worthington)

Hot Dogs

- Yves Tofu Wieners, Chile Dogs and Veggie Wieners (Yves Fine Cuisine)
- White Wave Hot Dogs

Sausage

- Meat of Wheat, sausage style (Ivy Foods)
- Gimme Lean, sausage style (Lightlife)
- Not So Sausage mix (Knox Mountain Farm)
- Prosage Patties, Prosage Links (Worthington)
- Dry sausage mixes (various brands)

Tofu

- Baked and savory baked (Tree of Life)
- Other tofu (White Wave, Nasoya, Mori-Nu)
- Tofu crumbles (Marjon Specialty Foods)

Turkey
❧ ❧

❧ Meat of Wheat, Beyond Turkey (Ivy Foods)

Milk Substitutes
❧ ❧

Soy milk, rice milk, rice-soy blend, Better Than Milk, or Darifree. Use lite when ever possible

Ricotta Cheese Substitute
❧ ❧

Drain tofu and crumble with a fork.

Salt Substitutes
❧ ❧

Braggs Liquid Aminos, tamari sauce (low sodium), miso, dulse, kelp, nori flakes, lemon juice, or umeoshi plum paste. The use of herbs and spices, especially cayenne pepper, lessens the need for salt.

Sour Cream Substitute

See recipe page 361 or check with health food stores for nondairy sour cream. I like the Tofutti brand.

Sugar Substitutes

For 1 cup sugar, substitute one of the following:

- ½ cup honey*
- ¾ cup maple syrup*
- ¾ cup liquid barley malt sweetener*
- ¾ cup frozen juice concentrate*
- ¾ cup Liquid Fruit Source (reduce the liquid and fat called for in the recipe by 50%)
- 1 ¼ cups granular Fruit Source
- Dr. Bronner's Barley Malt Sweetner (a powder), one dash = 2 teaspoons sugar

Tartar Sauce

Combine

½   cup dairy-free, fat-free mayonnaise
¼   cup relish
1   tablespoon lemon juice

Makes ³/₄ cup

Tomatoes, Organic

❧ ❧

See recipe page 388. Muir Glen's line of organic tomato products are excellent.

Worcestershire Sauce

❧ ❧

Use a vegetarian Worcestershire sauce. I recommend The Wizard's Stir Krazy.

*Reduce the liquid called for in the recipe by $1/4$ cup

General Nutritional Information

This section highlights some important vitamins, their function and vegetarian sources. Check out the anticancer pharmacy for the most up-to-date information available—these foods delay the aging process and promote optimum health.

We all know the benefits of exercise, but you know the importance of breathing? All this and 32 weight-loss tips!

Alkali/Acid-Forming Foods

Anticancer Pharmacy

Good Fat vs. Bad Fat

Legume Cooking Chart

Whole Grains Cooking
Chart

Measures

RDAs

Vitamins and Minerals

Weight-Loss Tips

Some Benefits of Regular
Exercise

Light

The Air We Breathe

Alkali/Acid-Forming Foods

To have beautiful, lush plants we know the soil should fall within a certain pH range for optimum health. Just like plants, our bodies need to fall within a certain pH range for optimum health. We thrive between pH 7.35 and 7.45, which is close to neutral. This level is accomplished by eating 75% to 80% alkaline foods and 20% to 25% acid-forming foods.

SOME ALKALI-FORMING FOODS

Almonds	Grapes
Apples	Lettuce
Apricots	Lima beans
Bananas	Peaches
Brazil nuts	Pineapple
Cabbage	Potatoes
Cantaloupe	Raisins
Carrots	Soybeans
Celery	Spinach
Coconut	Tomatoes
Cucumber	Turnips
Dates	Watercress
Figs	Watermelon
Grapefruit	

SOME ACID-FORMING FOODS

Cheese	Nuts (except almond
Chicken	and brazil nuts)
Eggs	Organ meats
Fish	Oysters
Fowl	Peanuts
Grains	Rice
Lentils	Rye bread
Liver	Veal
Meats	Whole wheat bread

To determine your level of acidity, urine can be applied to litmus paper in order to obtain a pH reading. You can find litmus paper at drugstores.

Anticancer Pharmacy

Listed below are fruits and vegetables with their respective phytochemicals or phytomins. Phytomins, a contraction of phyto (plant) and vitamins, protect plants from environmental enemies such as radiation, viruses, bacteria, and bugs. Plants have been on this planet a lot longer than we have so they are way ahead of us on survival techniques. We can learn from Mother Nature.

Research has indicated phytomins are real cancer-busters. High intakes have been associated with lower risks of all cancers, but especially colon and breast. Eating lots of vegetables can cut your risk of cancer by half.

- **Bok choy** carotenoids
- **Broccoli** carotenoids, dithiolthiones, indoles
- **Brussels sprouts** carotenoids, indoles
- **Cabbage** carotenoids, dithiolthiones, indoles, genistein
- **Cauliflower** carotenoids
- **Carrot** carotenoids, phenolic acid, monoterpenes, phthalides, polyacetylenes, triterpenes
- **Celery** phenolic acids, monoterpenes, phthalides, polyacetylenes, triterpenes
- **Chile peppers** phenolic acids, glucarates, monoterpenes, triterpenes
- **Citrus fruits** carotenoids, phenolic acids, glucarates, monoterpenes, coumarins, limonene
- **Cruciferous vegetables** (broccoli, kohlrabi, cauliflower, bok choy, kale, turnip, radishes, rutabaga,

cabbage, watercress, brussels sprouts, mustard greens, horseradish) carotenoids, phenolic acids, glucarates, indoles, isothiocyanates, monoterpenes, sulfides, triterpenes

- **Cucumber** coumarins, phenolic acids, monoterpenes, triterpenes
- **Cucumber skin** sterols
- **Eggplant** flavonoids, phenolic acids, glucarates, monoterpenes, triterpenes
- **Fennel** monoterpenes, phthalides, polacetylenes
- **Flax** flavonoids
- **Flax seed** lignans
- **Garlic** monoterpenes, sulfides, triterpenes, allium
- **Greens** carotenoids, phenolic acids
- **Melon** carotenoids, phenolic acids
- **Onion** sulfides, allium
- **Parsley** coumarins, phenolic acid, monoterpenes, phthalides, polyacetylenes
- **Parsnip** coumarins, phenolic acids, monoterpenes, phthalides
- **Pumpkin** phenolic acids
- **Scallions** allium
- **Soy products** (tofu, tempeh) flavonoids, lignans, phytates, isoflavones
- **Soybeans** flavonoids, phenolic acids, lignans, phytates, triterpenes, isoflavones (only good source), genistein
- **Squash** phenolic acids, monoterpenes, triterpenes
- **Tomatoes** carotenoids, phenolic acids, glucarates, monoterpenes, triterpenes
- **Whole grains** glucarates, phytates, triterpenes
- **Winter squash** carotenoids

Allium   Produces anticancer enzymes, protecting against stomach and intestinal cancer.

Carotenoids   Contain antioxidants able to block damage to RNA.

Coumarins   Inhibit tumor growth by promoting production of detoxifying enzymes.

Dithiolthiones   Same benefits as coumarins.

Indoles   Promote production of detoxifying enzymes and inhibits tumor growth.

Isoflavones (phytoestrogens)   Restrict growth of some enzymes that activate carcinogens. Could reduce estrogen-related cancers in women.

Limonene   Enhances production of anticancer enzymes.

Phenols and Polyphenols   Very powerful antioxidants. Enhance the production of anticancer enzymes.

Good Fat vs. Bad Fat

Our bodies do require some fats—the right amount and the right kinds. Excess fat is stored in the liver, arteries, and around the heart. High fat consumption is linked to cancers of the breast, colon, and prostate, not to mention obesity. At this time the recommended amount of fat consumption is 25% (and less) of the total calorie intake. Some feel 10% is more accurate.

When oils are heated above 320 degrees F, they become harmful to our bodies by forming free radicals. Think about it—the fat used in frying foods reaches a temperature of 428 degrees F. and most of these fats are reused, making them rancid also. Think about all those French fries, potato chips, crackers, and cereals!

Eliminating cholesterol in the diet alone will not reduce elevated cholesterol levels in your blood. Saturated fat is a major culprit. Avoid saturated fats (the bad fat). The worst fats are coconut oil and palm oil and they are classified as vegetable oils! Saturated fats are what elevate cholesterol levels, clogging arteries (one of the causes of heart disease). It's easy to eliminate cholesterol from your diet. *Only animal products contain cholesterol.* None of the recipes in this book contain cholesterol.

In making margarine, oils are hardened by hydrogenation, making a product that does not belong in our bodies. Avoid foods that list the word hydrogenated as one of their ingredients. Always be sure to *read labels.*

BAD FATS (SATURATED FATS)

Beef Lard	Coconut	Palm kernel oil
Butter	Coconut oil	Pork/bacon
Cheese/milk/cream	Processed cheese	Poultry skin

GOOD FATS

Safflower oil—polyunsaturated   Flax oil—vegetarian omega 3
Olive oil—monounsaturated

Use cold pressed or expelled pressed oils and store all oils in the refrigerator. Unrefrigerated oil can become rancid.

FIGURING OUT FAT CONTENT

What is the percent of calories from fat if a food label states 200 Calories, 5 Grams of Fat?

Listed below are two ways to figure fat percentages. The first one:

1. Multiply the grams of fat by 9

$$9 \times 5 = 45 \text{ fat calories}$$

2. Divide fat calories (45) by total calories (200)

$$45 \div 200 = 0.225$$

General Nutritional Information

3. Multiply by 100 = the percent of calories from fat

$$0.225 \times 100 = 22.5\%$$

4. So, of the 200 calories shown on the label 22.5% of the calories are from fat.

A quick way to figure 25% calories from fat

1. Take total calories   =   200
2. Drop the last digit   =   20
3. Divide by 4   =   5

If the label shows total grams of fat more than the answer in step 3, then the food contains more than 25% fat.

The above amounts of fat are acceptable according to the American Heart Association. Many experts feel the fat in our diets should be a much lower percentage.

Legume Cooking Chart

Dry Legumes (1 cup, dry)	Cooking Water (cups)	Cooking Time (approximate hours)	Yield (cups)
Adzuki beans*	3¼	1	3
Anasazi beans	2	1	2¼
Black beans	3	1–2	2¼
Black-eyed peas	3	1	2
Chickpeas	4	2–3	2
Great Northern beans	3½	1½–2	2⅔
Kidney beans	2¼	1½–2	2¼
Lentils, brown*	3	½	2¼
Lentils, red*	3	½	1⅔
Navy beans	3	1–1½	2⅔
Pinto beans	3	1½–2	2⅔
Split peas	3	1	2

Soak legumes with seasonings at least 8 hours before cooking.

*do not require soaking

Whole Grains Cooking Chart

Grain (1 cup dry)	Cooking Water (cups)	Cooking Time (minutes)	Yield (cups)
Amaranth	1½	20–25	2
Barley	3	45–70	2½
Basmati rice (brown)	2¼	35–40	3
Basmati rice (white)	2½	20–25	3
Brown rice	2	45–60	3
Buckwheat (kasha)	2	15–20	2½
Cornmeal (polenta)	4	25–40	3
Cracked rye wheat	2	25–40	2½
Millet*	2½–3	35–45	3½
Quinoa*	2	15–20	3
Rye berries	2½–3	60	2
Wild rice	3	50–65	3½
Whole wheat berries	2½–3	120	2¾

*Millet and Quinoa are even more flavorful if dry-roasted prior to cooking in water. Spread grain over the bottom of a heavy skillet and cook over medium heat until you begin to smell the grain's aroma. Transfer to water and simmer according to the chart above.

Measures

1 Cup	=	16 Tablespoons	=	8 Ounces
¾ Cup	=	12 Tablespoons	=	6 Ounces
½ Cup	=	8 Tablespoons	=	4 Ounces
⅓ Cup	=	5⅓ Tablespoons	=	2⅔ Ounces
¼ Cup	=	4 Tablespoons	=	2 Ounces
⅛ Cup	=	2 Tablespoons	=	1 Ounce

10 Tablespoons	=	⅝ Cup
5 Tablespoons	=	⅜ Cup
1 Tablespoon	=	3 teaspoons
1 Teaspoon	=	60 drops

General Nutritional Information

½ Pint	=	1 Cup	=	8 Ounces
1 Pint	=	2 Cups	=	16 Ounces
1 Quart	=	4 Cups	=	32 Ounces
4 Quarts	=	1 Gallon	=	128 Ounces

16 Ounces	=	1 Pound

RDAs
(Recommended Dietary Allowances)

Protein	50–63 g
Vitamin A	800–1000 µg
Vitamin C	60 mg
Calcium	800 mg
Iron	10–15 mg
Vitamin D	5 µg
Vitamin E	8–10 mg
Thiamin	1–1.5 mg
Riboflavin	1.2–1.7 mg
Niacin	13–19 mg
Vitamin B_6	1.6–2.0 mg
Folate	180–200 µg
Vitamin B_{12}	2.0 µg
Vitamin K	65–80 µg
Phosphorus	800 mg
Magnesium	280–350 mg
Zinc	12–15 mg
Iodine	150 µg
Selenium	55–70 µg

The above is a summary for adults over the age of 25. The high range is for males, the lower is for females. RDAs are based on how much of a nutrient you need to consume in order to avoid a severe deficiency. In most cases this is far lower than what is required for good health.

µg (microgram) = 1 millionth of a gram
mg (milligram) = 1 thousandth of a gram (1,000 mg = 1 gram)

Vitamins and Minerals

This section highlights some important vitamins, their function and vegetarian sources.

BETA-CAROTENE—ANTIOXIDANT/VITAMIN A

Beta-carotene converts to vitamin A in the body.

Assists:

- Bone growth
- Eyesight (especially night blindness)
- Fighting the effects of air pollution
- Fighting infection
- Gall bladder function
- Healthy skin
- Protein synthesis
- Reproduction
- Sexual functioning
- Slowing the aging process

Some sources:

Sweet potatoes, carrots, butternut squash, papaya, kale, spinach, apricots, cantaloupe, broccoli, pumpkins, turnip greens, watermelon, tomatoes, avocado, nectarines, tangerines, asparagus, alfalfa, beets, Swiss chard, dandelion greens, garlic, parsley, peaches, red peppers, spirulina, and watercress.

Antibiotics, laxatives, and some cholesterol-lowering drugs interfere with vitamin A absorption. Beta-carotene needs a little fat to enable it to pass through the intestinal wall, so for optimum absorption take with a food containing a little oil. Do not take large doses of vitamin A supplements.

General Nutritional Information

Vitamin B-1 (Thiamine)

Assists in:

- Blood formation
- Increasing carbohydrate metabolism
- Circulation
- Liver health
- Nervous system maintenance
- Normal growth
- Muscle building
- Respiration

Some sources:

Whole cereal grains, fresh green vegetables, potatoes, dried beans, brewer's yeast, wheat germ, brown rice, peanuts, peas, soybeans, asparagus, broccoli, brussels sprouts, nuts, plums, dried prunes, and raisins.

Antibiotics, sulfa drugs, and birth control pills reduce thiamine levels.

Vitamin B-2 (Riboflavin)

Assists in:

- Cataract prevention
- Cell respiration
- Fat and carbohydrate metabolism
- Formation of red blood cells and antibodies
- Health of skin, liver, nails, hair, and eyes
- Kidney and heart health
- Protein metabolism
- Reduction of eye fatigue
- Resistance to disease

Some sources:

Brewer's yeast, wheat germ, green leafy vegetables, beans, lima beans, asparagus, avocados, broccoli, brussels sprouts, currants, and nuts.

A deficiency of riboflavin sometimes appears as cracks and sores in the corner of the mouth. This vitamin can be destroyed by light, cooking, alcohol, and antibiotics.

Vitamin B-3 (Niacin)

Assists in:

- Carbohydrate, fat, and protein metabolism
- Cholesterol reduction
- Circulatory system
- Nervous system health
- Skin health

Some sources:

Yeast, broccoli, carrots, wheat germ, nuts, soybeans, brewer's yeast, dates, figs, prunes, corn flour, tomatoes, and potatoes.

Niacin has been used successfully in the treatment of mental illnesses. Avoid high doses if suffering from gout, peptic ulcers, glaucoma, liver disease, diabetes, or if pregnant.

Vitamin C—Antioxidant

Assists in:

- Adrenal gland function
- Bone cartilage development

- Collagen formation
- Fighting infections
- Iron absorption
- Mental health
- Pollution protection
- Removal of free radicals
- Sex glands
- Strengthening capillary tissue, gums, and bones
- Tissue repair (heart)
- Tooth formation

Some sources:

Kale, broccoli, turnip greens, strawberries, citrus fruits, cantaloupe, spinach, apricots, brussels spouts, papaya, kiwi, cauliflower, bell peppers, mango, tomatoes, asparagus, beets, and rose hips.

Vitamin C is reduced in the body by aspirin, alcohol, smoking, analgesics, anti-depressants, anticoagulants, birth control pills, and steroids.

VITAMIN E—ANTIOXIDANT

Assists in:

- Blood clot prevention
- Building healthy blood cells
- Circulation
- Pollution protection
- Removal of free radicals
- Selenium and phosphorus absorption
- Slowing the aging process
- Tissue repair

Some sources:

Almonds, wheat germ, sunflower seeds, kale, nuts, spinach, whole grains, turnip greens, brussels sprouts, cornmeal, sweet potatoes, and asparagus.

Do not take iron supplements and vitamin E at the same time. Do not take large doses if suffering from diabetes, rheumatic heart disease, or overactive thyroid.

CALCIUM (CA)

Assists in:

- Blood clotting
- Building healthy bones and teeth
- Heart rhythm
- Improving metabolism
- Muscle function
- Strengthening nervous system

Some sources:

Sesame seeds, collard greens, figs, almonds, seaweed, watercress, turnip greens, black-eyed peas, chicory greens, kale, beet greens, tofu, walnuts, and peanuts.

A calcium deficiency may result in: muscle cramps, nervousness, heart palpitations, brittle nails, eczema, hypertension, aching joints, increased cholesterol levels, rheumatoid arthritis, tooth decay, insomnia, or numbness in arms and legs.

IRON (FE)

Assists in:

- Increasing energy level
- Formation of hemoglobin (carries oxygen from lungs to every part of body)

General Nutritional Information

- Resistance to diseases
- Stress reduction

Some sources:

Dulse, kelp, wheat and rice bran, wheat germ, beans, apricots, figs, dates, peaches, prunes, green leafy vegetables, whole grains, lima beans, lentils, millet, parsley, raisins, and pumpkin.

High iron intake can lead to the production of free radicals in the system and increase your need for vitamin E.

POTASSIUM (K)

Assists in:

- Acid/alkaline balance in blood and tissues
- Endocrine production
- Healthy nervous system
- Kidneys in detoxifying of blood
- Proper muscle contraction
- Regular heart rhythm

Some sources:

Kelp, dulse, almonds, apricots, apples, dates, citrus fruits, bananas, avocados, potatoes, figs, lima beans, soy beans, mung beans, and wheat bran.

PHOSPHORUS (P)

Assists in:

- Acid/alkaline balance
- Building healthy bones and teeth
- Increasing carbohydrate metabolism
- Heart muscle contractions

- ☞ Healthy nerves
- ☞ Kidney function

Some sources:

Wheat and rice bran, almonds, Brazil nuts, pine nuts, walnuts, sesame seeds, asparagus, corn, brewer's yeast, whole grains, and beans.

MAGNESIUM (MG)—THE "NATURAL TRANQUILIZER"

Assists in:

- ☞ Acid/alkaline balance in body
- ☞ Elimination
- ☞ Raising energy level
- ☞ Increasing enzyme activity
- ☞ Healthy muscle tone
- ☞ Heart health
- ☞ Utilization of vitamins B, C, E, fats, calcium, and other minerals

Some sources:

Kelp, almonds, cashews, beans, spinach, Swiss chard, tofu, pumpkin seeds, sunflower seeds, okra, acorn squash, figs, lemons, and grapefruit.

New studies show a deficiency of magnesium will cause bone-loss density

SODIUM (NA)

Sodium with potassium and chlorine maintains proper electrolyte balance.

Assists in:

- ☞ Keeping body fluids normal
- ☞ Nerve and muscle function

☞ Production of hydrochloric acid in the stomach

☞ Transportation of nutrients from intestines to blood

Some sources:

Apples, apricots (dried), asparagus, carrots, beets, artichokes, celery, cabbage, water chestnuts, garlic, peaches (dried), radishes, broccoli, and brussels sprouts. Virtually all foods contain some sodium.

Excess table salt may result in edema, high blood pressure, potassium deficiency, and liver and kidney disease.

Antioxidants are important to the diet because they destroy free radicals. Free radicals weaken cells, making them more susceptible to cancer. Recently some new substances have been added to the list of beneficial antioxidant nutrients. These include CoQ_{10}, selenium, and melatonin. Melatonin is a hormone produced in the pineal gland and, as we age, our bodies can become deficient in this important antioxidant. It has been recommended that people under 40 years of age not take this supplement on a full-time basis.

Weight-Loss Tips

Being overweight is not considered to be in one's best health interest. I have included this list of hints for those of us that need a little extra help.

1. When having a salad in a restaurant, order the dressing on the side. When eating the salad, lightly dip your fork into the dressing then pick up some salad. You'll be surprised how much dressing you will have left when the salad is finished.

2. Keep a food diary and write down everything you put into your mouth.

3. When you crave a particular food, wait 20 minutes. While waiting, do something to get your mind off the food—take a walk, make a phone call, do a craft, take a bath, etc. If after 20 minutes you still want the food, eat it (in moderation).

4. Drink 8 (8-ounce) glasses of water each day. This is very sound advice nutritionally with the added benefit of being very filling.

5. Do not eat anything after your evening meal. If hunger gets to you, eat a piece of fruit.

6. Keep busy so your mind will not dwell on food. Replace eating with something enjoyable like a hobby or sport or whatever brings you pleasure.

7. Never reward yourself with food. Unfortunately we learned this from childhood—instead reward yourself with tangible things. This can be as little as a new bottle of nail polish to as large as a new car, depending on your budget and the size of the accomplishment.

8. When you have a craving for something sweet, try a pickle. I also find that a few pickled cucumbers do the trick. If all else fails, eat a piece of fruit or drink a cup of hot herbal tea.

9. Freeze leftovers immediately. This way you won't be tempted to snack on them.

10. If you feel a feeding frenzy coming on, do your nails. It's hard to eat with wet nails.

11. Every time you eat something, brush your teeth. You'll put that bite down, if you have to brush your teeth again.

12. Don't shop for food when you're hungry.

13. Make a weekly menu and stick to it.

14. Always have a bowl of cut-up raw celery, carrots, bell peppers, broccoli, cauliflower, or any other live foods. This is a nutritional bonanza and will keep you away from no-no foods. Once a week after grocery shopping, prepare your veggie bowl. What's handy is what is usually eaten first. This is also a wonderful way to get children to eat vegetables.

General Nutritional Information

15. Reduce protein and fat intake. Complex carbohydrates are a better choice and they give you more energy.

16. When having a sandwich, cut it into thirds. First cut a small pyramid, then half what's left. A quartered sandwich goes down like finger food, too fast, but thirds seem more filling.

17. Remember fat makes you fat!!!!

18. If you have a vegetable juicer, drink cucumber juice in the morning, it is a wonderful diuretic that flushes toxins from the body.

19. All that glitters is not gold—it's probably fat. Beware of shiny foods. Foods that shine and glisten usually do so because of their fat content.

20. Do not eat standing up or in a car. Make your meal an event. Sit at the table, turn off the TV and don't talk on the phone. Give your food your full attention and savor each bite.

21. When restaurant servings are more than you should eat, get a doggie bag and remove the food from your plate before you start eating. If you think you will only eat the food when you get home, leave it at the restaurant or find a hungry animal.

22. Set realistic weekly weight-loss goals for yourself. It's easier to lose one pound than 150.

23. When viewing TV commercials, use reverse psychology. Think of that burger bun as being wet and soggy or that candy full of nasty wax (as it is).

24. Out of sight—out of mind. If you have to have no-no foods in the house (why, do you?), put them where you won't see them.

25. If you weigh yourself, do it the same day of the week, the same time of day, wearing the same weight clothes.

26. Manifest your weight loss. Visualize yourself the size you want to be.

27. Give yourself something to work towards, put a picture on the refrigerator of how you want to look.

28. Use small plates. This makes smaller portions look larger.
29. Eats lots of vegetables, steamed with fresh herbs or cooked a favorite way as long as no or very little fat is used. A tomato sauce is good. This is not only a healthful way of eating, it is very filling. You will never feel hungry or deprived.
30. Bypass shops that cause you to buy foods you shouldn't—like bakeries, for instance.
31. When you think you are hungry, try drinking a glass of water. Sometimes we are not really hungry, it's our body signaling for more fluids.
32. Exercise on a regular basis. Exercise speeds up your metabolism, thereby burning calories and reducing hunger and stress. Walking is an excellent form of exercise.

Some Benefits of Regular Exercise

- Exercises the heart muscle
- Improves circulation
- Improves digestion
- Improves function of all organs and glands
- Improves tissue oxygenation
- Keeps the elimination organs functioning
- Makes you feel good and prevents premature aging
- Reduces stress
- Speeds up the metabolism, aiding weight loss

Light

It is very important for your well-being to be outside in *indirect* sunlight (shade), without eye glasses or contact lens for at least 15 minutes a day. Without light, plants can not survive and neither can you.

General Nutritional Information

The Air We Breathe

Our homes can be filled with formaldehyde and many other un-desirable chemicals that can effect our health. Plants are won-derful air cleansers. According to recent tests, the best plants for cleaning air are: Peace lily, Lady palm, Areca palm, and the Ficus plant. The study recommends 2 to 3 good-size plants per a 100-square-foot room.

Clean air is certainly important but at this time I would like to talk about breathing. Being a student of Yoga, I have learned the importance of proper breathing. We just don't breathe enough or deep enough. Prana, our life-force is stimulated by breathing. With proper breathing, yoga prana circulates through-out the body in a system of 72,000 nerves to remove blockages caused by stress, toxins, or improper diet.

When deep-breathing, inhale through the nose, slightly blowing up your stomach like a balloon. Give a long exhale through the mouth, contracting the stomach, forcing all the stale air from the body.

You will find the brain oxygenated, allowing for clearer thought and a reduction of the killer . . . stress.

Mail-Order Directory

All-One-God-Faith

P.O. Box 28
Escondido, California 92033
619-743-2211

Manufacturer of Dr. Bronner's Barley Malt Sweetner, soaps, and health foods.

Apple Valley Market

9067 U. S. 31-33
Berrien Springs, Michigan 49103
800-237-7436

Free catalog. Sells various health foods; supplier for Worthington Vegetarian Luncheon Meats.

Arrowhead Mills, Inc.

P. O. Box 2059
Hereford, Texas 79045
806-364-0730

Sells grains, flours, tahini, and other fine products.

California Olive Oil
134 Canal Street
Salem, Massachusetts 01970
800-FUN-OILS

Non-aerosol vegetable sprays.

Diamond Organics
P. O. Box 2159
Freedom, California 95019
800-922-2396

Free catalog. Specializes in fresh organic fruits and vegetables.
Shiitake mushrooms also available.

Dixie, USA
P.O. Box 55549
Houston, Texas 77255
800-347-3494

Free catalog. Source for many fine vegetarian foods including
Burger 'n' Loaf and TVP.

Eden Foods
701 Tecumsek
Clifton, Michigan 49236
517-456-7424

A wide range of high-quality products including soy milk, barley
malt syrup, sea vegetables, and grain coffees.

Ener-G Foods, Inc.
P.O. Box 84487
Seattle, Washington 98124-5787
800-331-5222

Manufacturer of Egg Replacer, baked goods, pastas, and flours.

Great American Natural Products

4121 16th Street North
St. Petersburg, Florida 33703
800-323-4372

Catalog available. Bulk natural foods including herbs, spices, grains, seeds, vitamins, and more.

Harvest Direct, Inc.

P. O. Box 4515
Decatur, Illinois 62525-4514
800-835-2867

Free catalog. Many vegetarian foods including Protean Meat Substitute and TVP.

Magic Chain

2598 Fortune Way, Suite F
Vista, California 92083
800-622-6648

Free catalog. Carries Dr. Bronner's Barley Malt Sweetner as well as unique and hard-to-find health products.

Muir Glen Organic Products

424 North 7th Street
Sacramento, California 95814
800-832-6345

Complete line of excellent organic tomato products including pizza sauce, pasta sauce, salsa, crushed tomatoes, and tomato sauce. If your health food store doesn't carry this product, call for help.

Morinaga Nutritional Foods

2050 W. 190th Street, Suite 110
Torrance, California 90504
310-787-0200

Aseptically packaged silken tofu.

Macrobiotic Mall

18779C North Frederick Road
Gaithersburg, North Dakota 20879
301-963-9235

Free catalog. Produce, grains, beans, books, vitamins, and more.

Nasoya Foods, Inc.

23 Jytek Drive
Leaminster, Massachusetts 01453
508-537-0713

Water-packed tofu, salad dressing, and vegan mayonnaise.

Sovex Natural Foods

P.O. Box 2178
Collegedale, Tennessee 37315

Manufacturers of Better Than Burger?, Better Than Milk?, and Tofu Ice-Cream Mix.

The Spice House

254 Granada
San Luis Obispo, California 93401

Large selection of dried mushrooms, dip mixes, and more.

Vogue Cuisine

437 Golden Isles Drive, #15G
Hallendale, Florida 33009
305-458-2915

Source for Vogue Instant Vege Base if not available at your health food store.

White Wave, Inc.

1990 N. 57th Court
Boulder, Colorado 80301
800-488-9283

Manufacturers of Meat of Wheat and many other vegetarian products.

Yves Veggie Cuisine

1138 East Georgia
Vancouver, BC
Canada V6A 2A8
604-251-1345

Contact customer service at above number for a distributor near you. Makers of excellent vegetarian hot dogs, hamburgers, and more.

Glossary of Ingredients and Remedies

༄ ༄

At this writing, many of the following items are available only at health food stores. I know sometimes this is not convenient or available in your area. More and more as consumer demands change, so do the items on the supermarket shelves. I have included a mail-order directory in this book for your convenience (see page 423).

Agar-Agar (AH-gahr)   A gelatin made from sea vegetables (regular gelatin is made from animals). It is tasteless, odorless, and rich in calcium, vitamins A, B complex, C, D, K, and iron. It comes in powder, flakes, or bars. I used the flake form in recipe testing.

Amaranth (AM-ah-ranth)   An ancient Aztec staple that has been reborn. It is used as grain although it is technically a fruit. It is high in protein, calcium, and fiber, nutlike in flavor and gluten-free.

Annatto/Achiote Powder (uh-NUH-toh/ah-chee-OY-tay)
This powder is used as a natural food coloring. It comes to us from the achiote seeds plucked from the annatto tree. Used in small amounts, the color yellow is obtained. Using larger amounts will give you a red color. You will have the best luck finding this powder in Spanish or Asian markets.

Apple Cider Vinegar   Use raw and unfiltered organic vinegar (available at health food stores). When vinegar is processed, the beneficial ingredients are removed. Raw apple cider vinegar is a wondrous food—2 teaspoons mixed with 1 teaspoon honey in a cup of distilled water, taken daily, is most beneficial to the body. There are books on the market describing benefits that range from arthritis-reversal to weight-loss.

Apples They are high in carbohydrates and calcium and are a good source of protein, iron, vitamin A, thiamin, riboflavin, and ascorbic acid. Apples are the best known source of vitamin B_2, which promotes digestion and growth. Apples are an effective blood purifier, are helpful in the treatment of hardening of the arteries, and are believed to be a good heart medicine (lowering blood cholesterol and blood pressure), blood sugar stabilizer, and virus fighter. They also aid in the elimination process of the body.

Arborio Rice (ar-BOH-ree-oh) A short-grain Italian rice used mainly to make risottos.

Avocado Rich in protein, it contains 14 minerals, vitamins A, D, and E. An excellent food for a healthy heart.

Baking Powder Use aluminum free. I use the Rumford brand.

Balsamic Vinegar (bal-SAH-mihk) A dark, mellow vinegar with a lovely sweet taste. It is also available in white, for those dishes where a dark color might ruin the appearance.

Bananas If you take diuretics or high blood pressure medication, you can benefit from the banana's high potassium content. If you take antacids, try reaching for a banana instead.

Basil Used successfully in the treatment of colds, flu, fever, stomach cramps, constipation, vomiting, headaches, and menstrual cramps.

Basmati Rice (bahs-MAH-tee)   A long-grain rice with a nutty flavor. Available in both white and brown.

Bee Pollen   Contains 22 amino acids, 27 mineral salts, all the vitamins, minerals, fructose, glucose, lecithin, hormones, carbohydrates, all the essential fatty acids, rutin, bioflavonoids, and over 5,000 enzymes and coenzymes. Truly a wonder food and perhaps a wonder medicine. If possible take local pollen, which sometimes can help immunize the allergy sufferer.

Bell Peppers   When available, red bell peppers, compared to the green, contain more carotenes, potassium, and vitamin C and have powerhouse beta-carotene. The green ones are good choices also, especially when eaten raw.

Beets   Beneficial in ailments of the gallbladder and liver. Do not throw away the greens—they are a nutritional powerhouse.

Beta-carotene   Vitamin A and beta-carotene are not one and the same—they are related but fulfill different functions. Beta-carotene is converted to vitamin A in the body. Biochemists have found that beta-carotene protects the cells against free radicals, which can cause cancer. It also appears to reduce the risk of some heart diseases.

Brewer's Yeast   A vegetarian source of B vitamins, this yeast can be added to just about any food. It is also good for animals. My cats love it so I keep some in a small bowl next to their food dish. It will also repel fleas if taken internally or rubbed into the animal's coat. Not to be confused with nutritional yeast.

Broccoli   Broccoli is rich in beta-carotene and vitamin C, is low in calories and very beneficial to the elimination system.

Bulgur (BUHL-guhr)   Wheat that has been hulled, steamed, and dried, retaining its nutrients. Virtually fat- and sodium-free, it makes for very healthful pilafs or other grain dishes.

Cabbage   Contains phytochemicals (phytomins) that boost the production of anticancer enzymes, enabling them to destroy cancer-causing substances.

Caffeine   Too much caffeine can cause osteoporosis by blocking calcium absorption in the body. The caffeine in two to three cups of coffee can draw 30 milligrams of calcium from your bones. Coffee is not the only culprit. Here are some other sources of caffeine:

Cola—35 to 47 mg.	Cappuccino—61 mg.
Tea —25 to 110 mg.	Hot cocoa—4 mg
Decaf. coffee—2 to 8 mg	Expresso—100 mg.

Cantaloupe   Vitamin-rich fruits have been associated with protection against cancer of the esophagus. Cantaloupe is low in calories and an excellent aid in elimination. Rich in both vitamins A and C as well as potassium; one half provides 825 milligrams potassium.

Capers   A condiment made from seed-like buds of a Mediterranean plant.

Carob   A chocolate substitute that is caffeine-free. Carob is made from the pods of the carob tree. It is available in powdered or chip forms.

Carrots   High in vitamin A, which aids in lowlight vision. Carrots are a wonderful source of beta-carotene—one cup (raw, shredded) provides 31,000 international units with only 48 calories. Fat-free and high in soluble fiber carrots make a good, nutritious diet food.

Cauliflower   Contains phytochemicals (phytomins) that boost the production of anticancer enzymes, enabling them to destroy cancer-causing substances.

Cayenne Pepper   Good for circulation, heart, and colon.

You might notice this spice in a lot of my recipes. The reasons are threefold; the spice lessens the need for salt, imparts a nice flavor, and is most healthful for the circulation, heart, and colon. When I started buying my spices at the health food store I noticed a big difference in the taste of various herbs and spices. I suppose it is because they are fresher. The cayenne pepper was much hotter than I had previously used. So, in the recipes adjust it according to your taste and the degree of hotness of your spice.

Cherries   Six to eight cherries a day might keep gout pain away. Cherries are a good source of magnesium (a natural painkiller) and potassium. For centuries, the Japanese have treated joint pain with a syrup made from cherry juice.

Chile Peppers   Chile peppers are rich in the anticancer, antioxidant carotenoids including beta-carotene.

Cilantro (sih-LAHN-troh)   These leaves of the coriander plant are also known as Chinese parsley. Very popular in Indian and Mexican cooking. A little goes a long way.

Cinnamon   In many countries, cinnamon is traditionally used to treat fever, diarrhea, menstrual problems, and postpartum bleeding and also as a digestive aid. In the United States, most of the cinnamon we use is actually cassia. True cinnamon grows in Sri Lanka and on the Malabar coast of India, and can sometimes be found in Mexican grocery stores. Its light yellowish-brown bark will be soft enough to crumble in your hands.

Coconut   Coconut has been a source of food for over 3,000 years. Coconut milk compares to mother's milk in its chemical balance and it is quite a complete source of protein when taken in its natural form. Although high in fat and calories, it is also high in carbohydrates, calcium, phosphorus, iron, thiamin, riboflavin, niacin, and ascorbic acid.

Coffee Substitutes   Usually made from grains and available at health food stores. Cafix and Roma brands were used in testing recipes.

Corn   Corn is one of the easiest foods to digest and high in roughage and carbohydrates—178 calories in 1 cooked cup. A source of iron, zinc, and potassium and is low in sodium.

Couscous (KOOS-koos)   Small grains of pasta made from milled wheat—a staple of North African cuisine. Whole wheat is now available in health food stores.

Cranberries   Cranberries have long been known as a treatment for urinary infections. They are also therapeutic for rectal disturbances. Due to their high acid content they should not be eaten too frequently.

Cruciferous Vegetables   The vegetables of this family bear flowers that resemble the cross or crucifix, hence their name. They are:

Broccoli	Turnips
Cauliflower	Radishes
Bok choy	Rutabaga
Kale	Cabbage
Brussels sprouts	Watercress
Mustard greens	Horseradish
Kohlrabi	

Cruciferous vegetables are important cancer and heart disease fighters that should be included in your diet.

Cucumbers   Cucumbers are cooling, good for digestion, alkaline in nature, and low in calories.

Cucumber Juice   Cucumbers are high in silica, which helps strengthen the elasticity of the skin and muscles, even in older skin. The best way to receive silica is through drinking the juice of unpeeled European cucumbers (those long skinny ones wrapped in plastic) and drinking the fresh juice daily. Be sure to clean the cucumbers with Veggie Wash (page xviii) before juicing. You will also find this juice will flush toxins from the system and is a wonderful natural diuretic.

Daikon Radish   See Radishes.

Darifree   A milk substitute sold in powdered form. (Formerly Vegelicious

Dairy-free Yogurt   A yogurt made without dairy products. White Wave brand was used in testing.

Distilled Water   Our bodies are made of 55 to 75% water. This body water must be replenished daily by drinking water or beverages, or by eating foods naturally containing water. The United States has an abundant water supply at this time, but the surface and ground water are being polluted by toxic chemicals which can get into our drinking water. Pesticides, fertilizers, and other chemicals are sprayed on our crops and ground. Underground storage tanks containing paints, solvents, petroleum products, and other chemicals are believed to be leaking and seeping into the ground.

For this reason I and many other concerned people interested in our health, recommend drinking and cooking with distilled water in place of the questionable water coming from our faucets and other bottled water. Drinking distilled water at room temperature flushes toxins from your body, helps relieve bloating, lubricates all your working parts, and moistures your skin. Just ask models, athletes and dancers, they will tell you "water is to the body as oil is to a squeaky, tight, dry hinge." It is very important to keep the body well-hydrated.

I have a portable water distiller I use in our home. Also, most bottled water companies deliver distilled water or it is obtainable at supermarkets. In recipes you will notice I recommend using distilled water.

Dried Fruits   Use unsulfured.

Dulse   This sea vegetable is mild in flavor and high in nutrition, containing protein, iron, chlorophyll, enzymes, and vitamins A and B.

Eggplant   The Chinese have long used eggplant in treating diseases of the stomach, spleen, and large intestines. Eggplant adheres to cholesterol in the intestines preventing it from being absorbed into the bloodstream thereby helping to reduce cholesterol levels. It is used in the prevention of atherosclerosis and convulsions and as an immunity enhancer.

Egg Replacer   An egg substitute made from potato and tapioca flours. Sold in powder form under the Ener-G Egg Replacer label, or see pages 365 and 394 for recipes.

Fiber   Fiber is to your intestines and digestive tract as a toothbrush is to your teeth. Experts say 20 to 30 grams of dietary fiber a day may reduce the risk of developing some cancers. The only source of dietary fiber is from the vegetable kingdom.

Flax Seed   Flax seed fiber is nature's richest source of lignins, which dramatically reduce the risk of breast and colon cancer. This vegetarian source of omega-3 fatty acids is essential in preventing cancer and heart disease as well as reducing joint pain from arthritis and helping with skin problems like eczema. New studies show daily consumption of ground-up flax seed in your cereal or juice can lower cholesterol and help the failing kidneys of people with lupus.

Garlic   A member of the lily family, garlic contains a compound called ajoene, which has been proven to be toxic to malignant cells. Garlic has long been considered medicinal, and has been used as a natural antibiotic.

Ginger   In India, the highly successful Ayurvedic system of medicine recommends eating ginger for the treatment of arthritis as well as many other ailments. Dutch doctors have found it beneficial in treating arthritic pain because ginger has the ability to increase blood circulation, carrying inflammatory substances from the affected area.

Grapes   High percentages of grapes in the diet have been linked to low cancer incidence. A good source of magnesium, they are cleansing to the liver and aid kidney function.

Green Beans   Alkaline in nature, high in protein and iron, and low in calories. One cup of fresh cooked green beans gives you 2 milligrams of iron and has only 20 calories. A 3 1/2-ounce T-bone steak has 2 1/2 milligrams of iron and 324 calories.

Green Tea   Because it is lightly processed, it retains many its phytochemicals like catechins. Studies show this plant nutrient can lower cholesterol helping to prevent atherosclerosis and can inhibit the growth of cancerous tumors.

Herbs and Spices   Use fresh and non-irradiated when possible. It's wonderful to have a little herb garden for cooking and medicinal use. If substituting dry herbs for *fresh* use 1 tablespoon fresh to 1 teaspoon *dry.*

Honey   Use pure and unheated. Honey contains over 25 different sugars, each one having a different function in the human metabolism. Honey is a unique food—a living organic, instant energy-building food containing all the essential minerals necessary for life: seven vitamins of the B complex group, amino acids, minerals, enzymes and other vital factors. Honey fortifies the heart, re-creates vigor, helps digestion, and reinforces the memory. Honey has been found to heal wounds where other methods have failed. Many health practitioners use honey in the treatment of difficult-to-heal wounds.

Juicing   After juicing vegetables, always try to use the left-over pulp. By discarding this precious substance you loose most of the fiber and, as new studies show, half the vitamins and phytomins.

Jicama   This root vegetable with a slightly sweet, nutty flavor is a good source of vitamin C and potassium. It remains crisp either raw or cooked. When raw, it is juicy, nutritious, and thirst quenching. A good substitute for water chestnuts.

Kale   High in calcium and iron. A ½ cup serving has as much vitamin C as an orange and four times as much beta-carotene as broccoli.

Kombu (KOHM-boo)   A wide, thick dark green seaweed which grows in deep ocean waters. Used to add nutrition and flavor to soups, rice and bean dishes. A nutritional powerhouse containing calcium, iron, magnesium, potassium, iodine, vitamins A, C, and D.

Kudzu/Kuzu (KOO-zoo)   This thickening agent is a natural wild mountain root starch native to Japan. It is rich in minerals and often is used medicinally for the digestive system.

Lactose Intolerance   If your body doesn't want dairy product, listen to it.

Lecithin, liquid   In some recipes it can be used as an emulsifying agent in place of eggs.

Leeks   Low in calories and considered therapeutic for throat disorders and good for the liver and respiratory system.

Lentils   These legumes are a very good source of protein, providing as much as many meats. They will help to build the glands and blood and are especially good for the heart.

Lettuce   The darker green the lettuce, the more beta-carotene it contains—iceberg lettuce is the lowest in nutrition.

Lima Beans   Limas are 18% protein. One pound contains as many nutrients as two pounds of meat.

Liquid Aminos   A liquid vegetable protein used as a salt substitute made by Paul Bragg, health pioneer.

Liquid Smoke   Not all liquid smoke products are the same. Read the labels. I prefer to use a natural product made by Nabisco Foods (Wright's Hickory Seasoning) that imparts a charcoal-broiled flavor to foods.

Margarine   I recommend Spectrum Naturals Spread brand. This is a nonhydrogenated, transfatty acid-free, 94% saturated, fat-free spread. In regular margarine the oil is heated which causes it to become rancid, forming free radicals, which are a cause of cancer.

Meat of Wheat   A meat substitute high in protein, low in fat, and chewy in texture—made by White Wave.

Meat Substitutes   The substitutes I have tried and like are:

Burger 'n' Loaf (Midland Harvest), Gimme Lean (Lightlife), Heartline Lite products (Lumen), Meat of Wheat products (White Wave), Worthington products (contain egg whites), seitan mixes by Arrowhead Mills and Knox mountain, TVP (textured vegetable protein), and tofu.

Milk Substitutes   Lowfat rice or soy milks are recommended. Powdered mixes are also available; Darifree, vegetable based or Better Than Milk? made with tofu. The powdered forms are very convenient when traveling.

Mirin (MIHR-ihn)   A slightly sweet Japanese rice cooking wine.

Miso   Miso is a salty fermented paste made by combining soybeans with rice, barley, or wheat and adding a bacterial agent called koju. It has been used by the Japanese for centuries for flavoring recipes and in some instances it is used in place of salt. It strengthens weak intestines, helps digestion, and discharges toxins from the body. High in protein, calcium, iron, and the B vitamins; a vegetarian source of vitamin B_{12}.

Mushrooms
Button mushrooms   Contain hydrazides, which are said to cause cancer. The hydrazides are killed by heat, do not eat raw button mushrooms.

Enoki   Stimulates the immune system, helping to fight viruses and tumors.

Oyster   In animal studies this mushroom has shown promise in fighting cancer.

Shiitake   Stimulates the immune system to produce more interferon, which fights cancers and viruses. Oriental mushrooms that can be purchased dried or fresh—Far Eastern markets stock both. I noticed in our local markets they have started to stock fresh shiitake and portabello mushrooms in the produce department. To reconstitute dried mushrooms see page 371.

Tree-ear   Can prevent heart attacks by keeping blood platelets from sticking together. In animal studies have been found to slow the growth of cancer.

Reishi   Used for thousands of years by the Chinese for health and well being, enhancing organic functions, promoting cosmetic rejuvenation and beautifying the skin.

Nightshade Vegetables   Named after one member of their vast family, belladonna (deadly nightshade). The food plants of this family are what should interest us. They are:

Tomatoes   Eggplant   Potatoes
Cayenne   Chile peppers   Paprika
Pimiento
Bell peppers (green, red, yellow, and cherry)
Hot peppers (long, red, and red cluster)

The nightshade family is high in alkaloids, which in *certain people,* for some reason, seem to remove calcium from bones and deposit it in the joints, kidneys, arteries, and other areas of the body where they don't want them. Eating nightshade vegetables seems to aggravate arthritic pain in these people and by elimination of these foods, aches and pains have completely vanished!

Non-aerosol Pan Sprays   For our environment's health use only non-aerosol. Pan Max brand made by California Olive Oil was used in testing.

Nutritional Yeast   High in B vitamins and protein. It can be added to most recipes for a cheesy flavor. Keep refrigerated.

Oils and Oil Replacers   Olive oil, safflower oil, flax seed oil, peanut oil, Wonderslim, tahini, applesauce, apple butter, prune butter (see page 375). Any oil should be stored in the refrigerator or it will become rancid.

Onions   This member of the allium family contains organo sulfur, a potent compound that researchers say helps to prevent cancer by enhancing detoxification.

Oregano   Used successfully for the digestion and as an expectorant for coughs, colds, and chest congestion.

Papaya   High in vitamins A, C, and E, potassium, calcium, phosphorus, and iron. Contains the enzyme papain, a veritable tonic to the stomach.

Parmesan Cheese Alternative　A soy product made by Soyco Foods.

Parsley　Has more iron than any other green vegetable. Parsley juice has been used as a treatment in the removal of small kidney and gallstones, ailments of the liver, and as a tonic for the blood vessels, capillaries, and arterioles.

Peaches　High in vitamins A and C, calcium, and phosphorus. The body assimilates peaches very easily because they are easy to digest.

Peas　The pea, alkaline in nature, is a good source of vitamins, A, B, and C. It has been used successfully puréed to provide relief for ulcer pains because peas consume stomach acids.

Phyllo (FEE-loh)　A pastry made of paper-thin dough. Buy whole wheat, if available. Usually found in the frozen foods section.

Pineapple　Contains bromelain, a protein-digesting enzyme that enhances digestion of all protein foods.

Pita Bread　Also called pocket bread, it is a flat, round, middle eastern bread.

Potatoes　The potato is a powerhouse food, nutritious and helpful in weight-loss programs. An excellent source of vitamins A, B, C, and potassium. One eight-ounce potato contains 0.2g fat, 3.6g fiber, 4.7g protein, 14 mg sodium, 1.1% calories from fat, 179.2 calories, and 0 mg cholesterol.

Potato Chips　Use baked chips. The Louise brand is very good.

Pumpkin　Rich in potassium and alkaline in nature. A good source of fiber, vitamins B and C, and beta-carotene. Low in calories.

Quinoa (KEEN-wah)   A staple of the ancient Incas, who called it the mother grain. It contains more protein than any other grain and contains all eight essential amino acids. A small round grain with a delicate flavor that cooks like rice.

Radishes, Daikon   A sweet, mildly spicy vegetable used in stir-fries, raw in salads, and shredded for moisture in loaves. A good diuretic, beneficial in ailments of the gallbladder and liver.

Salad Dressings   Use fat-free dressings.

Salt   Table salt is composed of insoluble inorganic elements, mainly a combination of sodium and chlorine with some additives thrown in. In the production of table salt, it is heated to very high temperatures to solidify the salt with additives that are used to make pouring easier. This process is said to cause the salt to become insoluble. It stays in your system, building up over the years, overtaxing your body. Salt can settle into your bloodstream hardening the arteries and contributing to high blood pressure. An excessive amount of salt can deplete the body's potassium.

The sodium found naturally in foods is organic and soluble. Nature provides all the salt our bodies require in the form of organic sodium.

Salt Substitutes   In place of the free-flowing table salts, I recommend using dulse, kelp, and nori flakes. These sea vegetables are mild tasting and very nutritious. Braggs Liquid Aminos as well as low-sodium tamari, salt-free Spike, salt-free all-purpose Parsley Patch, and miso are also excellent. If you still desire table salt I find coarse kosher salt fast dissolving, pure, and additive free.

Scallions   Along with garlic and onions, scallions contain a compound called allium, which blocks carcinogens that have been linked to colon, stomach, lung, and liver cancer.

Seitan (SAY-tan)   Seitan is a meat substitute made from whole wheat flour and is a good source of protein. It is very close to

meat in texture and taste, and is very versatile. It can be purchased boxed or prepared (in the deli department) of health food
stores. See page 376 for seitan preparation.

Shiitake (shee-TAH-kay)   See Mushrooms.

Soy Products   Recent studies have shown the soy bean to be
almost a miracle food. Soy is low in saturated fat and cholesterol-
free; it is high in fiber, protein, iron, calcium, zinc, and B-vitamins, contains all the essential amino acids, and is packed with
phytomins (the only good source of isoflavones).

Soy foods help prevent heart disease, breast and prostate
cancers, osteoporosis, gives relief from menopause problems,
and lowers cholesterol. It is almost the only source of genistein,
which blocks the process in which new blood vessels grow and
which is needed to nourish malignant tumors.

How much do we need? Experts don't all agree on this
point, but one of the top soy experts advises at least one serving
of a soy food daily. Examples of one serving:

1 cup (8 ounces) soy milk	½ cup green soy beans
½ cup (2 to 3 ounces) tofu	(sweet beans)
½ cup rehydrated TVP	3 ounces soy burger

Spiru-tein   A high-protein energy drink that can be mixed
with soy or rice milk. Available at most health food stores in individual packets.

Stripples   A vegetable and grain protein, made by Worthington Foods, that is a good substitute for bacon. Contains egg
whites.

Squash   Low in calories and are an excellent source of the antioxidant beta-carotene and potassium.

Stevia   A natural sweetener used for hundreds of years in
many foreign countries. It is sold in cut herb and extract form. In
testing recipes, I used the white powdered extract. It is very

sweet and a wonderful alternative to using chemicals. It only takes a little bit to sweeten a dish.

Sugar   The consumption of refined sugar, which is stripped of nutrients, is believed to be addictive because of how it affects parts of the brain. Have you ever had an urge for candy or other sweets?

Too much refined sugar can lead to health problems such as elevated blood triglycerides, chromium loss (which can lead to the onset of diabetes), depression of the immune system, and a slow-down of the mobility of white blood cells. A dysfunctional immune system can lead to diseases like rheumatoid arthritis and cancer.

Sweeteners   Barley malt liquid, Dr. Bronner's Barley Malt Sweetner (powdered; a 30-year-old recipe not only sweet, but nutritious), raw honey, date sugar, light maple syrup, brown rice syrup, chopped dates, chopped prunes, and Fruit Source (available both granular and liquid), stevia extract, and Devon Sweet (Devansoy Farms).

Sweet Potatoes   Rich in color, sweet potatoes are loaded with beta-carotene and have the potential to reduce the risk of lung cancer. A good source of niacin and beneficial to the eliminative system, one cup mashed provides 43,000 IU of vitamin A! That's eight times the recommended allowance.

TVP   Textured vegetable protein is a lowfat meat substitute made from high-protein defatted soy flour. It is available in chunks, filets, or granules.

Tahini (tuh-HEE-nee)   A paste made from ground sesame seeds.

Tamari (tuh-MAH-ree)   A natural soy sauce that is wheat-free. Buy low-sodium.

Tempeh   A chewy meat substitute that has a mild and nutty flavor. High in protein and low in fat, it can be substituted for meat in most recipes. Made from soybeans and/or grains.

Tofu (TOH-foo)   Made from soy beans, tofu is an excellent source of protein, calcium, and lecithin that is low in fat and cholesterol-free. Beneficial in the fight against cancer. Tofu for hot flashes? Yes, it is rich in natural estrogen which might explain why Japanese women, whose diets include many soybean products, report fewer hot flashes and other related menopausal symptoms. See also Soy Products.

Tomatoes   Tomatoes contain a compound called lycopene, which is thought to reduce the risk of cancer. People with low lycopene blood levels are considered a higher risk for pancreatic cancer. Watermelon and apricots also contain this compound. And for the gents, consuming 10 ($1/2$ cup) servings of tomatoes a week has been shown to reduce prostate cancer by 45%.

Tortilla Chips   Baked chips are available and recommended.

Udon Noodles (OOH-don)   Long, flat, wheat noodles that are used mostly in Japanese recipes.

Umeboshi Plum Sauce (oo-meh-BOH-shee)   A pickled plum paste made from the Japanese Ume plum and used to enhance the flavor of some recipes. It is also a wonderful digestive aid.

Umeboshi Plum Vinegar   A zesty vinegar made from Umeboshi plums.

Vege Base, Instant   An all-natural vegetable blend used for flavoring—made by Vogue.

Vegetable protein powder   A blend made from vegetables.

Vinegar   See Apple Cider Vinegar.

Vitamins (absorption)   Vitamins should be taken with food, otherwise they pass through the system too quickly.

Wasabi (WAH-suh-bee)   A Japanese horseradish powder. When made into a paste, it is eaten with Sushi. According to the Japanese, a spoonful each day will prevent allergies, especially hay fever. They only use when symptoms are apparent.

Water   See Distilled Water.

Wheat Germ   The core of the wheat kernel that is high in fiber, vitamin E, chromium and manganese. An excellent source of vitamin E. A British study has recently reported astonishing results indicating 400 to 800 IU's of vitamin E daily will reduce the incidence of heart attacks by 75%! Eating foods rich in vitamin E such as dark green leafy vegetables, whole grains, nuts, seeds, and legumes seems like a good idea.

Whole Grains   Whole grains are a good source of zinc. Zinc is needed by 100 enzymes in human cells to function properly. While a mild zinc deficiency may not produce obvious symptoms, it is thought to accelerate the aging process.

Wild Rice   Wild rice is actually a grass that grows in water. It is rich in protein, minerals, and B vitamins.

Worcestershire Sauce   The regular type contains animal products. A vegetarian brand I particularly like is called Wizard's Stir-Krazy.

Yuba   A Japanese delicacy made from the film that develops when heating soy milk. It is used in dishes where a skin, much the same as chicken skin, is desired. It can be found in health food stores or oriental markets.

Zinc   Whole grains are a good source of zinc.

Zucchini   See Squash.

Bibliography

Airola, Paavo, Ph.D. *How to Get Well*. Health Plus Publishers, Sherwood, OR, 1990.

Balch, James F., M.D. and Phyllis A. Balch. *Prescription For Nutritional Healing*. Avery Publishing Group, Inc., Garden City Park, NY, 1990.

Balch, Phyllis A. and James F. Balch., M.D. *Rx Prescription For Cooking and Dietary Wellness*. PAB Publishing, Inc., Greenfield, IN, 1992.

Carper, Jean. *The Food Pharmacy*. Bantam Books, NY, 1989.

Diamond, Marilyn. *The American Vegetarian Cookbook*. Warner Books, Inc. NY, 1990.

Geelhoed, Glenn W., M.D., Robert D. Williz, Jr., M.D., and Jean Barilla, M.S., *Natural Health Secrets from Around the World*. Shot Tower Books, Inc., Boca Raton, FL, 1994.

Gershoff, Stanley, Ph.D. *The Tufts University Guide To Total Nutrition 1996*. HarperPerennial, HarperCollins Publishers, Inc. New York, NY, 1996.

Hausman, Patricia and Judith Hurley. *The Healing Foods*. Dell Publishing, NY, 1989.

Heinerman, John. *Heinerman's Encyclopedia of Fruits, Vegetables and Herbs.* Parker Publishing Company, New York, 1988.

Herbst, Sharon. *Food Lover's Companion.* Barron's Educational Series, Inc., Hauppauge, NY, 1990.

Jensen, Bernard. Dr. *Foods That Heal.* Avery Publishing Group, Garden City Park, NY, 1993.

Kloss, Jethro. *Back to Eden.* Back to Eden Books Publishing Co., Loma Linda, CA, 1988.

Mindell, Earl, R.Ph, Ph.D. *Earl Mindell's Soy Miracle,* Fireside Books, Simon & Schuster, NY, 1995.

Panati, Charles. *Panatis' Extraordinary Origins of Everday Things.* Harper and Row Publishers, NY, 1989.

Prevention Magazine. Rodale Press, Emmaus, PA, 1996.

The Complete Book of Vitamins. Prevention Magazine. Rodale Press, Emmaus, PA, 1977.

Tofu Times. Morinaga Nutritional Food, Inc. July 1993.

Vegetarian Times Magazine. Cowles Magazines, Inc. Stamford, CT (various issues).

Index

International Conversion Chart

These are not exact equivalents: they have been slightly rounded to make measuring easier.

LIQUID MEASUREMENTS

American	Imperial	Metric	Australian
2 tablespoons (1 oz.)	1 fl. oz.	30 ml	1 tablespoon
1/4 cup (2 oz.)	2 fl. oz.	60 ml	2 tablespoons
1/3 cup (3 oz.)	3 fl. oz.	80 ml	1/4 cup
1/2 cup (4 oz.)	4 fl. oz.	125 ml	1/3 cup
2/3 cup (5 oz.)	5 fl. oz.	165 ml	1/2 cup
3/4 cup (6 oz.)	6 fl. oz.	185 ml	2/3 cup
1 cup (8 oz.)	8 fl. oz.	250 ml	3/4 cup

SPOON MEASUREMENTS

American	Metric
1/4 teaspoon	1 ml
1/2 teaspoon	2 ml
1 teaspoon	5 ml
1 tablespoon	15 ml

WEIGHTS

US/UK	Metric
1 oz.	30 grams (g)
2 oz.	60 g
4 oz. (1/4 lb)	125 g
5 oz. (1/3 lb)	155 g
6 oz.	185 g
7 oz.	220 g
8 oz. (1/2 lb)	250 g
10 oz.	315 g
12 oz. (3/4 lb)	375 g
14 oz.	440 g
16 oz. (1 lb)	500 g
2 lbs	1 kg

OVEN TEMPERATURES

Farenheit	Centigrade	Gas
250	120	1/2
300	150	2
325	160	3
350	180	4
375	190	5
400	200	6
450	230	8